Structures and Strategies

Structures and Strategies

An Introduction to
Academic Writing

Lloyd Davis and Susan McKay
The University of Queensland

First published 1996 by
MACMILLAN PUBLISHERS AUSTRALIA PTY LTD
627 Chapel Street, South Yarra 3141
Reprinted 1997 (twice), 2000, 2002, 2003, 2006

Associated companies and representatives
throughout the world.

Visit our website at www.macmillan.com.au
E-mail us at academic@macmillan.com.au

National Library of Australia
cataloguing in publication data

Davis, Lloyd (Lloyd Benjamin).
    Structures and strategies: an introduction to academic
    writing.

    Bibliography.
    Includes index.
    ISBN 0 7329 2929 6
    ISBN 0 7329 2930 X (pbk.)

    1. Academic writing. 2. English language – Rhetoric.
    I. McKay, Susan (Susan Beth). II. Title.

808.42

Typeset in Optima and Century Old Style
by Typeset Gallery, Malaysia

Printed in China

Cover design by The Incredible Sons of Hawaii Five-O

Contents

SECTION 2   ACADEMIC WRITING

SECTION 3   WRITING STRATEGIES AND REPRESENTATION

Acknowledgements

We would like to thank Peter Debus at Macmillan for supporting this project. We are also grateful to Elizabeth Gibson, Diana Giese and Glen Thomas for helping us to prepare the text.

The ideas and approaches we present here have been influenced by a number of past and present colleagues in the English Department at the University of Queensland, with whom we have taught and talked about the teaching of writing. They include Lesley Chase, Gail Craswell, Gay Crebert, Martin Duwell, Cath Filmer-Davies, John Frow, Harry Garlick, Tony Glad, Joan Mulholland, Jeff Pittam, Marie Siganto and Graeme Turner. Numerous post-graduate and part-time tutors have also informed our ideas in this area. We are grateful for their input, as well as for the responses of the many undergraduate students whom we have taught. We would also like to thank Birgit Culloty, in the University of Queensland Library, for her support and help over a number of years.

The notions of 'evaluative attitude and sense', which are introduced in Chapters 9 and 10, derive from M. M. Bakhtin's 1986 essay collection, *Speech Genres and Other Essays* (Austin: University of Texas Press).

The authors and publishers are grateful to the following for permission to reproduce copyright material:

Andre Deutsch for 'Racist arguments and IQ' by Stephen Jay Gould (from *Ever Since Darwin*; Blackwell Publishers for extract from *Critique of Commodity Aesthetics* by W.F. Haug; Sheryl Bagwell/ *Financial Review* for article 'Why women don't make it'; Basil Blackwell Publishers for extract from *The Fashioned Self* by Joanne Finkelstein; *Business Review Weekly* for article 'Argyle Diamonds sets shining example' by Jill Rowbotham; Chatto & Windus for extract from *The Great World* by David Malouf; The Conde Nast Publications/*Glamour* for articles 'Workplace don'ts' March 1992, 'Fashion workshop', May 1992; Greg Dening/*Meanjin*

41 for article 'Sharks that walk on the land: 'the death of Captain Cook' by Greg Dening, *Meanjin* 41:(4) Dec. 1982; Harper Collins Publishers Australia for extract from *My Brilliant Career* by Miles Franklin; Legal Service Company for article 'Discriminating—for women' by Bronwyn McNaughton, *Alternative Law Journal* Vol. 17 (2): 89–90 April 1992; Anne Lim/*The Weekend Australian* for article 'Desirable denim'; News Ltd./*The Australian* for article 'Forensic powers of the police'; *New Scientist* for article 'What we must do to save the planet' by Crispin Tickell from TALKING POINT, *New Scientist* 7 September 1991; Random House UK Limited for extract from *The Great World* by David Malouf; Sydney Cricket Ground for 'Dress Rules'; George Winterton/*The Australian* for article 'Removing the crown with light fingers'; The Honourable Justice M.D. Kirby/*Quadrant* for article 'A defence of the constitutional monarchy' September 1993.

Advertisements, cartoons: Matthew Martin, p. 30; NIKE Inc. Advertising, p. 218.

Reading this book

This book can be read in several ways, depending on the detail you are after.

> **Definitions** of key terms and concepts are placed in boxes, like this. Taken together, the boxes provide a glossary of basic terms, and direct you to fuller discussion in the main text.

The main text is unboxed, and in the same typeface you are reading now. It should be read in conjunction with the boxed definitions. Major occurrences of **key concepts** in the main text are indicated by **bold type**. Important *subsidiary concepts* are often in *italics*, as are other words which require special emphasis.

The whole text is broken up into fairly short sections by the use of descriptive headings and sub-headings, to enable you to locate particular topics as easily as possible. Exercises are included throughout the chapters, for further work in the classroom. At the end of each chapter is a listing of sources and references that have been used within it.

1 Structures, strategies and academic writing

The aim of this book is to offer students and teachers a semester-length program that studies a wide range of writing **structures** and **strategies**, with particular attention to **academic writing**. Structures and strategies are central to the idea of writing that is discussed throughout the book: writing involves organising and structuring texts strategically, thereby influencing readers' responses and understandings.

Writing texts comprises a number of activities. These include thinking and discussing; researching; planning and ordering; drafting and revising. These are all undertaken to a greater or lesser degree when we produce a text. We may be so familiar with some kinds of texts that we don't have to think very much before writing them. A short note to friends thanking them for a gift may seem pretty straightforward. Other kinds of texts demand more thought and planning. We are less confident about fulfilling their requirements or criteria and so take more care. Job applications or university and school assignments are a couple of familiar examples.

The effects on readers of the structures and strategies we end up using can also vary. We may expect certain results from our efforts but can't be sure that they will take place. The same text can be found extremely informative and persuasive by some readers but may leave others cold. Readers always bring their own opinions and views to texts.

Texts act as kind of meeting place between authors' and readers' ideas. In this sense, writing and reading texts is a process of *social interaction* between people's points of view, since the structures and strategies we use in writing are part of social communication. Writing is thus a structural, strategic and social activity.

Although we examine the structures and strategies at work in a wide range of texts, our focus is mainly on ones that relate to writing academic essays. Academic writing is only one kind that people do, though a vital one for students at university and college. These contexts set certain expectations and demands for writing. Many of these also exist outside education, especially in work

1

settings. The use of a formal style and a structured argument, and the need for research and documentation, are examples. Skills and techniques involved in academic writing are flexible and useable outside the classroom.

Furthermore, as we will repeatedly see, academic writing is not absolutely separate from many other types of writing, including fictional narrative, journalism and even certain sorts of advertising. Although each type of writing has different features from the others and we distinguish between them, the various forms do inter-relate. Often they seem to echo or imitate each other. For example, it can be surprising how often an apparently non-fictional or even scholarly type of writing, such as a history or a biography will use what might be thought of as fictional patterns, such as a heroic protagonist, narrative suspense or a contest between opposing moral values.

Academic writing shares certain features with other types but often uses them in different ways. A news report may summarise and present the comments of various experts, but it won't do so in as much detail as does the following example of academic writing, a paragraph from an essay by academic psychologist Brenda Major. It concerns the theory that men and women have different attitudes to work:

> It has frequently been proposed that differences in what men and women value or want from their jobs can explain their paradoxically similar levels of job and pay satisfaction (e.g., Crosby 1982, Sauser and York 1978). The logic of this argument is that women are 'contented' with their jobs and pay despite their objectively inequitable treatment because there is little discrepancy between what they want and what they receive. Three major assumptions are inherent in this explanation: first, that women and men value or want different things from their jobs; second, that women and men obtain from their jobs the things they want; and third, that sex differences in job values or wants explain the similarity in women's and men's job satisfaction. In support of the first assumption, a number of studies have found that men are more interested in pay and promotion than women are, whereas women value social relations on the job and 'comfortable' working conditions (e.g., good hours, easy transportation, pleasant physical surroundings) more than men do (see Nieva and Gutek 1981 for a review). With regard to the second assumption, there is ample evidence that men receive higher pay and more

promotional opportunities than women (Treiman and Hartmann 1981), and some evidence that women's jobs tend to be higher on comfort factors than men's (Quinn and Shepard 1974). There is no evidence, however, that women experience higher levels of positive social relationships on the job than men (Nieva and Gutek 1981). The third assumption, that sex differences in job values or wants explain women's paradoxically high levels of job and pay satisfaction, remains a *post hoc* explanation without direct empirical support.

This text has a number of features characteristic of academic writing: a clear pattern and development, with points numbered and ordered; a concern with logical and illogical argument; the use of research and evidence; and a formal, impersonal style and tone. A newspaper story might also use these features but would most likely be aiming to report on the differences between men's and women's attitudes, not to analyse different theories about them. It would accept differences rather than question them. The **point of view** of the academic and journalistic texts would be quite distinct.

The above features don't appear only in scholarly texts. They are, however, frequently emphasised in academic writing. Their effects are twofold, both structural and strategic:

1 They help arrange the text's information into an understandable sequence;
2 They create the effect of a well-researched and convincing summary of what is at issue on a topic.

In fact, the clarity of the paragraph's structure has the strategic effect of making it seem authoritative. In this sense, a text's structural features are simultaneously strategic. These two aspects of texts always work together.

We can start to consider the ways in which structures and strategies operate through closely analysing various texts, to identify their main features and effects. Having done this, we can try to imitate these features in our own writing, practising what other writers do and building upon the ways in which we already write. Hence the approach in this book combines the reading *and* writing of different kinds of texts.

The accent is on trying to think about what we and other authors are trying to achieve in our work. Asking why writers have selected certain strategies at certain places raises additional options and possibilities. This sort of awareness of how and why other writers structure their writing can help us in organising ours.

In line with this approach, each chapter presents three kinds of material: a discussion of key concepts on its specific topic; sample texts for analysis and class discussion; exercises for practice, and assignments. The extracts and exercises are meant very much as starting points rather than perfect models. We hope that readers will introduce their own textual examples and questions that develop and even revise the ideas presented here.

All the chapters have a double function. They aim both to cover a wide range of styles and strategies and to relate consistently to academic writing. They are grouped into three sections: **Writing Structures**, **Academic Writing** and **Writing Strategies and Representation**. The first section covers three modes of writing used in all social contexts, including the academic: description, narration and exposition. Each is seen as involving its own form of logic or way of thinking. Description focuses on spatial relations, narration on events occurring through time, while exposition seeks to explain, analyse or evaluate its subject matter. Variations in structuring each of these modes are considered. Finally, their functions in academic writing, especially as means of providing evidence, are examined.

The second section builds on this last point to focus more closely on academic writing, acknowledging its links and contrasts with other genres. Variations within academic writing are also stressed. As students realise, probably more clearly than their teachers, different subject areas have divergent conceptions of just what academic writing is.

There are, however, some structural and strategic continuities across subject areas, and these, along with the differences, are examined. These common features include the use of logic and research (in Chapters 5 and 7), and of the argument mode to present cases for or against specific issues and topics (Chapter 6). Academic argument, combining description, narration, exposition, logic and research, is seen as the central form of writing with which students and teachers are concerned.

The book's final section views all the preceding topics and modes of writing in a slightly altered way. It reviews the main points about modes and structures while also asking about their implications and consequences for authors and readers. Academic writing is seen as related to other genres not only in terms of the structures it uses, but also in the kinds of strategic effects it seeks. Because of this link, the way readers respond to texts becomes a central issue. When reading texts it is important to be aware of the sorts of effects they may be seeking and the way they are trying to achieve them.

The last section emphasises the importance of **textual analysis** in trying to work out what texts are doing. Analysis is initially seen as a means of critically reading and responding to research material (Chapters 8 and 11). A number of strategies through which texts may position readers to understand topics in certain ways are raised. These include figurative language (Chapter 9) and genre (Chapter 10). In these terms, academic writing is seen as a strategic mode which aims to convey a high 'truth' value.

At the same time, textual analysis is seen as an important part of our attitude and approach towards our own writing. Close analysis forms the basis of revising, editing and proofreading our work. By studying other writers' texts in detail we become able to view and review our own more carefully and thoughtfully.

Finally, textual strategies and analysis are considered central to recognising that texts work to **re-present** the world in certain terms to their audience. Texts are seen as setting up authority for themselves and positions of understanding for readers, in effect socialising them into adopting certain views on social ideas and events. The aim of analysing texts becomes to reveal the processes of socialisation and attitude formation that they construct. By reading texts critically, we are able to examine and question the social presumptions of different genres and their strategies of representation.

In the end, then, the study and practice of academic writing lead us to consider many of the key questions that come up in other literature, communications and cultural studies courses, issues of textual authority and genre, reader response, social position and representation.

Running through the different topics presented in the book are a number of central ideas or premises about writing in general and academic writing in particular. The first of these is that writing is a *process* which fuses language and thought. Writing doesn't simply reproduce abstract ideas on paper or on a computer screen. It is part of a process of working thoughts through and developing ideas. The connection between writing and thought is especially relevant to the central genre studied here: logical and persuasive academic argument.

For these reasons, the book includes numerous exercises that ask readers to revise and rewrite texts by other authors as well as by themselves, and then to consider changes to ideas that are introduced. At the same time, the importance of rewriting one's own work is constantly emphasised, not simply as a means of 'improving expression' or 'correcting grammar', but to clarify and reconsider the connections between expression and the ideas that are being presented. We try to encourage a view of writing as a continuing thought-and-language process that moves from:

1 outlining and planning (including research), to
2 drafting initial versions, to
3 revising, rethinking and rewriting the work, to
4 producing the 'final' text.

The goal of practising this process and approach to writing is to increase our understanding and self-awareness of the ways in which we write.

Using computers and word processors complements this view of writing. The great advantage of the technology is that it helps us rethink and rewrite our work. A printed version of an essay draft can be read and revised, the changes easily incorporated on to disk versions. Paragraphs and other sections of a paper can be smoothly moved to more suitable places. We can edit and proofread our work efficiently with the help of spell-check and grammar-check programs. The final presentation of a text can be polished through using a variety of fonts and type styles.

At the same time, computers significantly help in researching topics in all fields. From library catalogues to specialised indexes and bibliographies, computer and CD-ROM packages hold and provide access to incredible amounts of information. The material that is gathered can also be organised into personal databases which may aid in retrieving and using research in projects and assignments.

These kinds of keyboard and research skills are as important in the workplace as they are in education. The use of computers in academic writing and research exemplifies the way that many of the skills and knowledge acquired at college and university continue to be applied and developed in other situations.

The book's second premiss is that writing abilities only improve together with reading abilities. In reading and analysing texts written by others we become alert to a wide range of structures and strategies and their effects. We can then practise imitating as well as varying these processes in our own work. Hence many of the exercises ask readers to analyse examples and then write a related kind of text. Much of each chapter is also taken up with discussing specific features of sample texts and considering their impacts.

The aim of this approach is to enhance the dual skills of reading and writing. This double objective is especially relevant to university and college students since it helps refine the capacity not only to write essays and assignments but also to do related research. By reading attentively and focusing sharply on textual features, more information and insight can be gained from primary and background research materials.

The book's third and possibly most important premiss is that many of the crucial aspects of analysing other people's writing, plus producing and revising ours, revolve around the notion of textual point of view. As explained in later chapters, the concept of point of view or perspective involves a whole set of issues extending from an author's link to the subject matter, in terms of space or time, to his or her opinion.

The importance of focusing on questions of point of view and perspective is that they reveal that authors don't simply write about topics objectively or transparently but are constantly adopting certain positions or attitudes towards the material and ideas. Point of view operates across all the modes and genres of writing that we will be considering. An author's viewpoint can have a great influence on the ways readers respond to a text; it works as a kind of filter through which we see the subject. Hence we note the importance of always trying to identify authors' points of view when reading their work, and of clearly establishing our perspective on topics and issues in the texts we produce.

Perhaps the key idea that this books tries to convey is that writing and texts don't appear out of the blue. They are constructed and manipulated, sometimes by individual authors but more often according to structural, strategic and social conventions which affect the ways that different kinds of writing work. The aim is to recognise that such conventions operate in texts, by studying what some of them are, how they function, and with what results.

Work cited

Major, Brenda (1987) 'Gender, Justice, and the Psychology of Entitlement', in *Sex and Gender*, editors Phillip Shaver and Clyde Hendrick, Sage, Newbury Park.

Section 1

Writing Structures

2 Description

Description is one of the four modes of writing we will be discussing in this book. The others are **narration** (telling what happens), **exposition** (explaining something), and **argument** (presenting a case).

The four modes are ways in which writers transform their ideas into textual form. These modes involve **textual representations** because they *represent* (or more accurately *re-present*) the 'world' or some aspect of it in text. All writing is a process of representation, that is, when we write we are conveying something of the 'world', real or imagined, our experiences of it or our ideas about it, to the reader. This is not, however, without its problems. We have to filter out some of the complexity of this world and arrange the details so that they fit with the writing and reading process. In other words, we need to make choices when we write.

Description is the mode of writing that is used to *relate perceptions* to the reader. Usually, it is the appearance of something that is translated into words, so most description relies on the recreation of a visual image. We see examples of description which rely on visual perception every day: novels (the description of the physical appearance of characters and scenes); newspapers (the description of the appearance of a political figure, a court witness or a rock star, the setting of a crime or even a sporting match); advertising (the description of the attributes of cars, houses or the latest electrical appliances, etc.).

Descriptive writing, however, may involve more than an appeal to the visual sense. It can also provide images by referring to the other senses of touch, hearing, taste and smell: the description of the touch of a lover in a novel, for instance, or the feel of a towel that has been washed in a particular brand of fabric softener in an advertisement; the description of the sound of an orchestra or a heavy metal group in the review section of a newspaper; the description of the taste of a wine in a connoisseur's wine guide, or the taste of freshly picked fruit in an advertisement; the description of the smell of decay in a novel, or the smell of a perfume in an advertisement. Description thus covers a very broad sensory dimension.

> **Description** is the representation of sensory
> experiences in language.

Like the other modes of writing we will be introducing, description
acts as a process of representation which affects both the writer's
construction of a text and a reader's response to it. As we will see,
description is often associated with exposition—that is, we describe
in order to explain. But, for the moment, we are going to consider
description on its own.

As we have said, description is a process which represents
the world in a textual form. This produces three problems which
need to be dealt with by the writer:

1 **Perspective**
2 **Selection**
3 **Order**

First, there is a problem of **perspective**. Whose world are we
representing? Every time we write, we need to make decisions over
just where we, as writers, are positioning ourselves in relationship to
the material being presented, and where we want the reader to be
positioned. This perspective may be **spatial**, literally where we are
in the text, or it may be **attitudinal**, what we want to convey about
our attitude to the material. To a large extent, the choices in perspective will depend on what the author wants to achieve.

Second, since the world is necessarily larger and more complex than any of its representations, the process of representation
must be **selective**. Some details will be included at the expense of
others. The **focus** or emphasis in the description will affect the
selection of details.

Finally, the world and our experience of it are not linear in
form. Yet somehow we need to present our experiences in a
written structure which has a beginning, a middle and an end. We
will be imposing an **order** on material that may not have such an
order.

We will take these three problems, perspective, selection and
order, in turn and show how different writers deal with them. We
will be using extracts from a wide range of texts, including short
stories, non-fictional texts, newspaper articles and magazine items
as well as academic texts. Along the way, we will have the opportunity to practise descriptive techniques so as to develop our own
writing skills.

Perspective: personal and impersonal

Perspective is an appropriate term to use when talking about descriptive writing. It has several commonplace meanings, each of which can be applied to the construction of description texts. When we say that we need to 'put something into perspective', we are suggesting that we need to consider it in relation to other things. The notion of perspective as defining relationships is also evident in the way artists arrange objects in realist paintings using lines of perspective. Spatial relationships are not, however, all that can be inferred from the term perspective. When we express an opinion, we often suggest that we are using our own perspective. It represents our viewpoint. Each of these ordinary uses of perspective is valuable when thinking about the choices involved in descriptive writing. Each of them implies the position of the author in relation to the text, and therefore also implies a position for the reader. Hence, we can summarise our notions of perspective as:

1 The physical place constructed for the author in the text; and,
2 The attitude about the material conveyed by the author.

One way the author's perspective can be constructed is through the use of pronouns. Unlike some other forms of writing such as exposition and argument, description often involves the use of the first person pronoun, 'I', to create an individual or **personal point of view**. Travel writing, as an intensely personal type of writing, often uses the 'I' perspective to place the author into the description and to allow personal thoughts to be expressed.

In the following extract from a travel book, *Around the World in 80 Days*, author Michael Palin is describing his trip to the Pyramids. Since it is a personal account, the writer and his individual perspective are very much in evidence:

> Having arrived in Egypt six hundred years too late to see one of the Seven Wonders of the World—the Pharos lighthouse—I felt I couldn't leave without seeing one that still exists—the Pyramids. I had always presumed they were in the middle of nowhere, marooned in the desert. In fact they are within five minutes' walk of apartment blocks in the suburb of Giza. My first view of them is from a traffic jam on Pyramids Road. The 4,600-year-old apex of the Great Pyramid pokes up from behind a block of flats. My first full-frontal view of the Pyramids provokes a heretical comparison with the slag heaps which used to litter the South Yorkshire countryside where I grew

up. They had the same solid bulk, shape and immovable presence. Once free of the straggling suburb we are straight-away in desert. There's no transition through savannah and scrub-land, like in the geography books. The city ends, the desert begins, and it goes on until you reach Morocco. The dustiness of Cairo is explained. Every time a wind blows it dumps thousands of tons of desert on the city.

Closer now to the Pyramids and they are awesome. The blocks of sandstone at their base are twice as high as the small children playing around them. The structures rise serene and powerful above us, preserving an unmoving dignity, like great beasts surrounded by insects. Coaches ferry out an endless stream of human insects, deposit them at a tightly packed vantage point where they are assailed by camel-mongers, postcard salesmen, purveyors of trinkets and all the other free market forces which have ripped off tourists at this very spot for hundreds, if not thousands, of years.

In this extract, Palin describes his visit and in the process conveys something of his thoughts on the relationship between the ancient and modern, the monumental and the mundane. The author is very much part of this text as evidenced by the use of the first person. The 'I' pronoun makes the description personal and puts Palin at the scene. Consequently, the reader becomes a viewer, guided through the experience by the author.

However, this description does more than merely paint a picture. In a deliberate and meticulous way, Palin conveys his *attitude* towards the tourist experience. His previously held romantic notion of the Pyramids, surrounded by desert in grand isolation, has been overturned by the reality of finding them so close to Cairo suburbia. This closeness is constructed through the reference that 'they are within five minutes' walk of the apartment blocks in the suburb of Giza' and further emphasised by his first glimpse of them 'from the traffic jam on Pyramids Road'.

He continues in this vein by making the analogy, which he calls a 'heretical comparison', with slag heaps from the Yorkshire coal mines. This detail shows us something about Palin and how he wants his readers to see him. The similarities between the Pyramids and the slag heaps can be understood in terms of their size and shape and their obtrusive place on the landscape. Although Palin does not mention it, they also share similar origins as the results of human endeavour on a large scale. However, his use of the adjective 'heretical' frames the comparison and suggests that the Pyramids deserve more reverence than other more ordinary structures.

In the second paragraph, he continues to situate the Pyramids in the mundane world. He describes them as being 'like great beasts surrounded by insects', suggesting not only the size difference between them and the human visitors, but also their immovability and even their relative permanence. The extract ends with a reference to the 'camel-mongers, postcard salesmen, purveyors of trinkets and all the other free-market forces which have ripped off tourists at this very spot for hundreds, if not thousands, of years'. Once again, Palin is describing the experience of seeing the Pyramids in the context of the mundane world. However, this time he hints that perhaps this is the way the Pyramids have always been experienced.

The overwhelming impression conveyed in this extract is not so much the physical description of the Pyramids, and nor is it strongly related to their ceremonial place in Egyptian history; rather it demonstrates Palin's perspective on them as monuments swallowed up by modern civilisation. He seems cynical and more than a little disappointed by his experience.

Exercises

1 Write two or three paragraphs describing a tourist attraction which you have visited. You could choose a famous monument like the one Palin describes, or you could describe a theme park, a resort, a National Park or a public building. In your writing, try to convey the expectations you held before you visited the attraction and how you felt about it while you were there. Since it will be a personal account, use the first person 'I' point of view.

2 Re-write your description, but this time don't write yourself into the text. Without using an 'I' point of view, try to relate the same attitudes. What changes do you have to make? Is your second description as effective as your first? Show both pieces of work to a friend or classmate and let them be the judge.

Not all descriptions use such a personal perspective. The following extract has been taken from the news magazine *The Bulletin*. Here, Damien Murphy offers a less individual point of view. The street scene is described from a seemingly detached viewpoint:

> At dawn, bouncers toss two men into Adelaide's Hindley Street. They swear, beery-eyed and staggering, at their steroid-powered vanquishers. One is bleeding from a cut mouth. Other men spill from buildings. People push, people shove, while from speakers hung outside Rio's nightclub, American rap group Salt 'n' Pepa sing derisively: 'What a man, what a man, what a mighty good man...'

Some have ganged up on bouncers, others are fighting among themselves, a few are trying to restrain friends from joining the battle. Maybe 25 are fighting, 100 are watching. Somebody rings the cops.

The brawling dies when the blue uniforms arrive. Snarling bouncers are puffed up like territorial Dobermans, battered drinkers litter the pavement, bleeding, holding heads.

The detached style used in this piece does not place the author in the text. Instead, we are offered a perspective which encourages us to see the realism of the situation. We seem to be able to see the whole situation as if we were observing the street scene from above. This text uses an **impersonal point of view** and like many other examples of journalism is not constructed from a personal view-point in case it could be construed as biased or misleading. Rather, the reader is positioned to see the article as factual and truthful.

Exercises

1 Re-write Murphy's description as if you had witnessed the brawl. Decide where you were when the fight broke out and relate what you saw. What changes have you made and how do they affect the meaning of the text?
2 Using a detached, journalistic style, describe a street that you know well, perhaps a street where you have lived or worked (500 words). By describing some of the inhabitants, try to include something of the atmosphere of the street.

Selection and objectivity

As we have noted, the process of writing description is *selective*. Writers cannot possibly reproduce in words everything about a particular object, person or part of the world. The choices about what to include and what to leave out will depend on the **focus** of the description. By focus, we mean those aspects which are to be selected and emphasised. As we saw in the extract on the Pyramids, Palin chose to emphasise the modern context in which the Pyramids exist by describing the appearance of the Great Pyramid so close to a Cairo suburb, and further, by describing the tourists as insects and the tourist operators as 'free market forces'. Murphy's article about street violence suggests the reason for the violence with his emphasis on the appearance of the two men who seem to be the cause of the brawl as 'beery-eyed and staggering', and later on the 'battered drinkers [who] litter the pavement, bleeding, holding heads'.

In description, focus can also refer to the degree of **object-ivity** the author uses. In *objective* styles of description, the author will focus primarily on the object, the person or the scene, and describe them with little emotion or opinion in such a way as to represent them accurately. We see this style of writing in scientific texts. The following is a description of the first leg of a honeybee from *Animals Without Backbones* by Ralph Buchsbaum:

> The FIRST LEG has many branched feathery hairs for collecting pollen. Along one edge of the inner surface of the tibia is a fringe of short, stiff hairs which form an *eye brush* used to clean the compound eyes. The large first joint of the tarsus is covered with long, unbranched hairs, forming a *pollen brush* for collecting the pollen grains that become caught among the hairs of the fore part of the body when the bee visits flowers. This first joint also has a semicircular notch lined with a comblike row of bristles and known as the *antenna comb*. The antenna is cleaned of pollen by drawing it through the notch. As it is pulled through, it is held in place by a spur on the end of the tibia which fits against the tarsal notch.

The precision of this description through its emphasis on physical detail would enable an entomologist to identify the first leg of the honeybee and to differentiate it (presumably) from the hind leg of the same insect.

It is not only in scientific writing, however, that we find objective description. In the short story titled 'The Beach', Alain Robbe-Grillet describes the scene with equal attention to detail:

> The children are walking along a beach. They move forward, side by side, holding hands. They are roughly the same height, and probably the same age too: about twelve. The one in the middle, though, is a little smaller than the other two.
>
> Apart from these three children, the whole long beach is deserted. It is a fairly wide, even strip of sand, with neither isolated rocks nor pools, and with only the slightest downward slope between the steep cliff, which looks impassable, and the sea.
>
> It is a very fine day. The sun illuminates the yellow sand with a violent, vertical light. There is not a cloud in the sky. Neither is there any wind. The water is blue and calm, without the faintest swell from the open sea, although the beach is completely exposed as far as the horizon.

But, at regular intervals, a sudden wave, always the same, originating a few yards away from the shore, suddenly rises and then immediately breaks, always in the same line. And one does not have the impression that the water is flowing and then ebbing; on the contrary, it is as if the whole movement were being accomplished in the same place. The swelling of the water at first produces a slight depression on the shore side, and the wave recedes a little, with a murmur of rolling gravel; then it bursts, and spreads milkily over the slope, but it is merely regaining the ground it has lost. It is only very occasionally that it rises slightly higher and for a moment moistens a few extra inches.

And everything becomes still again; the sea, smooth and blue, stops at exactly the same level on the yellow sand along the beach where, side by side, the three children are walking.

The focus here is initially on the children, but it then moves on to the sea and then back to the children. However, it is the description of the sea, constructed objectively and from an impersonal perspective, that stands out. Using phrases like 'originating a few yards away', 'always in the same line', 'flowing and then ebbing', the author describes the waves with the precision and attention to detail of the scientist, creating a picture of the sea that seems convincingly real.

Exercises
1 Visit an art gallery or browse through some books on art. Choose a painting that appeals to you and describe it as objectively as you can. How does the style of painting affect the difficulty of this task?
2 Find a family snapshot (yours or someone else's) and describe the people in it with a similar degree of objectivity.

Subjective description

Not all description demands this level of objective accuracy. Other styles of writing rely on more **subjective** description in which the author attempts to focus on a feeling about the object, person or scene being described. To do this, certain aspects will be emphasised and others neglected. In this extract from *Johnno*, David Malouf describes his late father's garden:

It was September, and the roughstone terraces with their thickets of tiny white daisies were aswarm with insects. The whole garden sizzled and hummed. Big slow-flying grass-hoppers, so heavy they could barely stay airborne, barged across the lawn or lofted over a wall to the hibiscus. The air glittered, and bees were busy in the cups of creepers that were just bursting into flower, cascading over a trellis or choking a fence. Occasionally one of the local cats strolled through on its way to the waste ground next door and sniffed about for scraps; or a big waterbird floated in from the mangroves downriver and perched for a moment on a dahlia stake. Once I saw a good-sized goanna. Deserted for just a fortnight, my father's garden was already half wild. The darkness under the thickening boughs was alive with midges and heavy with the smell of rotting vegetation, jungle-damp and sickeningly sweet.

This paragraph relies on selected details about the plants, insects, animals and birds to convey the sense of wildness. The whole garden is 'aswarm with insects'. The description of the grass-hoppers as 'so heavy they could barely stay airborne' and of the bees as 'busy in the cups of creepers that were just bursting into flower' conveys something of the plenitude of spring. The arrival of the larger animals like the cat, the waterbird and the goanna suggests the absence of a human. Even without the sentence of explanation ('Deserted for just a fortnight, my father's garden was already half wild'), the overgrowth and increasing lack of control are apparent.

This approach can be used to add feeling or create impressions when describing people. In the following subjective description in *The Age* newspaper, Sarah Gristwood meets movie star Mel Gibson. The author not only describes Gibson's physical appearance, but conveys much about his character both on and off the screen:

He is best known for tough action pictures like the series of *Lethal Weapon* and *Mad Max* films. But Jodie Foster, who co-starred with him in *Maverick*, a remake of the '50s Western, describes him surprisingly as 'the kind of guy you just want to protect . . . I think that's his secret weapon, that he is so incredibly vulnerable and unaware of himself'. It's a quality that shows to advantage on the screen.

But if his celluloid persona is an odd mix of humor and hysteria, you get, close-up, a sense of steely control under the cheeriness. According to *Lethal Weapon* director Richard Donner, Gibson 'has a lot of anger and hostility. Under all the good-looking façade, he's a real tough son-of-a-bitch'.

He's not beautiful in the flesh in quite the way he is on film. But at 36, his famously boyish looks have not yet begun to ossify. His height (there's some debate about whether he's 170 centimetres or 178 centimetres) is unremarkable; what you do notice first are the extraordinarily active electric blue eyes. He is crackling with energy, striding along the terrace of the Hotel du Cap, chain-smoking and affecting to ignore the paparazzi clustered outside.

This description is full of apparent contradictions. On screen Gibson is described as tough but vulnerable. He exhibits humour and hysteria and is boyishly good-looking. The remarks from Donner that 'under all the good-looking façade, he's a real tough son-of a-bitch' seem to accord with Gristwood's own perceptions. Her description of Gibson as being less good-looking off screen and of unremarkable height supports the existence of a façade. His 'active electric blue eyes', his energy, his striding and the chain-smoking all denote toughness. Yet we are left with the image of him *'affecting* to ignore the paparazzi clustered outside' rather than *'ignoring* the paparazzi clustered outside'. Perhaps, after all, the toughness is only a front.

This distinction between objective and subjective description is difficult to maintain in practice. It is very difficult to write descriptions that are purely objective. Even the description of the leg of the Honeybee suggests the emotional involvement of the author with his topic. He clearly enjoys his work. Similarly, it is almost as hard to produce subjective descriptions that do not relate to objective reality. Gristwood's description of Mel Gibson suggests his personality through the details of his physical appearance.

Exercises

1 Write a 500-word description of a celebrity in the music industry. You could choose a rock star, a jazz singer, an opera diva or a famous conductor. Assume you are writing a feature article for a music magazine (which one is up to you), in which you describe the physical appearance of the celebrity in such a way as to demonstrate something of his or her approach to music.

2 Find a newspaper photograph of a well-known politician. Through the careful selection of detail, describe this person to emphasise some aspect of his or her personality (500 words).

Order

In the previous sections, we have discussed the importance of the perspective used in descriptive writing, and we have shown how the selection of detail affects the focus. Now, we need to consider how to translate these aspects of sensory experiences into writing.

What we may experience simultaneously cannot be written simultaneously. As we have said, the reworking of these experiences into a linear written form requires authors to impose a structure or **order** on their description. Since many descriptions relate to appearance (and the visual sense), the obvious way of imposing order is through spatial organisation that guides the reader's eye over what is being described. There are three main conventions of spatial organisation. We can describe what we see:

1 **Horizontally** (from left to right, or from right to left);
2 **Vertically** (from above to below, or from below to above);
3 **Diagonally** (from one corner to another).

Other possibilities include moving from the **foreground to the background** (or vice versa), from the **centre to the extremities** (or vice versa), or even **clockwise** (or anti-clockwise).

These kinds of spatial conventions are evident in the following paragraph taken from David Lodge's humorous novel on academic life, *Changing Places*:

When he drew back the curtains in his living-room each morning, the view filled the picture window like a visual *tour de force* at the beginning of a Cinerama film. In the foreground, and to his right and left, the houses and gardens of the more affluent Euphoric faculty clung picturesquely to the sides of the Plotinus hills. Beneath him, where the foothills flattened out to meet the Bay shore, was the campus, with its white buildings and bosky paths, its campanile and plaza, its lecture rooms, stadia and laboratories, bordered by the rectilinear streets of downtown Plotinus. The Bay filled the middle distance, stretching out of sight on both sides, and one's eye naturally travelled in a great sightseeing arc: skimming along the busy Shoreline Freeway, swerving out across the Bay via the long Esseph Bridge (ten miles from toll to toll) to the city's dramatic skyline, dark downtown skyscrapers posed against white residential hills, from which it leapt across the graceful curves of the Silver Span suspension bridge, gateway to the Pacific, to alight on the green slopes of Miranda County, celebrated for its redwood forests and spectacular sea coast.

Lodge uses **space words and phrases** to guide the reader's eye over this view such as 'foreground', 'right and left', 'beneath', 'bordered', 'the middle distance' and 'stretching out of sight on both sides'. He is carefully controlling the details in this text and their spatial relationships to each other. (What might he mean by 'the great sightseeing arc'?)

While these conventions apply well to the description of a fixed object like a painting in a frame, a photograph in a newspaper or a view out of a window, they don't apply quite as easily in other situations where the edges are not so well defined. For instance, how might we describe what we see on a trip or a journey? We can of course use spatial terms to structure what we describe, but we may also need to use **time** because what is seen changes as the trip progresses.

In the following paragraph, Donald Horne describes a car trip he made to Arnhem land in the Northern Territory:

> On either side of the Arnhem Highway the brown spear grass is bent, or flattened, or burned out, with the only green coming from the delicate, bright leaves of the zamia plant. The Adelaide River flood plains are still waterlogged from the wet season, and we stop for a while beside the sedges of a swamp, looking at waving green grasses where barramundi surface and bubble in the water, rocking the lilies. On the broad swamp plain, clusters of buffalo shine in the mud and the tropical bamboo flashes yellow and gold. After we cross the wide, tidal waters of the Adelaide River with its crocodiles and sawfish and sharks, we are consumed in a whole landscape of waving grass and shining water where buffalo rest like clumps of rock.
>
> The big, wet-green plains suddenly end in thickets of pandanus and we are absorbed back into the monotony of trees, broken only by a few creeks and the appearance of a miserably thin dingo, but as we approach the South Alligator River the plants get greener and richer. Another glistening, outstretched flood plain bursts in front of us, green with clumps of buffalo in the waving grass and hundreds of egret and magpie geese. This greenness stops in another line of pandanus thickets and we are back in the dullness of trees. Ahead of us, a distant blue, we see the Arnhem Land Escarpment.

Spatial description does not have to be static. Notice that Horne is describing the journey as it unfolds by using spatial constructions like 'on the other side' and 'beside', but because what he sees is changing, he signals the new scenery with 'after we cross' and 'as we approach'. In addition, he describes the views he passes as if they themselves were moving and stopping: 'The big wet-green plains suddenly end'; 'the plants get greener and richer'; 'another glistening, outstretched flood plain bursts in front of us'; and 'this greenness stops'. Spatial relationships are not the only way of representing images in description. Temporal relationships may be used as well to account for changes in spatial orientation.

Exercise

Reread your description of the painting to find out how you ordered it. List any spatial terms you might have used, such as 'above, beneath, on the side, at the bottom, at the top, in the corner, in the centre, at the edges, beside, nearby'. Explain how you guided the reader around the painting. What kind of spatial relationships did you construct for the elements in the painting?

Imagery and sensory language

Writers of description use perspective, selection and order to portray mental impressions in words. There is, however, another aspect which needs to be considered. Writers of description, particularly subjective description, can use **sensory language** to create the mood or feeling they want to convey about what is being described. They can use adjectives, adverbs, phrases and clauses to add to the impression they are attempting to foster. In addition, they may choose to use similes and metaphors. Some of the pieces we have looked at already include examples. David Lodge uses a simile to describe the view which 'filled the picture window like a visual *tour de force* at the beginning of a Cinerama film'. Donald Horne also uses a simile for the buffalo which 'rest like clumps of rock'.

An extended example of metaphor occurs in this explanation of Aboriginal bark painting from a gallery catalogue, *Power of the Land*. Here, the author describes the medium itself as a metaphor for Aboriginal philosophy:

The bark medium serves as a metaphor for the way Aboriginal people view the world. Almost no other painting medium shares its bare, organic properties. The surface splits and bends and the ochre itself is ephemeral and evades absolute permanence.

The art form has a singular aesthetic of reticence and spiritual resonance based on the subtle modulation of ochre tones. It achieves stasis because the artists transmit a vision of land as icon in terms of its elements: raw earth colours on living tree. The land is rendered human, yet celestial, and is revealed in symbols as if through its bones.

Each piece of *Eucalyptus tetradonta* (stringy bark) has its own irregular texture and dimensions; these determine the artist's subject matter. It is as if the subject is latent in the piece of bark. The bark support is sculptural, like an organism that still wants to be a tree. Each edge has a living line— crooked, not exactly square. The surface has an uneven texture, adding resonance to the paint layer.

This type of extended metaphor is difficult to maintain and quickly becomes tedious. In this case, the author manages to keep the metaphor going. What characteristics of the bark medium is the author associating with Aboriginal thinking? Is the comparison effective? Why?

Description and academic writing

When we think of academic writing, we may not immediately think of description. The kinds of emotionally charged literary passages full of metaphors and adjectives and adverbs commonly associated with description do not seem to have a place in the writing of the scientist, the geographer, the sociologist or the psychologist. Nevertheless, while description may not be the main means of representation in academic writing, it is often used to support exposition and argument.

In the following extract, taken from the cultural studies text *Myths of Oz*, the authors John Fiske, Bob Hodge and Graeme Turner analyse the various meanings of the beach in Australian culture:

> The move from culture, the city, on the right to nature, the sea, on the left is effected through a number of zones. First there is the road, the public site of transition, and the boundary beyond which the car, that crucial cultural motif, cannot pass. Next comes grass, or more typically and significantly, lawn. Lawns invoke the natural, not nature: so it is appropriate that on them we find 'furniture': benches, which are either painted green to look 'natural' or left as 'natural' wood. The lawn is

the most cultured bit of the beach and may be most typically used by the old, or families with young children, who need the security of culture, or perhaps some shade to protect them from the sun. We may also find those we could uncharitably type the incorrigibly suburban who import their chairs, tables, rugs, trannies and sometimes even television to make the outdoors as much like indoors as possible. Although we may find the occasional group of sunbathers here, for most of its users this zone provides an easy transition towards nature. At the edge of the lawn we meet the esplanade, a concrete flat-topped wall that marks the boundary beyond which the sea is not allowed to come: like all boundaries it is a popular place to walk, a moment of balance in a sacred no-man's-land outside profane normality.

The perspective used in this text is not typical of all academic writing. By using pronouns such as 'we', the authors write themselves into the text in much the same way as the authors of this textbook are doing. Why might they do so? What kind of perspective is created? The details used for comment in the analysis of the beach have been chosen selectively. What else could have been included? How would these other things have contributed to the overall meaning?

The authors organise their analysis in spatial terms by dividing up the beach and its immediate vicinity into zones. They then treat each zone in turn, locating it in relationship to others, describing its features and then analysing its meanings. Time seems to freeze to a standstill in this analysis; the only progression is through space. The description of the zones of the beach becomes 'typical' and representative of all beaches. This type of freeze framing of time occurs frequently in academic texts where *generalisations* are to be inferred. We have seen another example of this earlier in Buchsbaum's description of the leg of the bee.

In a different type of academic writing, this time a history text, *Australia: The Quiet Continent*, Douglas Pike is using time as well as space as an organising principle to describe Australia's place in the world. As we will see in the next chapter, the use of time is inevitable when describing and recounting historical events:

Twice as far from England as South Africa and with no near neighbour such as Canada has, Australia is geographically an extension of South-east Asia. In bygone ages when sea levels were low, Australia's northern shore was separated from the

Asian mainland only by narrow straits that hindered the passage of animals, but not of migrating tribes. East of the deep Timor Trench, the present Arafura Sea and Torres Strait were dry, and a few early arrivals even reached Tasmania by land. Some fifteen thousand years ago rising sea levels stopped migration and isolated Australia. While the old world progressed, the sea guarded the mystery of the southern continent and held its native people in stone-age bondage. When the sea at last gave up its secret, the first comers from Europe were not impressed by the uninviting northern front that Australia turned towards the old world.

This paragraph describes how Australia became increasingly isolated by the encroaching sea using both geography and history. The geographical details include the use of spatial relationships like 'twice as far from England as South Africa', 'an extension of Southeast Asia', 'separated from the Asian mainland only by narrow straits'; the historical details rely on the use of time words like 'bygone ages', 'early arrivals', 'some fifteen thousand years ago', 'while' and 'when'. This text shows how both time and space can be used to develop and depict complex ideas.

Description is more than a record of observations about the world. It is a particular representation of the world which relies on **perspective, selection** and **order**. Where the author is situated in relation to the text and its subject matter, whether the author chooses to use a personal or an impersonal point of view, which details are to be included and which are to be left out, and how those details are to be arranged, are all important considerations to make when writing or analysing a descriptive text.

Exercises

1 Choose an area of academic research that interests you from the following list: sociology, psychology, history, anthropology, physiology, chemistry, biology, physics or medicine. Browse through the academic journals which are the most prominent in your chosen field. (You may need to ask a librarian to recommend the relevant titles.) Try to get an idea of how description functions in the articles by writing one paragraph answers to the following questions: When is description used? How often is it used? What kind of perspective is taken? Does the author use 'I'? Is the description always objective? Can you find any instances of subjective description? What kind of structure or order is used in the descriptive passages?

Bring the results of your research to class so you can compare and contrast the various areas. Are there any differences between, say, the humanities and the sciences?

2 Repeat the exercise, but this time focus only on English as a discipline. (Note that the study of English can incorporate literature, drama, literary theory, cultural studies, communication studies, mass media and composition. There are journals attached to each of these fields.) Once again, choose one of the listed areas, survey the appropriate journals and compare your findings with those of the class.

Works cited

Buchsbaum, Ralph (1948) *Animals Without Backbones: An Introduction to the Invertebrates*, Vol. 2, Penguin, Harmondsworth

Fiske, John, Bob Hodge, and Graeme Turner (1987) *Myths of Oz*, Allen and Unwin, Sydney

Gristwood, Sarah (1994) 'Mad Mel', *The Age*, 2 July

Horne, Donald (1978) *Right Way: Don't Go Back*, Sun Books, Melbourne

Lodge, David (1978) *Changing Places: A Tale of Two Campuses*, Penguin, Harmondsworth

Malouf, David (1976) *Johnno*, Penguin, Harmondsworth

Murphy, Damien (1994) 'Nightmare on Hindley Street', *The Bulletin*, 3 May

Palin, Michael (1994) 'Around the World in 80 Days', *The Weekend Australian Magazine*, 15–16 October

Pike, Douglas (1962) *Australia: The Quiet Continent*, Cambridge University Press, London

Power of the Land: Masterpieces of Aboriginal Art (1994) National Gallery of Victoria, Melbourne

Robbe-Grillet, Alain (1993) 'The Beach', in *The Picador Book of the Beach*, editor, Robert Drewe, Pan Macmillan, Sydney

3 Narration

Time and narration

Whereas description frequently depicts spatial links in writing, we could say that **narration** represents time relationships in language. We saw with description that there is no single or correct way to write about space or sensory impressions. Rather, variations in perspective, selection and order are crucial steps that authors take to achieve certain effects in the different kinds of description that they write.

Much the same can be said of narration: in varying details and viewpoints authors produce quite different types of **narratives**. A narrative is **an account of events that occur over time**. When we read or watch a narrative, whether it's a fictional story, film or television series, a historical chronicle, a newspaper report or a documentary, we can analyse these variations in order to gain a clearer understanding of the significance of the time relationships and meanings that are being set up in the text.

There is, of course, more to narration than time relationships by themselves. Any story that we read also involves **characters**, **actions** and background **setting**. Further, narration necessarily implies that someone is doing the narrating. A story always has a **storyteller**; so too a narrative always has a **narrator**, a figure whose point of view towards the characters and action can be an influential factor for readers in understanding the text.

Unlike description, which often freezes time in providing spatial information, in a narrative the detail which the narrator provides about characters, actions and so on is organised along a time axis. As we will see, the passing of time, whether it's fast or slow (for the tempo of narration can also vary), propels narration. Thus these two elements:

1 The narrator's point of view on characters and events, and
2 The time pattern and tempo used in the narrative

are the crucial components which structure narration. By analysing texts closely, we can note the ways in which time and narrative viewpoint are used to organise texts, and can practise and follow these techniques in our own writing.

Narration represents time relationships in language.

Every **narrative** is told by a **narrator** from a particular **point of view**.

Key elements that structure narration include **narrative viewpoint** and **tempo**, **character** and **action**.

Because time is central to the way all narratives function, before trying to analyse narration in depth it will be useful to consider some basic notions of time and their connections to language and writing.

Social time

Although we constantly think about events and actions in terms of time, time is not simply a natural phenomenon but is *socially* made and moulded. One of the main ways in which time is made is through various types of writing. Later in the chapter we will consider some of these, such as fictional stories, and some non-fictional types such as history and autobiography. In all these forms of writing, the authors actively construct a model of time for their readers to follow and interpret. Time becomes an important way for them to structure and organise their works and so affects the ways we respond.

To say that time is socially moulded means that we don't automatically think about it in a certain way. We are in fact taught to think about it in ways that are culturally dominant. These ways might include noting changes in the seasons or alterations in the moon; measured cycles of domestic or agricultural jobs; preserving and retelling histories and legends; or regularly checking the TV guide. All of these techniques of noting time involve more than one person; they are processes in which a number of people take part and so share a common sense of time. We become conscious of time through our interactions with others.

Hence time operates on a social level, and it's from that level that we pick up our ideas about it. How might these social ideas occur in writing and other types of texts? We can start to see how they function by examining some visual texts, where spatial and temporal features interact. Indeed, one of the points which will emerge as this chapter progresses is the way in which descriptive and narrative elements in texts often work together.

The spatial organisation of texts often carries implications about time. Cartoon strips are one example of the way that spatial and temporal aspects of texts interact with each other. As a cartoon moves across the page from left to right we assume that time is progressing. Each frame or spatial unit is thought of independently, as showing one unit of time. This unit leads to the next, and so on. In cartoon strips space and time seem to work together to communicate the message.

Figure 3.1a

Figure 3.1b

The two aspects do not, however, always work in harmony. Sometimes space and time seem to come into conflict in cartoon strips, as in the examples by cartoonist Matthew Martin. In the first cartoon, an inexperienced or maybe a drunk pilot is trying to land a plane. The passing of time suggested by each frame finally turns our perception of space upside down. The strip's use of time reveals that our initial understanding of its space was wrong. Similarly, in the second, we see two office workers clock watching— maybe it's Friday afternoon. At first, the space and time of the cartoon seem to be working together. The ticks represent the passing of time spatially and visually; they seem to be symbols of time. However, the last frame reveals that these ticks are words written on the wall, not symbols of time at all. Each one isn't a different second going by, but the same word standing still. The space and time depicted in the strip work to question each other and to unsettle the way we usually read cartoons.

These kinds of trick cartoon strips are interesting because they reveal some of the things we take for granted about the ways space and time are represented in texts. They show that what we consider to be normal, even natural understandings of space and time are in fact social and textual **conventions** or patterns of usage with which we have become very familiar. We have mentioned some of these conventions are present already in cartoon strips, for example, that time is passing as we read from left to right, that each bit of the present is separate from the others. Yet as these two cartoons show, even our most basic ideas about space and time—up is up and not down, seconds pass and don't stand still, each second is new and different from the others—can suddenly be altered or challenged. So not only do authors and artists use time to structure and organise their work, but our understanding of time is also produced, reinforced and occasionally challenged by texts.

Another area where there are important links between time and language is in speech. Again, this importance is based on socially accepted conventions which we use when speaking. Time is manifested in spoken language in three main ways:

1 The speed at which we speak.
2 How long we speak for.
3 The timing of what we say.

First, in regard to speed, in different social situations different talking speeds are used. Contrast the tempo of a race-caller to the deliberate cadence of someone performing a marriage ceremony or an actor presenting a soliloquy in a play by Shakespeare. Often the seriousness of a situation demands that we speak slowly, or that we do so urgently. In another context, to speak quickly may be a sign of nervousness or anxiety and may undermine our intentions.

Different situations seem to require that we speak for varying lengths of time. An election campaign may call for long, or long-winded, political statements. In this context, short speeches may be a sign of ignorance. By contrast, in more informal social situations, we can easily offend people if we talk to them for too long or if we don't talk to them for long enough.

Finally, the timing of what we say—or *when* we speak—can be crucial in personal relationships. We cannot interrupt someone or talk out of turn. Often we might start to say something and then quickly stop, sensing that we have trespassed on to someone else's turf. The importance of timing to stand-up comedians exemplifies this link between time and language. If they measure their first punchline, the joke succeeds and a rapport develops with the audience, but if the first joke is mistimed the whole routine is in jeopardy.

Thus time can be central to some of the important social effects we create through language. Conventions of time and timing in spoken and written texts convey many ideas about the subject matter and the speaker or author to the audience. These ideas arise in addition to the structuring effects that time has in narrative texts. It is to these that we now turn.

Narration and chronology

We have seen that time can have various kinds of social implications and meanings in language. The dominant notion of time which affects the way we structure written texts is, however, that of **chronology**—that time moves through discrete periods from past to present to future. As we will see, chronological order plays an important role in many types of writing, which move from beginning to end.

Some cultures conceive of time in non-chronological terms. In his studies of Indonesian society, the American anthropologist Clifford Geertz noted that the Balinese idea of time is qualitative rather than quantitative: that is, people consider when it is a good time to do things instead of only calculating how much time will be needed for something. Nonetheless, chronological time is the dominant model of time in Western thinking, and our conventional understanding of it. Hence it plays an important role in narration, forming the structural basis of many different kinds of narrative.

> **Chronology** structures narratives as a progression of events from a beginning to an end.

The most obvious influence of chronology on narration is on basic plot structure. The progression of a story from beginning through middle to end parallels the sequence of past, present and future. An obvious instance of this structure is found in obituary articles in newspapers, commemorating a well-known person. Typically such articles recount the person's life and achievements, starting from their childhood and youth, moving through the middle and often most successful period of their lives, and then noting their last years. Colin Horne's obituary of the English professor and crime fiction writer J.I.M. Stewart, in *The Australian*, is a clear example:

> He was born in Edinburgh, the son of the director of education. As a boy Stewart studied both classics and English at the Edinburgh Academy before proceeding to Oxford in 1925. His distinguished undergraduate career led to his appointment as assistant lecturer in English at Leeds University (1930–35). There he was discovered by Sir William Mitchell, the ever-vigilant vice-chancellor of Adelaide, and imported as a fledgling scholar to succeed the august Sir Archibald Strong as only the second jury professor of English language and literature...

All of these events occurred in the past, and the narrative moves from earlier to later periods of Stewart's life in chronological order. Distinctions between events are made through the careful use of **time words and phrases** which, along with specific dates, order the sequence of Stewart's activities: 'was born ... As a boy ... led to his appointment ... to succeed'. All the verbs in the above excerpt are in the past tense, but the manipulation of time words and phrases enables readers to note the progression and changes in the subject's life.

> Narration uses **verb tense** and **time words and phrases** to structure and depict the time relationships between events.

Exercises

1 Write a 500-word biography of your favourite author. Try to establish a clear chronological order for the important events in his or her life.

2 Compose a short story in which a character travels back in time in order to prevent an accident occurring to his or her great-grandparents. Can you capture the character's mixed knowledge of the present and past?

Narrating time

Narrative fiction often makes careful use of time phrases. They serve numerous functions from structuring the text to giving insight into characters' feelings. Analysis of the following passage from David Malouf's novel *The Great World* reveals a range of these effects:

> All the months she was pregnant she had felt wonderfully separate and self-contained. She had eaten what she liked, slept till midday, spent her afternoons stretched out in the sun; with none of her usual restlessness, and none of the vexations either that went with her 'difficult' nature. And there was no selfishness in it, because she was no longer thinking only of herself.
>
> Separate, but at the same time connected and in the line of something: real *forces*, by which she meant forces that were outside her will.
>
> Time, for instance.
>
> The clock that had begun ticking in her, which was perfectly synchronised to the sun, was real time, not just clock time, and it synchronised her as well. It could not be stopped or slowed or quickened...
>
> One afternoon, in the dreamy state she fell into under the blazing sun, she had had a vision of herself as a cloud, so light and transparent that she might have dissolved or risen up and floated. But inside the cloud, far off in a spotlight at the very centre of it, a little figure was performing, not for an audience, not at all, but for himself...
>
> For months, with her eyes screwed up against the sun, her feet propped on the arms of a squatter's chair and a jug of Meggsie's lemon drink at her elbow, she had watched him perform. He was very small and far off at first, but the far-offness had to do with time, not space. He grew as he got closer; till he was so close she no longer had to squint to make him out.

Never for a moment in all this did she feel anxious for him, or for herself either. She would not float away and he would not fall. They were held, both of them.

And she did not have to feel impatient either. He was moving in his own time and would not be hurried. *He* was the clock. Somewhere up ahead, at a point they had not yet arrived at, he was already sitting up in his high-chair and banging with a spoon. All she had to do was wait the days out till they were there.

The focal character is Lucille, and during her pregnancy she experiences time in an intense way. The narrative registers this intensity through a combination of time words, phrases and verbs. It also follows a chronological order, tracing the build-up in Lucille's bond with the baby. She feels different emotions as time passes. Time is the pretext, the basic motive which underlies her changing thoughts, feelings and actions—from sleeping to eating to sensing the baby's growth.

This motive is represented through the careful use of time references, which can be very flexible in focus. They refer to the passing of seconds and minutes: 'the clock that had begun ticking in her', 'Never for a moment'; to the time of day: 'slept till midday', 'One afternoon'; to the time of year: 'All the months', 'For months'. The references create an awareness of the scene and context for readers, and this varies from a larger perspective—time of day and year—to perceiving the character's immediate experience moment by moment.

These two perspectives combine to convey a chronological progression through the narrative. This is represented in two ways: first, as the objective passing of time, day to day and month to month; second, as Lucille's personal impression of this period. Interestingly, these two notions of chronology are played off against each other: 'The clock that had begun ticking in her . . . was real time, not just clock time.' On the one hand, time is constant and cannot be forgotten, but on the other, it means far more than the continuous passing of seconds. It is her baby himself: '*He* was the clock.' The text contrasts the character's personal awareness of time against time as an abstract system.

Two further aspects of the narration-chronology connection should be noted here. The first involves comparing the time of events being narrated to the time when the narration is taking place. This relationship can be analysed by noting the tense of verbs being used. Is it past, present or future? As is the case with many novels, in Malouf's *The Great World*, the main tense used is the past: 'She *submitted* herself to it and *felt* no violation'—that is, the narration occurs after the events seem to have taken place. But narration can also occur as events appear to happen (an eye-witness account), or before events have occurred (a prediction, projection or 'guess-timate').

Distinctions between different kinds of narration can be made on the basis of verb tense. As will be seen in some later examples, history writing predominantly employs the past tense. By contrast, a fortune-teller uses the future tense to foresee any destined personal success and tall dark strangers; a campaigning politician's narrative of social success also uses the future tense, as does a doctor's prognosis of a patient's condition. Accordingly, we can say that the predominant verb tense may affect the certainty or assurance of both the narrative's subject matter and readers' responses. Texts about things that have already occurred seem, on the surface at least, to have a more definite tone than do forecasts of future events.

The second aspect of the chronology-narration link to consider here is the correspondence between the **tempo** of the narration and the events. In the Malouf excerpt, the speed with which events are recounted changes. The tempo varies according to the intensity of Lucille's experience. Contrast the openings of the fifth and sixth paragraphs: 'One afternoon . . . she had had a vision of herself as a cloud'; 'For months . . . she had watched him perform.' The first specifies a particular occasion, and the tempo of narration slows down to record the character's impressions at the same rate as they occur. In the next paragraph the narrative speeds up and generalises about Lucille's perceptions. The narrative moves much faster than the events it is recounting, for here the changes over time are more important than the one-off action of the baby.

The shifting tempo of narration is one of the main ways through which texts involve readers' own thoughts and feelings. Indeed, one of the important functions of time in narrative is *to propel the interest of readers*, to make them read on. Time creates **suspense**, a sense of something unknown or about to happen, as in this example from the opening of Jean Warmbold's novel, *Dead Man Running*:

> But when I tried getting in touch out of San Francisco, the number came up disconnected. And his address traced down to that deserted bungalow west of Colston this afternoon. How to add anything up? Especially when considering that Frank's wire arrived two short days ago with no hints whatever of an impending move.

> There is always the possibility that he is giving me the intentional slip. But then, why the telegram? That had never been Frank's style, to say one thing and mean another. Leastways, not the Frank I once knew...

Suspense is generated through the narrator's uncertainty about the discrepancy between her expectations and experience. It is captured by the verb tenses, which shift between past and present— 'tried, came, traced, arrived, knew' and 'is, is giving'—and the spectrum of time references, first to a more distant past, then to 'two short days ago', as well as to the present. These time variations also make *us* aware of what we don't know, and we read on, hoping that the text's future will reveal all.

To sum up the way time organises Malouf's and Warmbold's texts, we could say that the movement of time *drives* the narration. The continuity of events is based on the flow of time that is presented, but this flow isn't necessarily even and smooth. Time seems to speed up and to slow down. For authors do not always represent every instant of it. Time in narration is structured to depict what the author judges as the *significant* events. Some periods are omitted altogether. In the excerpt from Malouf's novel the important events occur when Lucille is conscious of her baby, and other events and phases during the nine months are omitted or only briefly mentioned.

We could compare this writing technique to the use of slow motion replays. In sport telecasts, for example, a replay is used to highlight the important moves; in films slow motion is used to let us see a dramatic scene clearly and to heighten suspense. The slowed-down parts of a written or visual text thus gain *meaningful emphasis*.

This pattern of omission and emphasis is sometimes called the 'telescoping of time'. Like selections and inclusions in descriptive writing, it is one of the chief ways that authors make distinctions in order to focus on the most important phenomena in a narrative.

Exercises

1 Write the opening paragraph to a mystery novel, in which you tell of a crime that has just been committed although its motive and the person who did it are unknown.
2 Compose a 300-word narrative in which a character 'flashes back' to recall an important past event in detail.

Point of view

We noted earlier that every narrative has a narrator. This is as much to say that every narrative is told from a *specific viewpoint*. As is the case in description, the notion of point of view in narration has a number of meanings. The first is linked to the time structure in a narrative:

1 Is the narrator's viewpoint before, after or simultaneous with the events being recounted?

The second is based on the narrator's involvement with the action and characters:

2 Is the narrator writing about events in which he or she or someone else takes part? (This relates to *first person* narration, '*I did it*', or *third person* narration, '*He/she/it/they* did it'.)

The third concerns the narrator's attitude towards or opinions on the events:

3 What kind of judgements about the subject matter does the narrator's viewpoint involve?

In this section we will examine the three aspects of point of view in narration, paying particular attention to the ways in which they can overlap. Each aspect affects our interpretations of the narrative.

Point of view combines the narrator's **involvement in** and **attitude towards** the subject matter.

Biography and autobiography are two of the main non-fictional types of writing in which features of narration such as chronological order and point of view play central structuring roles. Like obituaries, biographies tend to follow chronological order in recounting the experiences of their subject. This tendency often results in the use of the past tense to narrate events and thoughts in a person's life which have already occurred. Here is an example from David Marr's biography of Patrick White:

Belief came as a democratic revelation. White believed *everyone* had faith, even those who could not admit to it themselves. He held that this personal connection to God, admitted or denied, was the sustaining force in all lives. Such faith humbled him. His old fear and ridicule of the rough lives lived around Dogwoods was overlaid by a sense of common humanity under God, 'I felt the life was, on the surface, so dreary, ugly, monotonous, there must be something hidden in it to give it a purpose, and so I set out to find a secret core, and *The Tree of Man* emerged.' He saw the book as an expression of his new faith, but searched to find a new language in which to clothe this Christian impulse, 'to try to convey a religious faith through symbols and situations which can be accepted by people today'.

The narrator uses the past tense to set White's experiences back in time. Within this past setting, contrasts can still be drawn between what White has started to believe and what he used to believe: 'His old fear and ridicule . . . was overlaid'. The use of the adjective 'old' also helps this change to be noted, just as in the following lines, the adjective 'new' suggests the writer's ongoing efforts, 'to find a new language'. Hence, although the text is written fully in the past tense, time variations in the past can still be recorded.

In this passage the narrator's point of view is sympathetic to the subject matter. Marr does not assume an attitude to White's changed faith that differs from White's own opinion; he even uses the latter's words to explain what is involved. Here the biographer becomes a kind of channel for the character's viewpoint, though elsewhere in the book a separate perspective does come into play, 'As he grew weaker he shed his anger, but he remained entirely himself: curious, tart, demanding, very funny and alert.' In this instance, the narrator tells what is happening as well as suggesting his own view of White's personality.

The narrator's point of view may, however, have a more conspicuous role, actively judging and evaluating events and characters. The narrator in Dorothy Hewett's autobiography plays this kind of role:

I work a forty-five-hour week—five hours' compulsory overtime for £8; often not even that, because if I am five minutes late I am docked fifteen minutes by order of the bundy at the gate. As we eat our lunch, sitting out in the concrete yard, the cyclone-wire fence pressing its pattern into our shoulder blades, I try to raise the consciousness of my fellow workers. 'Get off your soapbox, Skin,' they call good-naturedly . . .

I have become the delegate on the job for a vicious, right-wing union who meet only once a year and if the rank

and file are seen at the union meeting, immediately report
them back to the boss.

In detailing working conditions at this factory, the narrator's viewpoint is implicitly critical. She does not openly say that she
objected to the conditions, but the selection of detail, especially the
loss of wages for being a little late, reveals her opinion. At the
same time, the narrator suggests solidarity with her co-workers
even if they do not share her commitment; they speak 'good-
naturedly' against her outlook in contrast to the 'vicious' opposition
of the union. The adverb and adjective are significant markers of
the narrator's viewpoint. They show that she is evaluating the
action at the same time as she recounts it. The narrative reveals a
political perspective on personal events.

The other aspects of point of view support these effects. In
contrast to the narration of Patrick White's life, this narrative uses
the past and present tense: 'I work...I am docked...I try...I
have become.' Although written years after the events have taken
place, the present tense gives the action a kind of immediacy, as if
it has just occurred. When combined with the first person pronoun
'I', the present tense also suggests that the author retains her
earlier viewpoint and opinions on events as she writes. The effect
is to reinforce the criticism of the working conditions and the
union by implying the consistency of the narrator's position.

At times, however, narrative point of view can also grow
more complex. A rift may appear between the narrator's perspective
and the character's, even if as here, they seem to be the 'same'
person or 'I' in the text. The viewpoint of Hewett's narrator becomes
self-critical or at least self-questioning:

> I was already well on the way to becoming that most
> dangerous and humourless of creatures, a martyr to a cause.
> I actually wanted to suffer in the cause of the working class.
> But I couldn't help lingering in front of shop windows, lusting
> after the latest fashions. Soon it would be too late and I would
> be too old to wear them. But then I would dismiss these
> thoughts as unworthy, the last twitch of a buried self...

The narrator reflects on the apparent contradiction between her
interests in fashion and in being a martyr to the workers. She implies
that both urges are linked to a younger self-indulgence. Hence
although the two figures of narrator and character are referred to
by the single pronoun 'I', they have different outlooks on 'themselves'.

This contrast cannot be registered by the one pronoun, so verb tense comes importantly into play. There is no present tense in this passage; instead, the past is used to suggest a gap between the narrator's earlier and current attitudes. Verb tense becomes the significant marker of the narrator's point of view on her own past behaviour.

The narrator can manipulate point of view by a combination of tense, pronouns, adjectives and adverbs. In doing so, the narrator establishes connections to the action and characters and also to the *readers*. For in most cases, a narrator invites or expects us to share his or her viewpoint. Thus the final effect of point of view we should note is that it works to **position** readers to understand a narrative in particular terms. In a way, readers find themselves included in the text, guided towards the narrator's perspective. As an example of this effect, here is Jack McPhee's account of working in the Pilbara in the north of Western Australia. Note the way the narrator creates a set of relationships between himself, his co-workers and hosts, before positioning the reader to join in the story:

> At night we'd all camp together and the Afghans would make a giant curry. When it was ready they would offer it to us first. We'd go over and help ourselves to as much as we wanted; we used to really pile our plates high because they were very good cooks. When we'd all finish getting our share they'd have a bit of a prayer, then wash their lips and fingers. Then they would sit round the curry and eat with their fingers from that one big bowl. That was their custom.
>
> They were very generous: you couldn't wish for better people. They wouldn't let you walk past without offering you something to eat or drink...

The direct appeal to the reader, as 'you', positions us to adopt the narrator's point of view. In telling its story, the narrative also becomes persuasive.

Exercises

1 Write a short narrative version of one of the cartoons included earlier in this chapter—one in the first person and present tense and one in the third person and past tense. What different effects and interpretations are produced by these variations?
2 Rewrite a newspaper report in the first person and change its verb tense from past to present (or present to past, depending on the original). Do these changes make the report seem less

or more reliable? Rewrite the first excerpt from Dorothy Hewett's biography as a news report on working conditions. Which aspects do you have to change and why?

Narration, grammar and academic writing

In analysing the various extracts in previous pages and doing some of the exercises, we have tended to focus on the way that grammar works to order and structure narratives. Every aspect of narration from chronological order to tempo to point of view is organised through points of grammar such as verb tense, pronouns, adverbs and adjectives. As we have seen, one of the important effects of these grammatical features is that they *position* readers to interpret the text in certain terms.

Hence an awareness of grammar helps us both to analyse narrative effects in other texts and write lucid narratives ourselves. For us to be able to perceive time in language it must be there, coded into the text. *Time is recorded in language through grammar.* Therefore we need to use the relevant parts of grammar consistently to ensure that the time relationships in our writing match our thoughts and are clear to the reader. Grammar allows us to put time down on paper.

In academic writing, the link between grammar and time becomes important whenever we wish to give *historical* details about the material we are discussing. History writing is another one of the main non-fictional types where narration plays a central role. But we use narration in our work even if we are not specifically studying history. Explaining the development of a psychological theory; interpreting the links between Victorian novels and society; analysing traditions in an indigenous culture—all these areas of study and writing (as well as many others) involve the techniques of narration that we have been observing throughout this chapter.

As an example of narration in academic writing we will focus on some history texts. In most cases, history depends on chronology in interpreting and explaining the order and influence of events. Here is a paragraph from G.C. Bolton's account of the white advance into north Queensland:

But the main trend of pastoral expansion was northward. Between 1873 and 1877 Greenvale, Cashmere and Gunnawarra stations were carved from outlying blocks of the Valley of Lagoons, and Kangaroo Hills and Christmas Creek were formed on its borders. Meanwhile Hann's discoveries and the

Palmer rush were attracting squatters to the country beyond. On the western side of the Peninsula the formation of Wrotham Park in 1873 was followed by the occupation of much of the Lower Mitchell, in several instances by pastoralists from the Bowen district. The Palmer rush attracted from 1874 several graziers hopeful of supplying the Maytown and Cooktown markets. Prospecting journeys by James Venture Mulligan in 1874 and 1875 drew attention to the lands on the Upper Mitchell, which were first occupied by James Fraser in 1876. The next year saw John Atherton overlanding with his family to take up Emerald End, near the present town of Mareeba. His run included a tableland, then almost impenetrably scrub-covered, to which his name was given. Close on his heels came George Clarke, one of the discoverers of Charters Towers, to claim for Frank Stubley, one of the new magnates of that golden city, much of what has since been known as the Evelyn Tableland. During the next three years there was a minor rush for country north and south of the Atherton Tableland.

Bolton places events in a temporal order, putting some before others or at the same time. He generalises about events, not referring to the specific hour or date of their occurrence but to a larger time pattern, over a period of years, when settlers and squatters were exploring and taking over the land. Verbs are consistently in the past tense, implying that these activities have long since finished, though their continuing impact is also recognised, at least in terms of placenames ('to which his name was given', 'has since been known').

Due to this perspective on the events, which is registered in the past tense, the historian perceives an order and pattern in them. His relative time and place in history seem to offer a perfect vantage point on the past. This vantage point might be questioned. Bolton could be seen as imposing a pattern on to events which may have occurred more randomly. Even if this possibility is not raised, we would still conclude that by ordering the action in this way the historian is able to write his history. In so doing he may create a chronology which is only one possible version of events relating to the white settlement of north Queensland.

The narrator's point of view can become more active in historical writing; it may start to evaluate or judge the narrated events. The effect is then similar to what we saw in Dorothy Hewett's autobiography, where the narrator offers a political interpretation of some of her experiences. Katie Spearitt's account of marriage in colonial Queensland also uses chronological ordering and the past tense to present information but then switches to the present tense when a conclusion is being drawn:

> Sex-segregation in the colonial Queensland workforce, as in other colonies, was acute. In 1891 women represented less than ten per cent of paid workers within each of the occupational groups of government, commerce and transport, and pastoral and agricultural. On the other hand, over 70 per cent of workers in the personal service sphere and over 65 per cent in the textile manufacturing sector were women. The plethora of women in the textile class as workers rather than dealers is a sobering demonstration of women's limited economic autonomy.

The present tense marks a point which the narrator is trying to make. It reveals a shift from recounting what happened to interpreting its significance.

In ordering events in time and interpreting them, history is similar to all narration. It gives certain emphases; selects, telescopes and compresses events; manipulates verb tense and point of view. The result of history writing is a particular narrative, involving character and action, viewpoint and tempo. Chronological ordering is only one part of its narrative process, and the other aspects and effects can be ascertained by considering its use of the main features of narration.

Time is not simply a natural condition but is produced through social conceptions of order and patterns in events. Time is not a given, but is constructed in various ways. In writing, time is represented and used in ways that match the understanding of it that is dominant in the author's social context. For most Western writers, the dominant understanding of time is based on chronological order.

Chronological order is therefore employed as a structuring principle in many types of writing such as fictional narratives and non-fictional autobiography, history, and journalism. In all of these types, time is not represented or used as a continuous, even flow, second by second. Instead, it is altered and manipulated, sped up or slowed down, as a means of emphasising certain events and actions which the author judges as significant. Through time the author can present an order or pattern of significance in the subject matter.

In representing all these possible patterns and variations, authors impose certain time structures and orders on the material they are writing about. Because of this imposition, the differences between fictional and non-fictional narration or writing is less than we might automatically assume. The word *history* has 'story' inside it, and this hints at the similar sorts of temporal patterns which factual and creative writing use.

As academic readers and writers, it's important that we pay attention to these features—the use of verbs and time words and phrases—so as to note the organisation of time in texts. Time patterns and order don't appear magically in writing but are generated by an author's use of grammar. Therefore if we wish our readers to be clear on the order of events and actions we must represent them in consistent grammatical terms.

Exercise

In an 800-word essay, compare the narrative techniques used in a short story and a newspaper report. Which text gives you a stronger sense of 'being there'? Explain the reasons for your choice.

Works cited

Bolton, G.C. (1963) *A Thousand Miles Away: A History of North Queensland to 1920*, Jacaranda Press, Brisbane

Hewett, Dorothy (1990) *Wild Card: An Autobiography 1923–1958*, McPhee Gribble, Ringwood

Horne, Colin (1994) 'Revered Don of Crime Fiction', *The Australian* 30 November

Malouf, David (1991) *The Great World*, Picador, Sydney

Marr, David (1992) *Patrick White: A Life*, Vintage, Sydney

Martin, Matthew (1985) Cartoons, in *Probably The Last of Stay in Touch*, editor, David Dale, Horan Wall and Walker, Sydney

Morgan, Sally (1989) *Wanamurraganya: The Story of Jack McPhee*, Fremantle Arts Centre Press, Fremantle

Spearitt, Katie (1990) 'The Market for Marriage in Colonial Queensland', *Hecate* 16: 23–42

Warmbold, Jean (1991) *Dead Man Running*, Virago, London

4 Exposition

Chapters 2 and 3 reviewed two ways of representing ideas in writing. We saw that **description** translates sensory impressions into language and that **narration** transforms events into stories. Whereas descriptive writing usually relies on space as its organising principle, narration uses time. In this chapter, we will be introducing a third mode of representation, **exposition**, and discussing its functions and main methods of organisation.

The primary purpose of exposition is to provide information through explanation. Accordingly, we can define exposition in the following way:

> **Exposition** is the representation of explanation in language.

As such, it is a mode of writing we come across very often in our everyday lives, in texts of all kinds from daily newspapers and textbooks to operating manuals.

Explanation

Articles in newspapers use exposition to **explain** the news. This is particularly evident in feature articles where significant events are given more attention than is possible in news stories. In these articles, personality profiles and interviews may used to explain the behaviour and attitudes of prominent people from rock stars to royalty; scientific research may be used to explain natural disasters like droughts, floods or earthquakes; expert opinion may be used to explain trends evident in crime outbreaks, traffic patterns, television watching, shopping habits, or educational opportunities.

Textbooks, too, convey information to their readers through explanation. Introductory textbooks often endeavour to explain a whole discipline to students. The following extract from *Psychology* by Henry Gleitman, a textbook for first year students, explains the breadth of inquiry covered by the field of psychology:

> What is psychology? It is a field of inquiry that is sometimes defined as the science of mind, sometimes as the science of behavior. It concerns itself with how and why organisms do what they do. Why wolves howl at the moon and sons rebel against their fathers; why birds sing and moths fly into the flame; why we remember how to ride a bicycle twenty years after the last try; why humans speak and make love and war. All of these are behaviors and psychology is the science that studies them all.

Not all textbooks will be so general in scope. More advanced textbooks will confine themselves to explaining just one part of a particular field. If we stay with the example of psychology, we could expect to find other textbooks (for second year students and later) devoted to narrower topics like personality disorders, childhood behaviour, experimental design and the like. All of these texts would be expository because they would all intend to explain details and information.

Operating instructions are also examples of exposition. They differ from the previous examples in that they explain a *process* rather than a field of inquiry or a news event. Whether we are trying to find out how to operate a new toaster or a new computer, we will be expecting to find an explanation of the process involved. However, this is not confined to the operating instructions of machines. Other examples of this kind of exposition, where explanation of a process is involved, include many other texts like 'how to vote' pamphlets which explain procedures at elections, or 'new student' guides that explain enrolment procedures at tertiary institutions, or even recipes.

Structuring exposition

So far, we have given examples of exposition without saying anything about how it may be organised or structured. Just like description and narration, exposition relies on logical organisation for **unity** and **coherence**. Unlike description and narration, however, which each use one main method of organisation, exposition has several. The choices available will depend on the nature of the subject that is to be explained. Some of the techniques we have already covered in description and narration may be useful in certain circumstances.

Sometimes the best way of explaining something is to describe it. In the next example from another textbook, *Physiology of Behavior*, Neil Carlson is explaining the principles of a cathode ray tube in an oscilloscope. This piece uses spatial relationships to explain how the machine functions:

> This device contains an electron gun, which emits a focused stream of electrons toward the face of the tube. A special surface on the inside of the glass converts some of the energy of the electrons into a visible spot of light. Electrons are negatively charged and are thus attracted to positively charged objects and repelled by negatively charged ones. The plate arranged above and below the electron beam, and on each side, can be electrically charged, thus deflecting the beam and directing it to various places on the face of the tube. The dot can thus be moved independently by the horizontal and vertical deflection plates.
>
> The deflection plates that move the beam horizontally are usually attached to a timing circuit that sweeps the beam from left to right at a constant speed. Simultaneously, the output of the biological amplifier moves the beam up and down. We thus obtain a graph of electrical activity as a function of time.

Like the examples discussed in the chapter on description, spatial organisation is a feature of this text. References to the horizontal and vertical directions, to left and right and up and down orientations, are all 'space' words. Certainly this text is descriptive, but because it has an over-riding function of explanation, we would classify it as exposition.

For some other texts, the best way to explain might be to use chronological order, that is, to provide a narrative. The following extract explains the usefulness of Windows software by tracing the development of the PC revolution:

> In 1981, IBM released its first personal computer, Microsoft released MS-DOS, and the PC revolution began. Throughout the 1980s, millions of users learned to issue a variety of MS-DOS commands and to use a variety of applications.
>
> By the end of the decade, most users had a word processor, a spreadsheet, and possibly a database application they used regularly. In fact, most users were seeking an easy way to exchange information between applications—a method that would eliminate the need to end one application before

looking up information stored by another.

In 1990, Microsoft introduced Windows 3.0, a program designed to maximize productivity. Windows 3.0 made computers easier to use, applications easier to learn, and allowed several applications to run at the same time. And—perhaps more importantly—it provided a simple means of information exchange between applications. Windows is a *graphical environment*: its menus, icons (meaningful symbols), and dialog boxes replace the often cryptic commands that MS-DOS requires.

In 1992, Microsoft released Windows 3.1, which provides object links to help applications share data: TrueType fonts, which you can size to any height and print exactly as they appear on the screen; enhanced help; and even an online tutorial. Windows 3.1 brings multimedia to the PC world. If your PC has a sound board, a CD-ROM, and a MIDI device, Windows 3.1 provides you with the ability to record, edit, and play video and sounds. In addition, Windows 3.1 lets you assign specific sounds to various system events.

Just as the 1980s saw the PC revolution, the 1990s are seeing the Windows revolution.

This example reads like a narrative, but narration is not the main function here. Once again, the most important function is explanation. How well does this example explain the usefulness of the software product? Is it effective? There are other ways the writer could have given the same information. The writer could have just listed the uses for Windows. Would such a list convey the same amount of information? What would be missing?

Although descriptive and narrative techniques can be used in writing expository texts, spatial or temporal logic will not be appropriate for all instances where an explanation needs to be constructed. Once again, the nature of the subject matter often suggests the most appropriate means of structuring and developing an explanation. Before we can expand on the various ways of developing exposition, however, we need to think about some of the basic structural elements of texts: sentences and paragraphs, the building blocks of exposition and indeed all modes of writing.

Sentences

Sentences are the primary structures we use to present ideas in written texts such as essays. A sentence can be defined as a sequence of words which forms a grammatically independent unit.

There are three basic types of sentence: the **simple** sentence, the **compound** sentence and the **complex** sentence. Each uses a different grammatical structure. They also present ideas in varying ways and relationships to one another.

A **simple sentence contains one independent clause**, that is, it contains a single subject-verb connection which expresses one main idea. The following sentences are all simple sentences:

The wombat fell asleep on the road.

Licensed restaurants serve alcohol on their premises.

You can put your groceries in a supermarket trolley.

A **compound sentence contains two or more independent clauses**. It is usually a string of simple sentences linked together with co-ordinating conjunctions like 'and, but, or, nor, for, yet':

The wombat fell asleep on the road and the truck nearly ran over it.

Licensed restaurants serve alcohol, but unlicensed establishments do not.

You can put your groceries in a supermarket trolley or you can stagger around with them in your arms.

The co-ordinating conjunction is used to allow ideas of equal significance to be expressed. In the first sentence the 'and' suggests the sequence of events, in the second the 'but' demonstrates a contrast, and in the third the 'or' provides an alternative.

Note that we need to be careful about the over-use of co-ordinating conjunctions, especially the over-use of 'and' to join separate ideas. People often say 'and' to link separate ideas or thoughts in conversations. Compound sentences which use 'and' to join strings of independent clauses can sound colloquial or even simplistic since this structure is similar to the way we talk. Consequently, a sentence which consists of a series of 'and' conjunctions will sound spontaneous rather than planned and should be used sparingly in academic writing.

Another way of linking independent clauses in a compound sentence is with the correlatives 'either...or, neither...nor, both...and, not only...but also'. Just as with the co-ordinating conjunctions, these constructions link **equivalent** ideas.

The **complex sentence has one independent and at least one dependent clause**. This type of sentence develops more complicated relationships than is possible with either the simple or the compound sentence. It relates ideas in terms of their *relative significance*. The main idea is expressed in the independent or **main** clause and the related but less significant idea is expressed in the dependent or **subordinate** clause. Subordination in complex sentences has the opposite effect to co-ordination in compound sentences. Whereas compound sentences create equivalence, complex sentences create an **order of significance**.

The main subordinating conjunctions include words like 'because, if, until, after, before, while, although, though'. In the following sentences, the order of significance is created by the subordinating conjunctions (the main clauses are in bold print):

The students went to a party (*main clause*) although they had an assignment due (*subordinate clause*).

I stayed home (*main clause*) because I had a cold (*subordinate clause*).

After we visited the art gallery (*subordinate clause*), **we went shopping** (*main clause*).

Other types of subordinating relationships are constructed in complex sentences using **relative pronouns**, 'that, who, whom, which' (again the main clauses are in bold print):

The actor, who had made so many movies, **died a lonely, broken man.**

My friend, whom I had met at school, **visited me in hospital.**

She bought the lap-top computer which came with a large screen.

Here the subordinate clauses are adding information to the main clauses rather than creating a sense of significance; nevertheless the information that is added is of a secondary kind.

Being able to recognise and write all three types of sentences is important in order to add variety to our writing and to enable us to develop and express ideas. The categorisation of sentences into simple, compound and complex is a grammatical one, but there is another way of thinking about sentences that will also help develop our writing skills. We can categorise sentences according to how they *create their meaning*, whether they make meaning by steadily adding information or whether they suspend their meaning until the end.

The first kind, the **loose** sentence, is one in which the main clause occurs at the beginning and is elaborated through the use of modifiers, co-ordinate or subordinate constructions. In this case, meaning is said to be constructed *cumulatively*. A good way to recognise a loose sentence is that we could stop reading it before its end and still have some sense of what it is about. Many types of writing uses sentences of this type. An example is:

> Politicians seek interviews during election campaigns, with those journalists who are most likely be sympathetic to their cause.

In this sentence the main idea, 'politicians seek interviews' is extended steadily through the sentence, but its sense is already apparent.

On the other hand, **periodic** sentences create suspense and add emphasis. This construction delays the final meaning for as long as possible, usually by placing the main idea of a complex sentence *after* the subordinate clause or clauses. In the next example, the periodic structure prevents the sentence from being understood until the end:

> Whatever discipline you choose to study, whatever sport you choose to play, whatever club you choose to join, you will find your time at university most enjoyable.

This structure sounds more dramatic than its alternative loose organisation:

> You will find your time at university most enjoyable whatever discipline you choose to study, whatever sport you choose to play, whatever club you choose to join.

The position of the main clause at the beginning of this sentence lacks the emphasis it had in the periodic sentence. As we said before, loose sentences are the standard form, and as such they represent the 'natural' way of representing information. Periodic sentences do not seem 'natural' and are meant to be noticed. We can often add variety and emphasis to our writing by deliberately including some periodic sentences.

Paragraphs

Sentences are important structural elements in both speech and writing, but paragraphs relate only to writing. We may speak in sentences, but we never speak in paragraphs, unless we are reading out something that has been written down. Paragraphs organise writing for both readers and writers.

For the reader, paragraphs *identify* related material and *guide* understanding. For the writer, paragraphs *break up* the subject and *aid organisation and presentation.* Paragraphs are a structural feature of written texts and as such are subject to established conventions and expectations. The conventions associated with expository paragraphs are as follows:

1 An expository paragraph consists of a series of sentences which develop a **main idea**.
2 An expository paragraph should show **unity**.
3 An expository paragraph should show **coherence**.

The main idea: the topic sentence

Lucidly written expository paragraphs do not just happen, but are a product of much thought and organisation. Part of that thought and organisation must go into determining what the main idea or thrust of the paragraph is to be. The expression of that main idea will be made in the **topic sentence**. The other sentences in the paragraph will elaborate the main idea, gradually refining it until all aspects have been explored and its meaning is clear. By convention, each paragraph contains just one idea, and so has one topic sentence.

> The **topic sentence** of a paragraph expresses the main idea.

Most often, the topic sentence will occur at the beginning of a paragraph to provide a clear focus for what is to follow. In the *Introduction to Personality,* Jerry Phares discusses the legacy of Freud:

> *There is hardly an area of life today that has not been touched by Freudian thought.* It is reflected in our art, our literature, and our cinema. One is as likely (perhaps even more likely) to encounter psychoanalytic discussion and analysis in English

departments as in psychology offices. Historians can be heard
talking about prominent figures from a Freudian perspective.
A whole new field of inquiry—psychohistory—is heavily dependent on psychoanalytic concepts. Many current child-rearing
dictums have distinct Freudian roots, and when we encounter
anxiety in our lives, we may well wind up consulting a psycho-
therapist whose practice has a robust Freudian flavor. Terms
such as *ego, unconscious, death wish*, and *Freudian slip*, have
become part of our everyday chatter. Even the ways lawyers
prepare their criminal defenses often carry the Freudian imprint.
In recent history, only Darwin's message that our forebears
were a bit gamey has had a comparable impact.

In this paragraph, the topic sentence is the first sentence and Phares
uses it to control the direction of the paragraph. He suggests that
most aspects of our lives have been touched by Freudian thought.
He then puts forward a number of examples to show what he means.

Exercises

1 Analyse how Phares varies the sentence structure in his paragraph.
2 Using Phares' paragraph as a model, write an expository paragraph
   which starts:

   There is hardly an area of life today that has not been touched
   by silicon chip technology . . .

   In your paragraph give examples to support this statement; then
   decide how many examples are needed to make the point clear;
   then put them in an appropriate order. Try to vary your sentence
   structure.
3 Bring your paragraph to class and be prepared to discuss the
   reasons for the choices you have made and the order you have
   selected. From the class discussion, what criteria can you use to
   determine the most effective number and type of examples?
4 Try rewriting your paragraph placing your topic sentence at the
   end. What effect does this have on the meaning?

Paragraph unity

We have discussed the role the topic sentence plays in providing a
focus for the paragraph. Since a paragraph develops a single idea,
the notion of **unity** is important too. Paragraph unity is achieved in
three ways:

1 Relevance
2 Consistent perspective
3 Consistent tone

1 Relevance

A unified paragraph develops its central idea by 'sticking to the point'. The topic sentence provides the focus for the paragraph and the reader should be able to expect the supporting sentences to be **relevant**. Digressions, no matter how interesting, should be avoided.

2 Consistent perspective

In the chapter on description, we mentioned two different kinds of perspective: physical and mental (or attitudinal). In expository writing, our physical place in relation to the subject is of less importance, so the mental perspective dominates. The author's attitude can be conveyed through the choice of **point of view** and **tone**.

Expository point of view may be **personal**, as indicated by the use of personal pronouns like 'I, me, we, us' in which case our role as writer is foregrounded. Alternatively, the author could use a more **impersonal** point of view and avoid all reference to him or herself. The choice will be determined by the occasion, the subject matter and the reader. An impersonal point of view is more formal than a personal one and implies **objectivity**. Academic subjects usually require objectivity and conventionally use the impersonal point of view. (For example, one effect of the personal point of view adopted in this book is a more or less friendly rapport between authors and readers. If we had avoided all references to ourselves, the text may have seemed more formal and distant.) The choice of point of view is a strategic one, but whether the personal or the impersonal perspective is used, we should aim for consistency.

3 Consistent tone

Choice of tone is also strategic and once again will depend on the occasion, the subject matter and the reader. With these three aspects in mind, tone can be formal or informal, serious or entertaining, authoritative or modest. Suddenly changing tone in the middle of a paragraph will confuse the reader and may affect our credibility as writers.

Paragraph coherence

Paragraph coherence is closely related to paragraph unity. By coherence we mean **logical order** based on recognisable patterns and closely linked structure. A paragraph that is coherently organised will help the reader understand the relationships between the central idea and the supporting points.

Each mode of writing, whether it is description, narration, exposition or argument, has its own pattern of organisation for paragraph development. In exposition, there are several conventional patterns that writers use to develop paragraphs:

1 Illustration
2 Definition
3 Classification
4 Comparison and contrast
5 Cause and effect

1 Illustration

Illustration is one of the easiest ways of developing an expository paragraph. The basic structure of a paragraph that uses illustration is a statement of the general idea followed by several examples. We have already seen this type of structure in Phares' paragraph on the impact of Freudian thought. (The exercise on silicon chip technology also used illustration as the main means of paragraph development.)

In the following example from his book *After Apartheid*, Sebastian Mallaby is writing about the changing political situation in South Africa, as apartheid was being dismantled. He uses several examples from other African countries to illustrate the revolutionary changes that are happening across the continent:

> Africa has had a fresh beginning. The collapse of communism in Eastern Europe sent a second wave of revolutions across the continent, with democrats rising against tired dictatorships in a dozen re-enactments of the Berlin Wall. From Ivory Coast and Zambia to Mali and Benin, people have demanded the political and economic freedoms that they were promised at independence in the 1960s. On the tip of Africa, the last bastions of white rule have given way. Namibia has gained its first sovereign black government. And South Africa's white rulers have lifted the restrictions on black movements that were banned for three decades; they have released Nelson Mandela, the most famous prisoner in the world. But, as in Eastern Europe, exhilaration has given way to bitter quarrels. South Africans are still struggling to replace white rule with something better. Nobody is sure what kind of country they will create.

Mallaby has constructed his 'fresh beginning' for Africa through the support of examples of countries where there have been recent revolutionary changes. He uses a geographical order of roughly north to south to progress to the final example and topic of his book, South Africa.

2 Definition
In contrast to illustration, definition is a more difficult means of paragraph development. Expository paragraphs which use definition are not merely repeating dictionary definitions but are trying to tease out the subtleties of meaning through examining particular *cultural or contextual connotations*.

Imagine a paper about urban society which needs to explain the concept of 'loss of community'. This is an abstract concept whose meaning varies depending on the purpose for which it is to be used. The meaning of 'community' will need to be defined before the implications of its 'loss' can be contemplated. The *Macquarie Dictionary* defines community as:

> a social group of any size whose members reside in a specific locality, share government, and have a cultural and historical heritage.

A dictionary definition like this gives the *denotative* meaning of 'community' but misses the *connotative* meanings that are needed to explain what a 'loss of community' means in the context of a paper on urban society.

A much more elaborate definition of 'loss of community' is developed in this paragraph from *The Problem of Sociology*, by David Lee and Howard Newby:

> It is a common observation that modern British society is characterized by a 'loss of community'. The phrase is often used in an oblique but poignant way to express the dissatisfaction which many people experience about the quality of life in the contemporary world. There is an implied antithesis between the past, when, so it is believed, the individual was integrated into a stable and harmonious community of kin, friends and neighbours, and the less palatable present, when all too often it is possible to feel like a piece of human flotsam, cast adrift in a sea of apparently bewildering social changes and buffeted by impersonal and alien social forces. The longing for 'community' therefore symbolizes a desire for security and

certainty in our lives, but also a desire for identity and authenticity. 'Real communities' are assumed to offer all of these qualities, while their absence is believed to induce a number of disquieting personal and social pathologies. The withering away of a 'spirit of community' as an apparently endemic feature of our social condition is therefore offered as the diagnosis of a wide variety of contemporary social problems, ranging from the incidence of juvenile crime to the loneliness of the elderly. More generally this sense of loss raises doubts about the validity of 'progress' and our fears concerning the direction in which modern society appears to be moving.

The authors have developed the definition well beyond that offered in the dictionary. It is important for them to point out to readers that there is a problem with the concept and then to clarify its meaning through its various connotations.

It is also possible to develop a definition through offering a series of examples. In the next extract from *Intergroup Behaviour* by John Turner and Howard Giles, the topic sentence is little more than a question and suggests that the answer will supply a definition. The authors then provide a number of defining illustrations:

> What is intergroup behaviour? Concrete examples are not difficult to recognize. Any daily newspaper provides plenty. For example, on just one day in 1980 (19 September) the British *Daily Telegraph* carried headlines which included: 'Iran and Iraq nearer to war', 'Israeli raid on Lebanon', 'Peace formula lifts dock strike threat', 'Electronics firms fear Japanese . . . competition', 'West Berlin link cut by strike', and so on. In fact, most of the political, economic and international news had to do in one way or another with intergroup relations. Nor is intergroup behaviour just to do with 'bad' news. There were just as many examples in the sports pages. Nearly all team games (football, rugby, cricket, baseball, etc.) are examples of pure intergroup behaviour. Indeed, this is a large part of their attraction for both players and spectators: to identify with one's own team or the representatives of one's own institution, area or country, empathize with their struggles and share vicariously in the emotions of victory or defeat.

The definition is constructed implicitly by the use and force of the examples. The situations quoted in the headlines and in the sports pages seem so familiar and occur so frequently that the reader has no trouble in deciding what intergroup behaviour is.

Exercise
Develop a 150–200 word definition for each of the following topics:

> nationalism
> friendship
> sub-cultures

You could try to work up a definition through a discussion of the various cultural uses of the word or you could use a series of illustrations to define the topic. Try to vary your sentence structure to add interest.

3 Classification
When we develop a paragraph using classification, we are organising information or ideas into categories or classes according to a particular purpose. Different purposes will yield different classification schemes and the choice is up to the writer. In the following example, Eleanor Blaurock-Busch and Lynda Wharton are explaining two types of migraine to the readers of a popular health magazine, *Nature and Health*. They classify migraine as either classical or common, based on whether or not the sufferers experience visual effects:

> There are two main types of migraine—classical migraine and common migraine. Classical migraine is preceded by a whole array of visual abnormalities. The sufferer may see flashing lights and curved bands of white or coloured light at the edge of their visual field. They become irritable and confused, and very sensitive to noise. When the actual headache arrives, it is an intense aching or pounding sensation, typically experienced on only one side of the head. Twenty per cent of all migraines fall into this category. More commonly, migraine is accompanied by nausea and vomiting. These 'sick headaches', or common migraines, are preceded by irritability and depression, rather than the spectacular light shows. The actual head pain is of the same intensity and type as a classical migraine.

This method of classification seems quite appropriate for its non-professional audience, but it may not be explicit enough for trained medical staff.

4 Comparison and contrast

Comparison and contrast are two other ways of developing an expository paragraph. While comparison focuses on similarities and contrast focuses on differences, both methods are structurally similar and are usually considered together. There are two ways to approach a comparison (or for that matter a contrast). The first is the *topic-by-topic* approach, sometimes called the *divided* approach. Here each topic is discussed separately. This can be represented as follows:

Topic-by-topic structure
    Topic 1
        point a
        point b
        point c

    Topic 2
        point a
        point b
        point c

The second is the *point-by-point* method sometimes called the *alternating* approach. Here, the first point is developed for each topic, then the second point for each topic, and so on.

Point-by-point structure
    Point A
        topic 1
        topic 2

    Point B
        topic 1
        topic 2

    Point C
        topic 1
        topic 2

Neither the topic-by-topic nor point-by-point structure has any intrinsic advantages over the other. Each topic and its related points can be covered by either method. The choice usually comes down to whether the writer wants to emphasise the topics as a whole or prefers to stress specific points. The point-by-point approach is more difficult to write because the writer needs to control the comparison (or contrast) very tightly, but it is often more interesting to read.

The following paragraph on twentieth century sculpture from *An Intellectual and Cultural History of the Western World* combines a topic-by-topic approach with a point-by-point approach in a complex and thoughtful way. Author Harry Elmer Barnes is comparing sculpture with painting and architecture:

> The development of twentieth-century sculpture is related closely to the history and aesthetics of modern painting. There are also certain parallels between recent sculpture and architecture. Each of these branches of the fine arts has strong affiliations with the styles of the past, yet extraordinary changes have taken place in all of them, sculpture by all means included. Like the architects of our century, modern sculptors have made ingenious use of new, exciting materials including plastics and metals. They have at the same time continued the ancient traditions of bronze-casting, direct carving in stone, and fired clay. Like the painters of this century they have reinterpreted the human figure geometrically or with emphasis on its emotional capacities, and they have shared in the creation of non-figural or abstract forms. Since the Second World War especially, sculpture has enjoyed, as have both painting and architecture, a vigorous and abundant expression carried out by many gifted, original personalities.

The author has announced the comparison at the start. He takes two sentences to announce that he sees similarities between sculpture and modern painting on one hand, and sculpture and architecture on the other. The rest of the paragraph structure then is broken up into two halves. The first covers the similarities between sculpture and architecture and the second between sculpture and painting.

Within each of these sections there is another comparison in a point form. The first relates to the similarities in the use of materials in both sculpture and architecture, and the second shows similarities in the interpretation of the human form. The last sentence ties the paragraph together.

Exercise

Choose two forms of music to compare or contrast. List their similarities and their differences. Using the alternative patterns described above, write two paragraphs: one which uses the point-by-point structure and one which uses the topic-by-topic structure. Are the paragraphs equally effective?

5 Cause and effect

Yet another method of paragraph development is based on causal logic where the writer creates a relationship between causes and effects. It is possible to do this either by first stating the cause and then listing the effects, or by listing the effects first and then stating the cause. This particular type of logic will be treated more fully in the next section on academic writing.

Linking ideas

The use of particular patterns of development is just one part of maintaining coherence in expository paragraphs. Another is the provision of **links** which connect various ideas together and which set up relationships between successive sentences. These are achieved mainly by careful organisation of the text, to clarify ideas and their relationships for readers. If a writer makes a generalisation, then the reader would expect to see some specific information to back it up. If the writer announces a problem, the reader would expect to discover the answer. If the writer states that a topic has several parts, then the reader would expect to see each of those parts discussed.

More overt relationships can be made using the following kinds of connectors:

numerical words such as 'first, second, third';

repetition of key words or phrases either in their original form or as synonyms;

connectives such as 'however, nevertheless, meanwhile, consequently, therefore, after, before, as a result, meanwhile';

pronouns, such as 'he, she, it, they, I, we, you';

demonstratives, such as 'this, that, these, those';

and

repetition of grammatical structures in successive sentences.

Most writers use a combination of these linking words to improve the coherence of their writing. In the next example taken from *An Introduction to Australian Society*, Donald Edgar has made some use of pronouns ('it' to refer to 'family') and connectives ('despite', 'because', 'yet'), but he also employs several repetitions of grammatical structure:

> Despite recurring fears that the family is dying, losing its functions and not socializing children properly, it is still the most basic institution for human socialization. Our first experience of social *others* takes place here; our first social *bonds* form here; our first experience of roles as patterns of expected behaviours is here; our early feelings of *power* and *authority* (in the shape of parental rights to control us) develop in the family. The structural location of our family in the wider society and the structure of relationships within the family will affect what we learn, how we learn and what sorts of persons we become. Because our class, status, religion and ethnic groups differ so much we should expect to see vast differences in the ways families socialize their young. Yet this should not blind us to the fact that such differences also reflect power differences of groups within the wider social structure. It is in that sense that the family remains a chief mechanism for the 'reproduction' of existing power relations in society and the *social distribution of competence.*

In the second sentence Edgar writes: 'Our first experience of social others takes place here; our first social bonds form here; our first experience of roles as patterns of expected behaviours is here.' Each of these clauses is deliberately identical in structure and gives emphasis to the idea of the family as a crucial institution in the socialisation of children. Are there other instances in the same paragraph where a grammatical structure is repeated?

Links like these and the others listed above should only be used to develop a logical structure which already exists in the paragraph. They should not be relied on to construct logic by themselves. The insertion of a few words like 'consequently' or 'however' may give a superficial appearance of a unified and coherent paragraph, but cannot guarantee or produce a logical discussion in itself.

Exposition is one of the four principal modes of writing. Although it often makes use of description and narration, it is also quite different in terms of structure and perspective. Exposition marks a move away from description and narration as experiential types of writing to more topic-centred writing. It also represents a move from a relatively intimate form of writing to a more formal one. In these changes, we see the effacement of the personal self of the writer and the downplaying of his or her individual thoughts and experiences. Exposition makes its subject matter central not in emotive or subjective terms for the author, but through the text's logical organisation. Hence, we have discussed several conventional patterns of exposition and shown their values for both writers and readers.

In the next chapter, we take up one pattern of expository paragraph development, cause and effect, as a special case. We show how this particular type of logical order is used as a key strategy of academic writing.

Works cited

Barnes, Harry, Elmer (1965) *An Intellectual and Cultural History of the Western World*, 3rd edition, Dover, New York

Blaurock-Busch, Eleanor, and Lynda Wharton (1993) 'Migraines', *Nature and Health*, May

Carlson, Neil R. (1986) *Physiology of Behavior*, 3rd edition, Allyn and Bacon, Boston

Edgar Donald (1980) *Introduction to Australian Society: A Sociological Perspective*, Prentice Hall, Sydney

Gleitman, Henry (1986) *Psychology*, 2nd edition, Norton, New York

Jamsa, Kris (1992) *Concise Guide to Microsoft Windows 3.1*, Microsoft Press, Washington

Lee, David, and Howard Newby (1983) *The Problem of Sociology: An Introduction to the Discipline*, Hutchinson, London

Mallaby, Sebastian (1992) *After Apartheid*, Faber, London

Phares, E. Jerry (1984) *Introduction to Personality*, Merrill, Columbus

Turner, John C., and Howard Giles (1981) 'Introduction: The Social Psychology of Intergroup Behaviour', in *Intergroup Behaviour*, editors, John C. Turner and Howard Giles, Basil Blackwell, Oxford

Section 2

Academic Writing

5 Cause and effect

This chapter begins the second section of the book which is composed of a more specific focus on academic writing. In the following three chapters we will consider:

1 the use of **logic** in writing, especially in academic texts;
2 different ways of constructing a written **argument;**
3 the role of **research** in academic writing.

We will also review and expand some of the ideas that have come up in the earlier chapters on description, narration and exposition. In particular, we will try to explain how these ways of structuring ideas of space and time, as well as comparing and contrasting, explaining, defining and classifying material, are very important aspects of producing academic texts.

One of the conclusions you might have drawn from the first section of the book was that it's very rare for a text to be pure description or narration, or 100 per cent exposition. Most (if not all) texts use a combination of these three modes. They mix description, narration and exposition to convey a range of different sorts of information. Thus, while we read and analysed descriptive, narrative and expository *paragraphs* in the first section, we did not really think about how *complete texts* were put together, or how the different modes might connect with one another in the one text.

In these three chapters we will want to examine these kinds of questions, especially in relation to the ways academic texts combine different modes of writing in presenting their logic, argument and research to readers. To do this properly we must examine some whole texts to see the different means they use to organise their material and writing modes, including the handling of point of view. Throughout this section, then, we will be primarily dealing with the structure and logic involved in the academic essay.

> **Academic writing** combines description, narration and
> exposition with research to present a logical argument
> in response to certain questions and topics.

Logic and writing

The three modes of description, narration and exposition all contain
and present varied sorts of thinking. Indeed, we might say that
each one involves getting down on paper a different kind of logic
or thinking: spatial-descriptive, temporal-narrative and analytical-
expository. Because of this, we can claim that writing is very much
a thinking process. We not only use it to represent our attitudes
and perspectives on different places and events to others. We also
use it to organise our thoughts about topics into certain orders.
Writing about something often helps to clarify ideas about it for
ourselves as well as for readers.

Quite specific kinds of thinking go on in writing as well.
Often they might be rather abstract, as when a scientist attempts
to explain a particular theory. Here is Charles Darwin summing up
his ideas on the extinction of species:

> From these several considerations I think it inevitably follows,
> that as new species in the course of time are formed through
> natural selection, others will become rarer and rarer, and
> finally extinct. The forms which stand in closest competition
> with those undergoing modification and improvement, will
> naturally suffer most. And we have seen in the chapter on the
> Struggle for Existence that it is the most closely-allied forms—
> varieties of the same species, and species of the same genus
> or of related genera—which, from having nearly the same
> structure, constitution, and habits, generally come into the
> severest competition with each other. Consequently, each new
> variety or species, during the progress of its formation, will
> generally press hardest on its nearest kindred, and tend to
> exterminate them.

Darwin is trying to explain his reasoning. He uses the text to recap
and reflect on what he has already said, 'we have seen in the
chapter...'. However, he is not simply describing or summarising
what he has written before. Nor is he using the kind of direct
exposition that we saw in the last chapter, where authors illustrated,

compared or classified various points. Instead, the extract builds upon that kind of writing and *draws conclusions from it*. The use of the words 'it follows' and 'Consequently...', like 'therefore, thus, hence, so, as a result', is a key sign that conclusions are being made. The author is taking his thinking one step further than exposition. In fact, he uses the earlier exposition as the basis for presenting his theory. It provides the building blocks of his judgement.

What we see here is that the author has moved from using a logic of exposition to a logic of **cause and effect**: that is, the earlier descriptions of the phenomena of natural selection are now set up as *causes* which produce certain *effects or results*. Rather than simply explaining particular conditions and changes, the author is beginning to make an *argument* about their origins and outcome. This shift in emphasis—from descriptive and expository logic to causal logic and argument—is one of the most important features of academic writing. It enables the author to make a case for or against a topic or proposition. **Causal logic** is thus one of the fundamental strategies we use in writing academic texts.

> **Causal logic** establishes and explains the links between situations and their outcomes, events and their results, evidence and its proofs.

This chapter focuses on the functions of causality in thought, language and writing. We will consider causality as readers and writers: that is, how others use it in their writing and how we might use it in ours. First of all, we will consider a number of examples of the way causal logic works to structure texts. Next, we will turn our attention to one of the more important writing styles used repeatedly in assignments for many subjects—the presentation of an argument for or against some topic. The idea of causality, of distinguishing between the causes and effects of a situation, is very often a central step to take when trying to argue clearly about a topic.

Exercise

Re-read the comparison and contrast between two forms of music which you wrote in Chapter 4. Now, write a paragraph in which you sum up your opinion about the comparison.

Evidence

Before developing the concept of causality, we can briefly reconsider the topics of space, time and exposition which have already been dealt with. As noted above, many university or academic assignments involve making an argument—a case for or against something. Where do description, narration and exposition fit into such writing?

Our answer would be that in effectively presenting a case or argument it is crucial to offer readers **evidence** of what we are talking about. Description and narration—the organising of ideas into terms of space and time, along with analysis and explanation of their order—are some of the main ways in which evidence can be presented. Consider the classic courtroom question, 'Where were you on the night of...?' The lawyer is looking for details concerning the space and time of the witness's actions: when and where was she? Sitting with a mysterious stranger on a still summer night, sipping a mango daiquiri, as the cloudy atmosphere intensified? Explanation and analysis of such evidence will then follow. The disclosed details are linked together to prove the prosecution's claims.

In trying to make a case for or against a complex topic or issue, we have to *combine* a number of different writing strategies: descriptive, narrative, expository. Although they provide details and evidence, these need to be supplemented by an account of the logical structure and order of the material we are investigating. It is on this point, in presenting the logic that supports our evidence, the set of concepts and premises which underlies the issue being considered, that questions of causality become important.

Causality

Some initial definitions of the notions of cause and effect will aid our analysis of their roles in texts. Most generally, **a cause is something which produces some change**. From this broad definition come three other points which, while philosophers may not all agree on them, are useful for our purposes. Implicit in the definition that a cause produces change are the following ideas:

1 A cause has the power to do something.
2 There is a necessary connection between a cause and the change it produces.
3 A cause comes before its effect (or at least it doesn't occur after its effect).

Thus a cause has power to act, is connected to its effect, and happens before the effect. How do these ideas come into play in different types of texts and writing?

Advertisements are an interesting example. They present the product or service as *the* cause of a successful or useful outcome, as the following ads suggest:

ACADEMIC success in Chem, Maths, Biol., Phys. to Yr 12. Excellent Teacher. Qual. and very experienced. 533 8391

LEARN TO DANCE
Rock-'n'-Roll and meet new friends with K O Rockers Dance School at Italo-Australia Centre. Full course structure, singles, couples, families. No partner reqd. Phone 419 0723

GUTTERS repaired and cleared. Year-round protection from leaf litter. Unique mesh system. Keep those shade trees. Most homes under $150. Phone Bailey, 563 4322

In each case, the offered service seems to guarantee personal or social, academic or domestic success. The first sentences clearly state the effects that can be achieved, and the texts then provide supporting explanations of why they will be effective or why the causal process will do what it claims: due to an excellent teacher, a unique system or a complete course. Although it provides little text or explanation, the following magazine advertisement similarly implies that if we wear this particular perfume we cannot avoid becoming a 'playful, vibrant' woman. Her pleased, sophisticated appearance seems to offer visual proof of the product's success.

Figure 5.1

The persuasiveness of many ads derives from an impression that they create of *inevitable causality*. The product or service seems destined to improve our circumstances. This impression reflects the three aspects that define a cause: the product alone has the power to change our situation; it will necessarily be effective; and we need to buy the product before we can produce the change.

Often advertisements must convince us that our circumstances need changing, that a case exists in which a causal remedy should be applied. They set up a context for change that only the product can bring. 'Before-and-after' ads are a classic example. The product in question enables us to get from the past, when something is wrong, to the future—a thinner, prettier, happier future.

Advertisements first create a conscious or semi-conscious need for change in their audience and then offer the means of change. Of course the accuracy of a product's efficiency is often exaggerated or misrepresented by ads. One of the ways that such overstatement occurs is through a technique that we will see used throughout many different types of causal arguments, from the informal such as ads, to the formal such as academic texts. This involves limiting the possible effects that a single cause might have.

Causality frequently works through strictly defining the process of events in which it occurs or to which it applies. It sets up what we can call a **causal chain**, an exclusive sequence of causes and effects. Advertised products represent an ideal future by bracketing any other events which might be involved. These events are placed outside the causal chain along which the product functions, and so its effectiveness seems unequivocally positive (for example, the above ad for school tutoring does not mention either the extra hours of work that the student will have to do or the cost). One of the main tactics of the anti-smoking movement has been to redefine the causal process which cigarette ads represent, by drawing attention to, and commenting on the negative effects which will accompany sailing a yacht, riding a horse, skiing, or wining and dining while we smoke.

The limited definition of a cause's effects is a basic stage in putting together a case through causal logic. The effects that we wish to acknowledge as being desirable or correct are underlined and other possibilities are downplayed or ignored. As we will see, the streamlining of logic into a causal chain is one of the main strengths of using causal explanations and analysis in our work. At the same time, it also opens our writing and that of others to charges that we are being too selective in drawing conclusions. In this sense, analysing the logic of causal chains becomes an important step in reading academic and other texts critically.

Exercises

1 Write a 150-word script for a radio or television commercial which is promoting the benefits of a luxury-resort holiday. Try to use causal logic to structure your ad. Next, write a parody of the ad which details some of the holiday's potentially negative effects.

2 In a short essay explain and analyse the causal logic used in a selection of magazine advertisements for men's and women's fashions. What are the common features of the ads? Do they all set up causal chains of positive results? Do they exclude similar kinds of negative effects?

Priority

Another important aspect of causality is an obvious feature of before-and-after ads—its relationship to chronological order. Remember, a cause is defined as coming before or prior to its effect in time. This idea of **priority** is both a temporal idea and a causal one: 'the state of being earlier in time, or of preceding something else; precedence in order' (*Macquarie Dictionary*). We gain a fuller understanding of narrative texts that employ time structures (like stories and histories) by noting the ways that this organisation also grants a logical, causal order to their events.

> Narratives employ **causal** as well as **temporal** structures.

Thus we can rethink the temporal order of events in a narrative as also being a causal order. This double process can be observed even in quite simple narratives, such as those written for small children. The uncomplicated language and order of events does not mean that causal logic is not at work, as the following story by Tohby Riddle about a dog called Fletcher shows:

> Fletcher was a rather unusual dog. It wasn't just that he preferred pancakes to dog biscuits ... it was that he cooked them himself. Nor was it that he lived in a kennel. That was quite common ... except that he built it with his own two paws. Not only was Fletcher allowed on the couch, he had chosen the upholstery. While other dogs barked at the moon, Fletcher studied it through his telescope, such was his interest in astronomy. For many dogs, a visit to the park would mean chasing cyclists ... but not for Fletcher. If the neighbours had a complaint to make about Fletcher, it wasn't that he kept them awake all night by barking ... but that he played his Bing Crosby records too loud.

Such a dog inevitably attracted a lot of attention. Overnight Fletcher became a star... even a movie star. His picture was everywhere. Soon everyone wanted to know Fletcher or at least be seen with him. He became the favourite of every society hostess. So while most dogs spent their evenings rummaging through garbage bins or chewing on a shoe... Fletcher was visiting clubs... presenting awards... or attending the opera.

But things change. One evening, while Fletcher was special guest at a dinner on a harbour cruise... he was spotted by someone from the dog pound. There was a brief scuffle... but Fletcher swam to freedom.

As for the rest of the story, no-one really knows. Some say he went on to become the first dog in space... while others say Fletcher ended up in a cottage somewhere on the coast with an old fisherman... and a most unusual cat.

These fantastic events are related in chronological order, as they happen to Fletcher. Although about a world which seems to have little rational order, the story uses a chain of cause and effect to amplify its opening descriptive and narrative sentences. The first paragraph begins by making a proposition, that Fletcher is unusual, and then offers descriptive and narrative *evidence* in support of the claim. The second and third paragraphs, however, develop in a different way. They no longer merely provide evidence but trace the *positive and negative effects* of Fletcher's extraordinary abilities. These talents become *causes* which drive the narrative's changing action until it reaches its conclusion.

We perceive a causal chain even within a humorous children's story like this one. That we can do this has two implications: first, that as readers we are socially and textually conditioned from childhood to look for causal connections between ideas; and second, that even our humour is not totally lacking in causal logic—instead it tends to combine unusual or surprising elements into a causal chain.

History is one of the most prominent narrative genres, so we might expect to see similar causal chains accompanying chronological patterns in history texts. If we consider a paragraph on the beginnings of modern thought in the sixteenth century, from Bertrand Russell's *History of Western Philosophy*, we can again note the use of causal logic:

The period of history which is commonly called 'modern' has a mental outlook which differs from that of the medieval period in many ways. Of these, two are the most important: the diminishing authority of the Church, and the increasing authority of science. With these two, others are connected. The culture of modern times is more lay than clerical. States increasingly replace the Church as the governmental authority that controls culture. The government of nations is, at first, mainly in the hands of kings; then, as in ancient Greece, the kings are gradually replaced by democracies or tyrants. The power of the national State, and the functions it performs, grow steadily throughout the whole period (apart from some minor fluctuations); but at most times the State has less influence on the opinions of philosophers than the Church had in the Middle Ages. The feudal aristocracy, which, north of the Alps, had been able, till the fifteenth century, to hold its own against central governments, loses first its political and then its economic importance. It is replaced by the king in alliance with rich merchants; these two share power in different proportions in different countries. There is a tendency for the rich merchants to become absorbed into the aristocracy. From the time of the American and French Revolutions onwards, democracy, in the modern sense, becomes an important political force.

There are a number of significant features in this extract. It begins with what is called a **thesis statement**, a sentence which concisely presents the writer's position on the topic. A thesis statement near the beginning of an essay or chapter is a very clear way of letting readers know where we stand. (We could say that a thesis statement does for an essay what a topic sentence, discussed in Chapters 4 and 6, does for a paragraph.) It establishes the author's point of view concerning the subject matter. Thus Russell writes: 'The period of history which is commonly called "modern" has a mental outlook which differs from that of the medieval period in many ways.' Immediately we know *what* Russell's argument is going to be, though we don't yet know *why* he has this viewpoint.

> A **thesis statement** puts forward the point of view or organising idea for an essay.

In a way, then, a thesis statement demands that authors provide both evidence and a causal explanation to back up and prove their position. Thus by including a clear thesis statement in our essays, we not only signal our viewpoint on the topic to readers, we also prepare and position ourselves to support and explain our perspective.

Russell takes these steps in the following sentences which begin to expand on the 'many ways' that the modern period differs from earlier ones. The details he lists comprise various political, religious, economic and social changes, all of which take place through time. They are presented in the text through descriptive, narrative and expository writing. Russell is not merely constructing an historical outline or portrait of different events, however; these details are the *causes* of the historical change for which he is arguing. The occurrences described by him take place in time and produce historical change. They are both temporal and causal factors.

In fictional narratives, histories and in most types of writing which use a firm time pattern, the time order of events also becomes a causal order. Chronological order is deepened in meaning and significance through its causal development. The connection between chronology and causality thus becomes an important tactic we can use in trying to present a strong argument. For instead of only giving an outline of when events happen so as to illustrate a situation—for example, that with its many political, economic and religious events in Europe the Renaissance seems very different from the Middle Ages—we can go on to argue that these events *cause* important, distinctive changes in the sixteenth and later centuries. By arguing for a causal change, we gain an explicit thesis concerning the topic, and we increase the force with which our viewpoint strikes the reader.

Exercises

1 Reread the biography of a favourite author that you wrote in Chapter 3. Write a short analysis of the events in his or her life in which you explain their causal connections. Can you also distinguish the different modes you used in the biography by dividing the text into sections of narration, description, exposition and causal logic?

2 Make up a random list of ten nouns. Swap your list with someone else and then try to link the new words into a short chronologically ordered narrative. Can you find causal links between the story's events?

3 Write one paragraph which develops three or four changes in your life caused by starting to study at university. Begin with a thesis statement which establishes your point of view towards these changes.

Causal logic and essay structure

The shift from narrating when events occur to arguing that when they occur they produce certain changes is crucial to developing an effective form of analytical writing. Such writing is effective for a number of reasons. The first reason relates to the link between temporal and causal priority:

> 1 Chronological order itself becomes more meaningful when events are represented in a causal connection, as the events do not seem to occur randomly or coincidentally.

The second develops the logical effects of the temporal-causal connection for supporting our thesis:

> 2 We can argue our thesis upon the basis of causal logic instead of relying merely on circumstantial evidence.

In both these cases, as mentioned earlier, causality allows us to narrow down and define the possible effects, reasons and details which are most relevant to our position (establishing a causal chain).

The third reason relates these logical benefits to ways in which we can order and construct our essays:

> 3 Causal logic can be used clearly to plan and organise an argument as a written text.

Causal logic is closely tied to the grammar and structure we use in analytical writing. We can demonstrate its usefulness by considering a couple of examples. Let's begin with an excerpt from an essay by Ronald B. Scott on pop singer Madonna's 1989 hit video, *Like a Prayer*:

> The video images presented in this initial scene are significant for two reasons. First, the church is presented as a zone of safety, and the function of black religion as a sanctuary from the immoral behavior of the outside world is made manifest. Madonna's articulation of the line 'feels like home' underscores the safety that the church provides to all who are in need. Second, the church is seen as a sanctuary for *all* people, regardless of, in this case, race, which underscores the doctrine of the equality of all people that is fundamental to black religion. In effect, Madonna presents a narrative that affirms the comfort and safety provided by the black church by stating that the experience feels like returning to the safety of one's own house.

In the first sentence the author states his general position on the significance of the video images. He then offers two causes for it. The first is more narrow or specific—the church signifies a sanctuary for black people; the second presents a wider reason for the image's relevance—the church suggests a sanctuary for all people. Lastly, Scott notes a further universal cause for the image's significance: it evokes connotations of 'home'.

It would be quite easy for the author of this paragraph to have planned out its structure and content. He could have used a simple diagram to do so:

Significance of video images
1 church as black sanctuary;
2 church as sanctuary for everyone;
3 church as home.

From this list we can see the kind of clear patterns of organisation that causal logic may provide. It allows authors to develop a plan for their essays which can then be filled out. The causal chain provides the basis of the paragraph and essay structure. (Of course, some readers might point to effects that this causal chain has *excluded*: the church may be seen as oppressive institution rather than a sanctuary, with the video finally endorsing a conservative Christian message. As noted earlier, we often need to be ready to question the effects emphasised in any causal chain.)

We can also note that Scott has ordered his causes in a climactic way, building up from the specific to the universal. Through being able to list and distinguish between causes, a writer can 'rank' them in terms of importance and then decide the most effective order to put them in for his or her readers. Often a build-up to the most widely applicable point or cause, as in this example, is most informative and noticeable for readers.

A more complex application of causal logic can be seen in the following paragraphs from an essay on Australian cinema in the 1980s by Elizabeth Jacka:

So far I have been discussing only cultural arguments for regulation of Australian content, but of course there are a couple of different though related arguments. One is the economic argument; the other the need to safeguard employment. One of the reasons for regulating for Australian content is to help counteract the economic imbalance that exists between the scale of overseas industries, especially of course the US industry, and the local one. Product, both film and television, is much more cheaply acquired from overseas (though this is said to be changing) and without some special requirement at least on television stations to broadcast Australian material, the economic logic of the situation would suggest acquiring all products from overseas ...

The second argument is the need to safeguard Australian employment. This requirement is explicitly embodied in Section 114 of the Broadcasting and Television Act and it is also found in the 10BA Australian content requirements for film ... The unions and associations have been active to varying degrees in ensuring that Australian production does use Australian actors and other creative personnel as far as possible ... However, the employment argument is in a sense also part of the cultural one. The very existence of the professions covered by the various unions (the actors, writers, directors, designers, photographers, etc.) depends on the prior existence of the various forms of cultural production, and their expansion depends on the growth of the various cultural forms.

These paragraphs demonstrate some other ways in which causal logic can help us to plan essays clearly. Generally, such logic seems to suit the grammar and word order that we use, for a cause is like the subject of a sentence and an effect is like the object. When a series of cause and effect explanations becomes the primary means of arguing our case, each one can clearly fit into a separate sentence, or perhaps be the topic for a couple of sentences or paragraphs.

In the above passage, Jacka uses both possibilities. She begins by noting two additional reasons why local content in Australian TV and film should be regulated—economic and employment. Then follows a single sentence which explains the economic reason: 'One of the reasons for Australian content is to help counteract the economic imbalance that exists ....' Having described this effect, Jacka expands on its implications in the following sentences (as well as in another paragraph, not quoted above). The economic cause provides the key theme for this part of her essay. When she turns to the issue of employment, Jacka uses it as the subject for a whole paragraph. Note that she expands on employment as a cause for regulation by narrating the actions of government and unions as supporting evidence.

So by presenting more evidence or an explanation, each cause and its effect(s) can be used as the basis for a number of paragraphs in the body of an essay. **Causality has a structure that closely fits the way we put sentences, paragraphs and even whole essays together.** As Jacka's text shows, causes and effects can be counted or numbered—'there are a couple of different though related arguments. One is . . . the other . . .'—and then used as the building blocks of an essay. From there, we can consider the relationships between the different causes, perhaps contrasting or combining them to make an even stronger case. Jacka first distinguishes the economic and employment factors from the cultural arguments for regulation that she has already used. She then shows that these two new arguments are ultimately related to her first ones, reinforcing them and requiring them to be expanded: 'Thus in order to protect the film and television industry as local industries and to give employment, some national regulatory policy which protects Australian-based companies and workers is appropriate. But what of the arguments on the cultural level? What *is* the thing called "Australian content"?' By distinguishing and then connecting the various relevant causes and arguments, the author is able to strengthen her case.

Exercises

1 Newspaper editorials are a well-known format which present a position and then try to explain supporting causes, reasons and effects. Select three recent editorials and write a 500-word expository essay, analysing their causal logic and structure.
2 Choose one of the editorials and write a response that opposes its position. State your own thesis clearly and then support it through causal logic and explanation. Before writing up your response, map out a full plan of the text's causes, reasons and effects (as was done above for the paragraph on the Madonna video). How do your reasons relate to one another? Are you going to use a climactic order to present them?

Logic and persuasion

For various reasons—its definition of relevant events and issues and its structural clarity—causality forms an influential style of thinking and writing. Especially in an academic context like the one we write essays in, causal logic has a value, almost a traditional one, that makes it all the more convincing for readers. We can consider the importance causality has assumed in Western thought and writing by looking at two long-established instances: the image of God as cause of the universe, and the syllogistic mode of argument. Together they illustrate the traditional cultural significance which causality holds for us.

When we think of causal logic in terms of its traditional value, we start to see that just as there is no one correct way to describe or narrate details, so there is no single or perfect means of proving a thesis or position. Causal logic is effective because, like chronological order in regard to time, it is widely accepted as the conventional way to present and support a position or thesis. However, it's not the case that causal logic is always 'true'; rather, readers often find the causal approach highly **persuasive**.

We have seen that one of the basic assumptions about a cause is that it comes before the change it produces. This assumption suggests that our culture imagines causality in parental terms, often as the 'father' of a family of effects. This paternal idea of causality is exemplified in the Bible, where God is the cause and father of creation: 'In the beginning God created the heaven and the earth.' The opening chapter of Genesis also suggests that God's causal function is realised as much through his actions as through his speech: 'And God said, Let there be light: and there was light.' God does things by language. His words have a causal power that produces results.

The idea that words have causal effect extends to our thinking about ordinary language. We can also do things with words. If you say to someone: 'I promise', as you say it you also do it. When a dignitary smashes a bottle of champagne against a ship and says: 'I name you the good ship Whatever', his or her saying so gives the ship that name. Everyday speech, like the word of God, can have direct results.

But it can also work less directly. As we saw in advertising, language can cause people to do things through its **persuasiveness**. In this case, the causality of language is not immediate, but is delayed until the audience responds in a certain way. The idea of persuasion is based on the effectiveness of language to move our *emotions* through a rather loose and sometimes even deceptive causal logic. In both these ideas about the way language works— its power to do things directly and through persuasion—notions of causal logic are at work.

Perhaps because of its links to religious-cultural ideas like God, causal logic is a basic part of Western society. However, causality also has traditional value as a means of reasoning in academic and intellectual discourses. Here, the causal chain known as the **syllogism** is an established method. Basically, a syllogism contains two pro-positions from which a conclusion can be drawn; for example:

All persons are mortal.
Charlie Chaplin is a person.
(Therefore) Charlie Chaplin is mortal.

The propositions combine to cause or produce the conclusion, and the implied 'Therefore' signals that the third step is the conclusion.

In its own terms, the syllogism does seem a foolproof logical method, a clear causal chain. Once again, however, these features may be a function of its narrowness. If a syllogism is persuasive, it may be because of verbal smoothness rather than any absolute truth. Such smoothness—in the neat, simple flow of the sentences and the apparently obvious meaning of each term—can divert us from complex or arguable definitions which might be involved in its starting premisses. What is meant by 'Charlie Chaplin'—the person, the 'little tramp' character in films, or the legendary star and director? What does 'mortal' mean—subject to physical death? In another sense, that of cultural reputation and fame, Chaplin is obviously an immortal figure. In what sense, then, are these key words being used? The syllogism doesn't really tell us.

Syllogisms exemplify some of the strengths and weaknesses of causal argument. On the one hand, they bracket or exclude issues we might wish to raise, and they may use and appeal to ideas without always carefully defining them. On the other, the conciseness and clarity of this form of reasoning make it a useful writing and arguing technique. A syllogistic pattern of reasoning can often persuade us to adopt its point of view on the topic.

Exercises

1 Expand the above syllogism into a paragraph by explaining the logical connections between the three steps and defining the key terms.
2 Try to come up with three more syllogisms yourself. Are there problems of definition with the key terms you have used? What ideas must these terms presuppose for the syllogism to produce its conclusion? Choose one of the syllogisms, and use it as the basis for a 400-word essay, which you develop by defining the key terms and explaining the causal connections.

Causal logic, point of view and academic writing

Like the modes of writing and logic we considered earlier, essays using causal logic attempt to set up a point of view which readers will adopt as their own. The sense of correctness and factuality may persuade readers to accept the premisses and conclusions of the causal and logical chains. These lines of reasoning work in two related ways: they present and explain their own set of causes, reasons and effects, and they silence or exclude other views or questions which might be put forward on the issue. As seen in the previous section, the direct and rapid steps of the syllogism allow it to fulfil both of these conditions, making it a widely used model for causal argument.

The readiness of readers to accept a text's logical viewpoint depends on a number of factors. The various steps in the causal chain must be accepted as validly leading to one another (for example, they shouldn't contradict themselves). They must be explained in sufficient detail and, if necessary, provided with adequate supporting evidence through descriptive, narrative and expository writing.

If we want to evaluate a causal explanation or argument in some detail, we will have to try to judge the way it uses all of these aspects and conditions. However, there is no set formula that measures whether the steps in an essay lead to each other validly, or if there is enough evidence, and so on. We have to think about these elements and whether they help constitute an acceptable explanation or argument.

The point is that causal logic in itself cannot ensure that an argument is a valid one. It is not possible to appeal to an abstract notion of pure logic that will somehow guarantee the truth of a text's thesis and point of view. Truth in texts, including academic texts, is a slippery quality. It changes for different groups of readers depending on their points of view and backgrounds. **For any argument to be effective and persuasive it must appeal to the social and intellectual perspective of the audience.**

We can see truth's slippery qualities in an academic context by briefly considering an essay that examines the development of the discipline of psychology. The author, Carolyn Wood Sherif, argues that despite its claims of scientific accuracy and truthfulness, psychology has regularly produced biased results. Even if we don't fully accept her discussion, it still suggests that the use of apparently logical techniques and arguments does not automatically produce factual conclusions:

> Undeniably, the prestigious and successful sciences in the late nineteenth and early twentieth century were those securely focused on the physical world and the physical processes of the organic world. Psychologists, in their strivings to gain status with other scientists, did not pause long on issues raised by the differences between studying a rock, a chemical

compound, or an animal, on one hand, and a human individual, on the other. Instead, methods that had been successful in the physical and biological sciences were embraced as models for psychology. Researchers were soon deep into analogy, comparing the human individual to the chemical compound or to the animal as the subject of research, with all the power that such an analogy gives to the scientific investigator, at least if the animal is captive and small. Unlike the natural scientist, however, the psychologist had only social power over the research subject, not the greater power to explore, observe, and analyze that had unlocked so many of nature's secrets for the physical sciences.

The methodology promoted in psychology, in its strivings for social acceptability and prestige, rested on the assumption that the causes of an event can be determined by breaking down the event into component parts, or elements, and studying those parts and their relationships to one another. The more 'basic' these parts or elements are, the more 'basic' is the inquiry.

What psychology defined as basic was dictated by slavish devotion to the more prestigious disciplines. Thus, a physiological or biochemical part or element was defined as more basic than a belief that Eve was created from Adam's rib, not because the former can necessarily tell us more about a human individual, but because physiology and bio-chemistry were more prestigious than religious history or sociology.

Here, Sherif begins to outline a number of reasons why psychological methods produce biased findings. She uses causal logic to reveal and conclude that these methods cause flawed results. The analogy with physical sciences, assumption of 'basic' elements, and imitation of acclaimed disciplines meant that techniques and ideas suitable for certain kinds of research were applied to different, in fact unsuitable, experimental subjects (i.e., people).

The essay also suggests that these methods were taken up by psychology less because they were objectively judged appropriate than because of rivalries and concerns over the legitimacy of psychology as a new field. Sherif implies that procedures were accepted as correct on account of their familiarity and reputation rather than any intrinsic analytical value. This social and intellectual perspective determined what was thought of as 'logical'.

All this is to say that early psychology did not proceed in a purely logical way. It used techniques that seemed persuasive because they reflected approaches in other more prestigious areas. The approaches may have been logical in those contexts, but that did not mean it was logical to apply them directly to a new field.

Of course, Sherif herself does not argue in a purely logical way. She too attempts to position readers to accept her point of view by emphasising details, such as the 'strivings' of psychologists to 'gain status'; by using phrases such as 'slavish devotion'; and by drawing analogies, 'studying a rock . . . and a human individual'. These textual and stylistic moves support her case, making the logic of her position seem more persuasive.

Causality, like description, narration and exposition, is an important strategy to be used in making an argument for or against something. It can help us to construct an ordered perspective since the movement from cause to effect has a grammar which is similar to the way we structure sentences, paragraphs and even whole essays. Causality allows for the strict definition of the process of events and effects in a causal chain, so helping us to present and order our ideas. By using a thesis statement we can clearly establish the key issue in our argument for the reader.

While it is carefully structured, causality does have a traditional value in our culture. The appeal to clear logic is an influential strategy in our writing. At the same time, if we inspect a causal argument carefully we may see that it breaks 'pure' logic in appealing to readers' social and intellectual perspectives. Causality is not simply an abstract ideal but is closely related to authors' and readers' **points of view**.

Thus we need to keep a double perspective on causal logic. First, as writers we should appreciate its usefulness in organising and presenting our thoughts. But secondly, as readers, we ought to remain alert to the way that causality can persuade and manipulate us by presenting debatable ideas and values as logical and objective conclusions.

Exercise
Write a 800-word essay on the benefits of one of the following topics:

- A university education
- Listening to live music
- Overseas travelling
- Playing sport

Try to explain the positive effects of the activity you choose.

Works cited

Darwin, Charles (1859, 1985) *The Origin of Species by Means of Natural Selection*, Penguin, London

Jacka, Elizabeth (1993) 'Australian Cinema: An Anachronism in the 1980s?', in *Nation, Culture, Text: Australian Cultural and Media Studies*, editor, Graeme Turner, Routledge, London

Riddle, Tohby (1992) *A Most Unusual Dog*, Macmillan, Melbourne

Russell, Bertrand (1946, 1991) *History of Western Philosophy and its Connection with Political and Social Circumstances from the Earliest Times to the Present Day*, Routledge, London

Scott, Ronald B. (1993) 'Images of Race and Religion in Madonna's Video *Like a Prayer*: Prayer and Praise', in *The Madonna Connection: Representational Politics, Subcultural Identities, and Cultural Theory*, editor, Cathy Schwichtenberg, Allen and Unwin, Sydney

Sherif, Carolyn Wood (1987) 'Bias in Psychology', in *Feminism and Methodology: Social Science Issues*, editor, Sandra Harding, Indiana University Press, Bloomington

6 Argument

One of the most common kinds of assignments set in university and college courses asks students to **argue** for or against a certain proposition. Such topics may be more or less complicated. Some may expect the writer to base the essay mainly on his or her own ideas, building a case through logical structure. Other topics, indeed most of the ones set in academic courses, expect writers to develop and expand a logical case by integrating research and analysis of other people's ideas with their own.

In this view, academic argument stands at the centre of the writing structures and strategies that we are examining. Because it involves presenting a logical case, supported with evidence and explanation, academic argument makes use of all the *descriptive, narrative, expository and causal structures* that have been discussed in previous chapters. Since it also incorporates research, academic argument employs various methods of *locating and then applying and presenting research material*, as considered in the following chapter.

At the same time, academic argument frequently entails evaluating and judging the theories and research of other writers. Accordingly, it often requires the use of critical perspectives to analyse the functions and effects of *textual strategies* such as figurative language and genre. A number of these kinds of strategies are studied in the book's final section.

Because many different types of writing, research and analytical activities contribute to presenting an academic argument, writers also have to pay close attention to organising all the material into a coherently constructed text. The essay structure established in academic argument is crucial to its ability to make a convincing and persuasive case. An unclear structure can weaken an argument no matter how deeply its author has researched and pondered. **Academic argument synthesises all the writing structures and strategies covered in this book.** We can determine the roles of the various strategic and structural features by observing and analysing the component parts of academic essays and other argument texts.

Propositions

When someone writes a description or a narrative, their raw material is either a set of things in a particular space, or one or more events occurring over a period of time. They adopt a certain perspective towards the things and events, which becomes apparent through the patterns of selection, emphasis and omission of detail which are used in the text.

In writing an argument essay we adopt a similar approach. The raw material is, however, no longer things or events but **propositions**. The *Macquarie Dictionary* defines a proposition as 'the act of proposing... something to be considered, accepted, adopted, or done', where 'the act of proposing' means 'to put forward (a matter, subject, case, etc.) for consideration, acceptance, action'. Hence, in academic argument essays, we debate *for or against* matters or subjects which are put forward for consideration or acceptance (only sometimes do academic essays call for action, though other kinds of texts, like newspaper editorials, often make that sort of move, as in the last exercise in this chapter).

Our decision whether to argue for the proposition or against it, as well as the strength of our support or opposition (total or partial, for instance), determines the selection and emphasis of detail and so reveals our perspective on the issue. The raw material of the proposition is transformed into the particular case we are trying to make. In this process, the **point of view** we adopt towards the proposition is crucial.

Like the other modes of writing we have considered—description, narration and exposition—argument also works through *establishing a specific point of view and arranging details to support or confirm that viewpoint.* What distinguishes argument from the other modes is the deliberate way it sets up and expresses its viewpoint. For while descriptive or narrative viewpoints often remain implicit, argument essays tend openly to announce their perspective on the proposition before proceeding to defend and support it through evidence and other details.

Theoretically, a proposition functions in an argument essay as a kind of 'pre-thesis' statement. It indicates the issue which is to be debated; it does not, however, necessarily identify the author's position on the topic. In many essay questions, a proposition is provided. Initially, then, it's not even the writer's own idea (for example, many assignment questions offer a proposal or quotation which students are invited to discuss). It's then up to writers to decide which side of it they will defend, or where they will position themselves in relation to the proposition. Having taken a stance on the topic, authors can then announce their thesis. The point is that in themselves propositions can always be argued either way, for or against. They are never automatically true but require support and explanation.

When we read articles and books, the proposition's role as a 'pre-thesis' statement tends to be elided—that is, the author has already decided which aspect of the proposition he or she is going to defend. There is no need to present the issue as two-sided. In this respect, published papers as well as completed essays typically read as though their proposition or thesis were indisputable. The fact is, however, the authors still began with a debatable proposition and then made up their own minds in the process of planning and writing the argument. And, of course, this isn't to say that authors are always right. It's possible that readers may question or even reject an author's position.

Consider the following extract written by the historian Christopher Hill. It begins with a debatable proposition—yet clearly Hill has already decided where he stands:

> The Bible was central to all intellectual as well as moral life in the sixteenth and seventeenth centuries. Controversies between Presbyterians and Episcopalians from Elizabeth's reign onwards turned on arguments about Biblical texts. For Walter Travers, for instance, the relationship of church and state was determined by the fact that Old Testament prophets had found it necessary to admonish even godly rulers like David and Hezekiah. But it was not only in religious matters that the Bible was regarded as authoritative. The great Puritan oracle, William Perkins, declared that Scripture 'comprehendeth many holy sciences', including ethics, economics, politics, academy ('the doctrine of governing schools well'). Take the apparently secular sphere of political theory...

The first sentence could be accepted or contested in a number of ways. For example, certain readers (or other authors) might contend that the Bible was *not* central at all; others might suggest that it was central but not to *all* life; still others might claim that the Bible was central to moral life but not to all *intellectual* life. A range of positions may be adopted about the two centuries Hill suggests as well—that the Bible was central in the sixteenth but not the seventeenth century, or vice versa. Each of these objections could also combine with one or more of the others to dispute Hill's claim.

As it stands, however, the text accepts its proposal as true and proceeds to offer supporting examples of the Bible's intellectual and moral implications. The examples clarify the opening proposition. They are written in narrative mode, telling us what people said and thought (since the text is a historical study, we would expect narration to be used). However, they aren't included simply to tell a story but to support and explain the author's position, so they have expository and argument functions as well. Like other texts that use causal logic, argument texts employ description, narration and exposition to offer evidence of their claims.

As Hill moves in this paragraph from asserting a proposition to defending and illustrating it, we can see a mini-version of how argument texts work:

1 A **proposition** is offered.
2 Supporting **evidence** is provided, through description, narration and exposition.
3 **Logic** is used to develop the proposition and evidence into a **case.**

These are the three basic steps in building an argument. While we can glimpse their effects in the above example, we need to examine them more fully in order to see how they contribute to the organisation of an argument, for in longer texts, each step is an important facet of essay structure.

> An **academic argument** is constructed by developing a **proposition** into a **case** through using **description, narration, exposition** and **logic.**

Planning, structuring and drafting

Questions of structure, planning and drafting arise for all forms of writing. In earlier chapters we saw the importance of these questions in descriptive and narrative texts. It was apparent that authors must consistently follow certain spatial and temporal logics if descriptions and narratives are to be clear. These logics rarely spring fully formed from an author's head but have to be planned out—a simple example would be drawing up a chronological list of events before attempting to write a narrative.

A similar process of structuring and planning is needed in texts that use exposition or causal logic. The author has to decide how to arrange the explanation, comparison or causal chain into an order which will strike readers as reasonable (for example, structuring the three key statements in a syllogism). Again, it is usually best to think the arrangement through before starting to write.

Argument essays require careful planning if they are to come across as logical and convincing. Because they start with a proposition which is itself open to debate, arguments must try to proceed fluidly and clearly so as to anticipate and dispel the reader's doubts, difficulties and objections. In this section, we will describe a way of planning argument essays that can help to realise these goals. Subsequent sections will then focus in more detail on the structure of various segments of academic argument and the relations among them.

Let's start by assuming that we want to use Christopher Hill's proposition: 'The Bible was central to all intellectual as well as moral life in the sixteenth and seventeenth centuries', as the basis for an academic essay. How can we turn this one statement into, say, a 1,000-word essay of about seven paragraphs, in which we back up and develop the proposition with evidence and logic?

Obviously we would have to have some knowledge of the period, gained from lectures and tutorials, and from reading books and articles on church and society during the Renaissance, and perhaps some religious texts from the time as well. Assuming we already have or can gain this awareness (and the next chapter considers some approaches to academic research), how can we organise it into an argument?

The first step, as noted earlier, is to establish our position on the topic: do we concur or disagree with the proposition? Once we have staked our position, it will form the basis of the introductory paragraph's **thesis statement**, the one sentence which conveys the author's viewpoint or organising idea for the whole essay. If agreeing with Hill's point, we could use his proposal or our own version of it as the essay's thesis statement.

The essay will have to argue for this position by introducing a number of subsidiary supporting points. Perhaps following Hill's reasoning, these points could be the Bible's relevance to religion, ethics or morality, economics, politics and education. To inform readers of these ideas and to follow up the impact of the thesis statement, each of the supporting points should be indicated in the introductory paragraph. They will then become individual ideas to be discussed and illustrated through the *body*, or middle section, of the essay.

In fact, each of these ideas will form the **topic sentence** for one of the central paragraphs—the sentence identifying what each paragraph is about and how it relates to the essay's thesis. In this case, after the introduction the essay will have five main paragraphs, all adding different details and information in support of both the thesis and each topic sentence. The argument will then close with a concluding paragraph that sums up our position and the reasons for holding it.

This approach thus generates a seven-paragraph argument essay, whose structure can be sketched out as follows:

Introduction	Thesis statement (Bible's centrality). Indication of supporting topics/ideas
1st paragraph	Topic sentence 1 (on religion). Explanation of supporting evidence and logic (using description, narration and exposition)
2nd paragraph	Topic sentence 2 (on morality). Explanation of supporting evidence and logic (using description, narration and exposition)
3rd paragraph	Topic sentence 3 (on economics). Explanation of supporting evidence, etc.
4th paragraph	Topic sentence 4 (on politics). Explanation of supporting evidence, etc.
5th paragraph	Topic sentence 5 (on education). Explanation of supporting evidence, etc.
Conclusion	Summing-up position

Within this outline, relevant items of supporting information for each paragraph might also be briefly noted (e.g., in the second paragraph, key points about the Bible's moral importance could be listed). In drawing up the plan we should also consider the most effective and interesting order in which to place subsidiary ideas.

In part this question of ordering the ideas depends on the strengths of our supporting evidence for each point. At times we need to be able to stand back from our research and try to weigh up its validity and persuasiveness. In most cases, a climactic order that builds to the most significant point is most effective. In the above scheme, then, religion is put first since it is fairly obvious that the Bible would be important for religious matters; education is placed last since it is vital in socialising and training people to accept the influence of the Bible in morality, politics and economics: it helps the system perpetuate itself.

This model can be used to plan and organise academic essays on all topics. It is flexible in length, since depending on the assignment's size, the number of central supporting paragraphs can be increased or diminished. Putting an **essay outline** together in this way provides an initial opportunity to think through the topic after our research is completed and before starting to write. As such, it is a kind of focused *pre-writing exercise*, which makes us weigh up our ideas and research (it might emerge at this stage, for instance, that more information is needed to support one of the points in similar depth to the others). It also helps us to envisage the shape and substance of the argument. Drawing up an essay outline is a vital step in academic writing. It should always precede any attempt at a **first draft**, the preliminary version of the argument that will be revised into the final essay.

With the research and outline finished, we are in a position to write the initial draft. At this stage, even though an outline has been structured, our ideas on the topic may still be developing. It's not until trying to put our ideas into essay form that we really see what our thoughts on the topic are. *Drafting an early version (or two) of an academic essay is part of the process of thinking the topic through.* It provides a basic form which we can rethink and rewrite, asking whether the ideas seem logical and clearly expressed: Have the main points from the outline been included? Are the thesis statement and topic sentences understandable? Does the evidence illustrate and support these ideas? These are the sorts of questions we can ask about a draft and set about improving or correcting in the essay's final version.

Exercise

Draw up essay outlines for the following topics:

- The role of news media on people's understanding of the world
- Social censorship of arts and media
- The relation of environmental conservation to economic growth
- Tertiary education as a user-pays system
- Government regulation of people's private habits and lifestyles

Formulate a proposition for each topic, and then develop five points that would support your thesis about the proposition. Try to evaluate these points in terms of their significance and so place them in a related order in the outline. (As this chapter continues, you will be asked to build some of these topics into complete argument essays.)

Introductions

The introduction to an argument essay is particularly important. It has a number of functions which include setting up the topic, laying out a plan for the paper, and conveying the validity of its thesis:

1 to raise the topic or subject matter;
2 to put forward the proposition;
3 to define key terms in the proposition;
4 to announce the thesis statement;
5 to indicate the main supporting points.

Since the second step has already been considered, we will now discuss the others and review the overall purpose of the introductory paragraph.

In the last chapter, it was suggested that by underlining causal links in narrative, a more compelling account of the details can be presented to readers: causal logic *supplements* narration. In a way the relationship between argument and exposition is similar. As we have seen, exposition works to explain, analyse, compare or contrast ideas and topics. It does not necessarily make a case about the topics—or at least doesn't always make a strong case about them.

Argument supplements these forms of exposition by turning their findings or results into a proposition to be defended. That is to say, **argument transforms exposition into a case**. The findings of exposition provide the thesis of an argument essay. This transformation occurs as the introductory paragraph or paragraphs carry out the above five steps.

Consider this introduction to the second chapter of Raymond Williams' study, *Marxism and Literature*:

> A definition of language is always, implicitly or explicitly, a definition of human beings in the world. The received major categories—'world', 'reality', 'nature', 'human'—may be counterposed or related to the category 'language', but it is now a commonplace to observe that all categories, including the category 'language', are themselves constructions in language, and can thus only with an effort, and within a particular system of thought, be separated from language for relational inquiry. Such efforts and such systems, nevertheless, constitute a major part of the history of thought. Many of the problems which have emerged from this history are relevant to Marxism, and in certain areas Marxism itself has contributed to them, by extension from its basic revaluation,

in historical materialism, of the received major categories. Yet it is significant that, by comparison, Marxism has contributed very little to thinking about language itself. The result has been either that limited and undeveloped versions of language as a 'reflection' of 'reality' have been taken for granted, or that propositions about language, developed within or in the forms of other and often antagonistic systems of thought, have been synthesized with Marxist propositions about other kinds of activity, in ways which are not only ultimately untenable but, in our own time, radically limiting to the strength of the social propositions. The effects on cultural theory, and in particular on thinking about literature, have been especially marked.

The key moments which should be of interest to Marxism, in the development of thinking about language, are, first, the emphasis on language as *activity* and, second, the emphasis on the *history* of language. Neither of these positions, on its own, is enough to restate the whole problem. It is the conjunction and consequent revaluation of each position that remains necessary.

In these paragraphs Williams is preparing the ground for a twenty-three page discussion of language. The material is complex, and the introduction moves carefully. It begins by discussing the broader subject area and explaining the important links between the chapter's key terms, Marxism and language, especially the former's recurrent inability to interpret the latter.

In these steps, Williams realises the major goals of an introduction. He raises the subject matter in a general way; that is, he doesn't leap immediately into a thesis statement but prepares the reader to accept its pertinence and value. Next, he shows the complexity of the subject matter, by defining and discussing its key terms and suggesting that misunderstandings of these terms frequently occur. (Although Williams doesn't do so, it is often a good idea to use a dictionary or thesaurus to help establish definitions of the argument's central terms.) By drawing attention to these misunderstandings Williams opens up space for his own proposition. Hence the initial paragraph of expository analysis and definition prepares the way for the chapter's thesis. It will be developed by that thesis into an argument.

By the end of the introductory section, Williams has moved from commentary and exposition to arguing a case that the 'key moments' for a Marxist theory of language are notions of language as socially active and historical. In so doing he identifies the three main points which the chapter will deal with: language as activity; language as historical; language as historically active. The introduction closes with the central concepts defined and related to one another, the author's position clearly marked out, the thesis proposed, and the main points indicated. The reader knows what he or she is going to read and why. A debatable proposition has become acceptable grounds for the ensuing chapter.

Perhaps the most important aim of the introduction in an argument essay is to secure the *empathy* of readers, in order to ensure that they will give the rest of the paper a fair reading (their full agreement can come later and may not be entirely necessary). By explaining the subject area, defining the terms, and then stating the thesis and main supporting points, this empathy can be produced before readers turn to the main section or body of the essay.

Exercise
Choose three of the topics from earlier in the chapter for which you prepared essay outlines and propositions. Using the ideas you have developed, write an introductory paragraph for each which fulfils all five functions discussed above. (Remember to look up the propositions' important words in a dictionary to help define them clearly.)

The body of an argument essay

The function of the central section or body of an argument paper is to provide evidence and logic that will illustrate and support the thesis statement. This section is the longest part of the paper. It provides the opportunity to show readers the results of the research and reasoning that have been done. As this material can be more or less complex and diverse, it's very important to structure this part of the paper lucidly and coherently, enabling readers to follow the flow of the argument. In line with these goals, the body of an essay has three important functions:

1 to present and explain **evidence and support;**
2 to make clear **transitions** between different points;
3 to **respond** to opposing viewpoints.

These functions concern both the essay's structure and its content or material.

Putting together an essay outline allows writers to sift through the evidence and research they have assembled and to consider in which order it is best presented. In effect, the outline provides a plan for the body of the argument. The general rule is that a climactic order, building up to the strongest points at the essay's close, is most effective. The main reason for this view is that a series of convincing points and reasons at the end of a paper leaves a strong impression that the whole argument is well-supported. The outline and planning stages of the essay, then, should be used to decide on questions of order as well as on the adequacy of research and information.

The body of the essay consists of a flexible number of paragraphs, all of which deal with a separate point that supports the thesis statement. Each of these points forms the **topic sentence** of one of the paragraphs—often the first sentence, informing readers of the paragraph's topic. (Another general rule is that each paragraph should develop one main idea; when a new idea is introduced it's time to start another paragraph.) The key point raised in the topic sentence should then be backed up and developed through evidence and explanation. Hence, **it is in the body of the argument that writers make most significant use of narration, description and exposition**—stories are told, things and places depicted, ideas clarified.

1 Evidence and support

We can see these strategies coming into play in a section of Ngaire Naffine's book *Law and the Sexes*, which argues that the law conceives of all people as if they were a certain kind of man. The author develops and upholds this thesis in the following paragraphs:

> The man of law is an interesting blend of characteristics, all of which, however, cast him in the mould of our society's view of the superior male. On the one hand there is the Hobbesian component. This aspect of the individual is 'acquisitive, competitive, tough, active and individualistic' (Coltheart 1986: 116). In this respect he is a hard-driving individualist: thick-skinned and assertive, a man with a purpose, an agent not a victim. It is this concept of human nature advanced by Thomas Hobbes in the seventeenth century, and endorsed by John Locke, which according to Coltheart (1986: 113) 'remains the model of the liberal citizen'. And it is this liberal model of the public person which has been directly imported into law by theorists such as Blackstone and Rawls...
>
> But there is also another side to the man of law which complements his rugged image of masculinity and demon-

strates his cultural superiority. This is the man of reason: the prudent maker of contracts, advancing his own interests, with rational calculation. His is a high-brow, cultivated form of masculinity which depends on an ability to think and act intelligently, not with brute force. And his is a middle-class intellectual conception of masculinity in the sense that middle-class, male intellectuals have tended to find these qualities in themselves. It calls to mind a comment of Sachs and Wilson (1978: 10) on the judicial view of the male sex: 'If anything, the judges attributed to men a superior spirituality rather than a greater physical prowess, as reflected in loftiness of mind, a capacity for reverence, and the ability to indulge in abstract thought.' It also reminds us of the thinking cultivated in our law schools and valued in the courts... An ability to reason dispassionately and articulately is deemed essential in legal man.

Naffine aims to defend her thesis through analysing the legal notion of 'the superior male' and by introducing evidence of its functions and effects. She divides the figure into two parts to consider it more closely: the Hobbesian individualist and the reasonable man. Each becomes the focus of a separate paragraph, and in order to uphold this division, Naffine quotes from and discusses the ideas of a number of legal and social theorists.

These paragraphs build a body of evidence in support of the thesis by using the full range of writing modes: portraying 'legal man' (description); recounting the figure's historical emergence and influence (narration and causal logic); explaining and analysing the concept from a number of angles (exposition and logic). Each paragraph also closes with a sentence that sums up and reiterates its main point. The evidence is presented and its key implication underlined.

2 Transitions

Authors of arguments must do more than simply assemble a pile of evidence. As they go from point to point, they must also produce a growing sense of the validity of their thesis. To do this, it is essential both to relate one's ideas to those of others (by citing and commenting on their work), and to show the connections between one's own ideas. Making these connections is another important facet of the body of an argument essay.

Because an essay's central section provides a range of varying points and research, clarifying their links and contrasts is vital. In moving from idea to idea, paragraph to paragraph, it is necessary to make **transitions** which clearly signpost for readers the essay's developing argument.

Naffine does this in the opening sentence of the second paragraph: 'But there is also another side to the man of law which complements his rugged image of masculinity and demonstrates his cultural superiority.' She distinguishes the next point from the previous one ('another side'), while suggesting they are tied to and reinforce each other ('complements'). This kind of explicit sequencing of ideas reveals the argument's continuity: it is not a combination of random points but a coherent structure whose various parts are related and ordered.

Transitional sentences, either at the end or beginning of a paragraph, are an essential part of organising evidence and reasoning for an argument. In addition to marking the flow of ideas, they bolster the impact of individual points by enabling evidence for one to relate to others. In the above example, the historical force of active masculinity as a legal factor is seen as more powerful because it is underpinned by a premiss of rationality. Transitions thus help readers follow an essay's line of argument and allow reciprocal support between the points being made.

3 Responding to opposing views

Since the proposition of an academic argument is always debatable, viewpoints opposing an essay's thesis inevitably emerge. They may be apparent in the research material one examines (for example, differing interpretations of a historical or a literary text), or authors may recognise them in the process of devising the paper's thesis. Accordingly, if there is enough room left in an essay after making one's case, it is often effective to try to anticipate and counter questions which some readers may raise. In the essay outline, a paragraph responding to other views can be placed before the conclusion, or responses may be distributed through the essay's central paragraphs.

Basically, there are two ways of handling views that oppose the thesis. The first is simpler but is not always applicable: to **refute** the views, to disprove the opposing arguments. Because it involves questions of proof, refutation works best if the other view is based on incorrect research or information. It can be less effective in disproving an interpretation of facts. In most cases, academic arguments are over questions of interpretation since writers try not to present a paper or thesis until research has been checked and confirmed.

In this case, the more useful strategy is often not to refute but to **concede:** to allow opposing arguments to stand but then *neutralise* them as misleading or incomplete in their claims through pointing out failures or limitations of logic and misinterpretations of texts. Conceding the opposing argument usually enables one to go on to supersede it.

Consider this example from Kay Stockholder's study of lovers and families in Shakespeare's plays, titled *Dream Works*:

> The love and family relationships that structure almost all of Shakespeare's plays are often taken as conventional or peripheral devices in the service of other concerns. In the early comedies they are often ignored as merely conventional background to satiric, moral, or philosophic issues. In the problem plays and tragedies they are obscured by their protagonists' existential or political fates, and in the romances the family structures are often taken as metaphorical expressions of spiritual transcendence. However, the persistence, of love and familial motifs suggests that more abstract concerns should not be seen apart from the frameworks in which they are articulated. Rather, as these frameworks become permeated with and representative of issues of commonwealth and cosmos, they enable a perception of the ways in which the conceptual systems draw their emotional power from the more immediate personal realm, and the way in which this augmentation of abstractions intensifies the import of the personal concerns that have been thus metaphorically extended.

The first half of the paragraph concedes and summarises the way most critical accounts of love and family in Shakespeare's work have tended to see them as minor affairs relative to moral, political and spiritual issues. Stockholder does not try to overturn these interpretations but instead points to their limited understanding of love and family. She then changes the perspective—the switch is marked by the words 'however' and 'rather'. Precisely because love and family arise in all of these complex areas, they *must* be a significant element of the plays. Stockholder thus uses the opposing perspectives against themselves and to support her thesis. Whereas refutation would have involved the hard task of trying to erase those interpretations, concession allows the author to adapt and recycle them into her own case.

A concessional response to opposing views produces two positive effects, an explicit and an implicit one. First, it shows authors building the argument in front of the reader: their position becomes clear through contrast with others. Second, authors themselves can compare their positions against others, sharpening up their own sense of the essay's point of view.

Conceding and adapting opposing views completes the functions of the central body of the essay. It is a final complementary step to presenting evidence in support of the thesis and making transitions between points.

Exercise
Using the outlines and introductions you have already devised, go on to write a 700-word central section for one or more of the topics. Pay close attention to organising evidence to support every paragraph's idea and to including transitions between the paragraphs. Do you wish to add a paragraph that responds to opposing arguments?

Conclusions

In contrast to an introduction, which sets out an essay's aims and ambitions, a **conclusion** offers the chance to reflect on what has been written. It should not simply repeat the introduction but explain why the thesis statement has been satisfactorily supported. In short, the conclusion works as a closing statement of what the argument has shown.

Sometimes writers are not exactly clear what their argument has shown until the conclusion is written—i.e., the conclusion seems to generate the thesis statement. If that occurs, it is best to rewrite the introduction to the essay, to set up clearly what is going to be concluded. A similar step of rewriting the introduction should be taken if the conclusion ends up differing from, or even contradicting the initial thesis statement. Writing a conclusion is often an important part of the drafting process.

That these changes to the essay's ideas can occur underlines the fact that writers continue to think their topics through long after they have finished planning and outlining them. The drafting and writing process is very much part of the thinking process. The conclusion provides the author as much as the reader with an opportunity to reflect on what the essay has been saying.

For example, in the following extract E. J. Hobsbawm reflects on the interconnections between social-political rights and labour movements which he has been arguing for in the article 'Labour and Human Rights':

Socialist movements of the late nineteenth [and early] twentieth centuries—particularly in the early days—thus provided one of the few environments in which, say, emancipated women, Jews, and people with coloured skins could except to be accepted on their merits as human beings and not suffer formal discrimination; perhaps the only such environments for those who had neither a great deal of money nor family connections. Perhaps they did not give the rights of such groups as exclusive a priority as their supporters might have wished, but they not only defended them, but actively campaigned for them, as part of the general championship of Liberty, Equality and Fraternity—slogans which early labour and socialist movements took over from the French Revolution—and of human emancipation. The struggle against social oppression implied the struggle for liberty.

The paragraph recapitulates both specific points about the egalitarian structure, tradition and activities of socialist movements, and the more general thesis concerning the link between labour campaigns and the drive for social freedom. It ends with a simple but striking statement that sums up and underlines the link between oppression and liberty, capturing the article's key point.

In some published essays and books, the conclusion also functions as an indication of future directions and ideas that the author hopes to pursue. This kind of conclusion is perhaps less effective in argument essays since it may distract readers from the thesis that is currently being endorsed. In this sense, the conclusion offers the author the final chance to impress his or her point of view on the reader.

Academic argument is the most frequently assigned kind of essay that students have to produce. It combines a wide range of writing structures and strategies in the attempt to present and support a coherent thesis with evidence. This kind of essay usually requires careful planning, organising and drafting in order to make its case as compelling and interesting as possible.

In a way, one can never be 100 per cent correct in an academic argument: rival views or interpretations can always be proposed. Hence the onus falls on producing a convincing and persuasive text. An important part of doing so is to express the ideas clearly and to structure the argument logically, drawing links between the thesis and supporting ideas. But as well as writing and organising essays clearly, authors must **research** topics in sufficient detail.

The following chapter discusses a number of approaches to academic research.

Exercises

1 Write a concluding paragraph for each of the essays you have produced through the chapter. Does the conclusion change or challenge the thesis statement and evidence you have already developed? Reread and revise the papers to ensure that their points of view on the topics remain consistent.

2 Analyse the following article into its component parts—i.e., write a comprehensive outline of the essay in which you identify the introduction, body and conclusion; the thesis statement; the main supporting ideas and topic sentences; its evidence and any uses of description, narration, exposition and logic.

Do you agree with the case that is presented? Develop an outline that opposes the article's ideas. Write a 500-word essay in which you challenge the main points that it makes.

What we must do to save the planet

Crispin Tickell

The world faces a growing list of problems: overpopulation, dwindling resources, environmental degradation, industrial pollution, ozone depletion, global warming and the rest. It is already too late to avert them. But we can still mitigate some of their effects and prepare ourselves for a different sort of world.

Over the last twenty years, there has been some progress towards this goal. A remarkable change in public awareness has led individuals, groups, governments and international bodies in their different ways to take the first steps towards wisdom. These are to recognise that these problem exist, and to begin—albeit in piecemeal fashion—to do something about them.

But in relation to the size and scope of the issues, we have hardly started. We are still at the beginning of the beginning, and must learn not only to behave differently but to think differently. This is most difficult of all, as it requires us to abandon assumptions, change habits, create new models of thought, accept different values, and see the world through other eyes.

To change our way of thinking, we first need to recast our vocabulary. Words are the building bricks of thought. The instruments of economic analysis are blunt and rusty. Terms such as 'growth' 'development', 'cost benefit analysis' and even 'gross national product' have come to be misleading. They are more than ripe for redefinition.

Secondly, we need to realise that 'conventional wisdom' is sometimes a contradiction in terms. Some trends—for example the consumption of non-renewable resources—point in the wrong direction. But, as the French writer René Dubos has well said, 'wherever human beings are concerned, trend is not destiny'. Nothing is inevitable unless we make it so.

Then there is the need to change our culture. The division between the cultures of science and the arts is rightly decried. But neither culture is now in charge. Our real bosses are the business managers. Even two centuries ago. Edmund Burke feared that the age of 'sophisters, economists and calculators' had come. Our problem is that their calculations are usually short-term.

Finally, we need a value system which enshrines the principle of sustainable development. The concept can mean different things to different people, but the idea behind it is simple: we must devise models for a relatively steady-state society, in which population size is in broad balance with the availability of resources.

Behaving differently follows naturally from thinking differently. Much of the new behaviour will come from individuals and groups. But it is governments that are best placed to exercise leadership and there are several areas in which they must act.

Taking the question of people first, government must support international organisations seeking to limit human population increase, to promote the status of women and family planning, and to anticipate and cope with likely displacements of human population.

Then there is the matter of energy. Social costing must be applied to different sources of energy; efficiency of energy use must be increased and energy conservation improved; and alternative sources of energy must be found so as to cut back on the consumption of

fossil fuels. Energy-efficient transport systems must be introduced and new building design promoted.

Concerning land use, action is needed to promote reforestation and agro-forestry; and to make more economical use of fresh water. Setting up ministries of land use would put an end to the division of responsibility between bodies representing vested interests, such as agriculture, forestry or town and country planning.

At the same time, industry must introduce cleaner production methods and learn to cope more effectively with the disposal of toxic and other wastes.

All this amounts to a refashioning of our society. But the size of the task need not stun us into inaction. There is a relatively short list of principles on which governments should learn to act, both individually and jointly.

First, the practices governments can adopt make sense not only for environmental reasons. Conserving forests and creating new ones to draw carbon out of the atmosphere will help to slow global warming. So will a shift to fuels which do not add to atmospheric carbon dioxide. But there are other excellent reasons for acting in this way, such as conserving our non-renewable resources of coal and oil.

A measure of internal reorganisation will also be necessary. This should include: tight co-ordination at the centre, to ensure the integration of policies; environmental auditing within ministries, as well as environmental accounting in annual budgets; proper environmental costing and pricing of government actions; the use of fiscal incentives and disincentives, for example covering the generation of energy; and ensuring clear ground rules for the operation of the free market.

Governments should insure against disaster. The premium for this is precautionary investment, such as improving coastal defences, building bridges and oil rigs higher out of the water, and planning for changing patterns of rainfall—and thus the availability of fresh water.

Governments should also re-target scientific research, provide more financial support for it, and co-ordinate the results, globally as well as nationally. At the global level, we need better means of observation from satellites and ground stations, as well as regular monitoring of changes in the condition of the land, the sea and the air.

Governments should work out an international strategy which sets the framework for collective action. It should take good account of equity, and must, above all, be founded on national as well as international interest. Lastly, governments should always consider environmental issues in a broad context. Isolated measures designed to cope with one problem can make others worse.

Above all, we must recognise that human society is more fragile than life itself. Ultimately we are as constrained by biological limits as any animal species. But, unlike them, we can consciously shape our future. If we fail to do so, there will be no one to blame but ourselves.

Source: New Scientist, 7 September 1991

Works cited

Hill, Christopher (1993) *The English Bible and the Seventeenth-Century Revolution*, Allen Lane, London

Hobsbawm, E. J. (1986) 'Labour and Human Rights', in *Politics and Ideology*, editors, James Donald and Stuart Hall, Open University Press, Milton Keynes

Naffine, Ngaire (1990) *Law and the Sexes: Explorations in Feminist Jurisprudence*, Allen and Unwin, Sydney

Stockholder, Kay (1987) *Dream Works: Lovers and Families in Shakespeare's Plays*, University of Toronto Press, Toronto

Tickell, Crispin (1991) 'What We Must Do to Save the Planet', *New Scientist*, 7 September

Williams, Raymond (1986) *Marxism and Literature*, Oxford University Press, Oxford

7 Research methods

The previous chapter stressed the importance of integrating research findings into academic essays. Indeed, as we will see, the presence of research findings is one of the most important generic markers of academic writing. In this type of writing, authors are expected to present more than their own thoughts and ideas. They are required to put forward a logical case based on verifiable evidence and explanation. This chapter deals with some of the methods which can be used to locate appropriate research material and then suggests how this might be applied and presented in an essay.

Locating research material

The first stage in locating appropriate research material involves becoming familiar with the library catalogue. The holdings of a library are catalogued using a system of card indexes, microfiches or online computer entries. Each method allows researchers to search the catalogue for information classified according to author, title or subject, and will retrieve books, journal titles, magazine titles, newspaper titles, collections of conference papers, theses, reference works, government publications and audio-visual materials.

The library catalogue has some limitations, however: a subject search on a given topic will provide titles of relevant books, journals and newspapers, but it will not help with information about chapters in books of edited collections, individual papers in particular volumes of journals, or articles in particular editions of newspapers.

Access to this information may be available through **reference lists** (or **bibliographies**) in books which are closely related to the topic, but this is an unreliable method of searching for information. A more systematic and consequently more effective approach is to make use of specialised **indexes** and **abstracts** held in the library.

Indexes and abstracts

Indexes and abstracts are publications which help to locate chapters in books, individual articles and conference papers. Often they cover specific disciplines. Some examples include: *Humanities Index, Social Science Index, Psychological Abstracts* and *Communication Abstracts*.

Not all indexes are so specialised. Information about current issues and events in Australia and overseas may be accessed via *APAIS (Australian Public Affairs Information Service)*. APAIS defines its scope as 'a subject guide to scholarly periodical literature in the social sciences and humanities published in Australia and to selected periodical articles, conference papers, book and newspaper articles on Australian economic, social, cultural and political affairs'. As such, it provides a valuable research tool for a variety of topics. A description of how *APAIS* is organised also illustrates the basic format for similar indices.

APAIS is divided into three sections: the Key to Literature Indexed, the Subject Index and the Author Index. The Key to Literature Indexed lists periodicals, newspapers, books and conference proceedings. The Subject Index is the main one, and is where articles are listed under specific subject headings. Sometimes the index will suggest preferred subject headings, more specific titles or related terms that direct the user to other relevant material. (For example, some of the articles included later in the chapter were initially looked for under the heading 'Equal Opportunity'; the Subject Index directed us to the heading 'Affirmative Action' where relevant articles were actually listed.) The Author Index lists the authors of the articles that are indexed.

Recently, many indexes and abstracts have been organised into electronic databases on CD-ROM. This means that many volumes of indexes and abstracts can be stored on a single compact disk, making searching much faster and easier. Conventional hard copy indexes and abstracts tend to be classified according to author or subject, but CD-ROM versions can be searched using keywords (or their combinations), titles or publication dates. *APAIS* is available in electronic form on the CD-ROM titled *AUSTROM* (which also includes other databases on education, leisure, family studies, law, criminology, consumer affairs, architecture and sport).

There are various other sources of research material. Depending on the topic, the following may be useful: encyclopaedias, dictionaries, atlases, government publications, yearbooks, films, videotapes, audiotapes, published bibliographies, newspaper clippings services. In addition, economic, social and demographic statistics can be found in Australian Bureau of Statistics publications, which are available in most large libraries.

Notetaking

Once the research material has been located, some record of it needs to be taken in order to keep track of it for future use. Two kinds of information need to be recorded:

1 the publishing details; and
2 the content of the material (and a critical response to it).

Publishing details

A record of the publishing details is necessary for the appropriate acknowledgement of the original author *and* for the location of the material, should anyone want to check it for themselves. The details needed will vary according to the form of the publication. A book would require the following details:

- full name/s of the author/s;
- title of book (including any sub-title) as listed on the title page;
- edition used;
- city of publication;
- publisher;
- year of publication.

A chapter in an edited collection would need a record of slightly different information:

- full name of author/s of pertinent chapter;
- title of chapter;
- title of book (including any sub-title);
- edition used;
- full name of editor/s;
- city of publication;
- publisher;
- year of publication;
- page numbers of chapter.

An article in a periodical would need:

- full name of author/s of article;
- title of article;
- title of periodical;
- numbers of volume or part;
- date of publication;
- page numbers of article.

There are several ways of keeping a record of this information. For a short list of references, notes of the details on a piece of paper would do. For longer lists, many researchers prefer to use a card file (either handwritten on 75mm by 125mm cards, or using a computer program like a database) where each 'card' is used for the details of one reference. This system enables the cards to be ordered and re-ordered: by author, by subject matter, or even chronologically. It can also become part of a permanent record of research, to be re-used and updated for other projects.

Recording content

Taking notes on the content of research findings involves not only summarising the main theme and direction of the author's line of thought, but also some kind of critical reaction to it. We need to list the major points which the author is making to show the development of the argument, *and* we should record our own critical evaluation of the individual points and the logic of the argument.

These two aspects—the summary and the evaluation—combine to make our notes a valuable resource when we come to write a research essay. Not only do we have a record of what others have said, and so can use their arguments to substantiate our own, but we can give our own position and point of view a critical edge by being able to respond to such arguments.

The method of recording the content and evaluation of published material is a personal choice. There are two main ways of going about it. The first is to take extensive notes while reading (and re-reading) the material, including a summary of the main points, word-for-word quotations of important points (using prominent quotation marks to identify them as the author's words), and of course the evaluation. The notes can be cross-referenced (or attached) to the cards which record the publishing details of the article or book.

The other commonly used method of recording content is to take photocopies. Photocopying every relevant article or chapter on the topic can be quite satisfying and certainly promotes a feeling of achievement as the pile of paper grows. The advantage of photocopying is that the copies provide a permanent record of exactly what others have said on any topic. The disadvantage derives from the passive, non-critical nature of the activity. Photocopies have value only if they are read critically. Highlighting relevant passages helps, but does not organise or evaluate the points. In addition, photocopying is subject to copyright provisions and may not always be possible.

Exercise

Using the library catalogue, make a list of twelve recent sources that would provide useful research material for one of the following topics:

- immigration debate in Australia;
- intellectual property;
- land rights;
- performance enhancing drugs.

Record the publishing details. Sources should be a mixture of books (from the library catalogue) and periodical articles (from indexes such as *APAIS*). Note down your search strategies and compare those used by others in your class.

Applying and presenting research material

There are several ways of incorporating other people's ideas in research essays: they include **summary**, **quotation** and **paraphrase**. These are not interchangeable options; each has a specific purpose. In practice, when writing an essay or assignment it's best to use a combination of the three methods.

Summarising another person's argument can be useful if an overview is required. For example, if we wanted to write about a particular social issue that was currently being debated, we might find it useful to summarise the main points of each side of the argument before putting forward our own position. The exact words used by each side may not be needed, and an overview would suffice.

Direct quotation of someone else's words should be used if the exact words need to be commented on. For example, in some academic arguments the definition of the terms can be a most important aspect of the case. Here, other author's definitions may need to be quoted and critically appraised. Direct quotations are also useful if an author is using a term in a particularly meaningful or innovative way.

Sometimes it is tempting to use many direct quotations in a research essay. The quoted material can sound very authoritative; however, it may be difficult to integrate a lot of material from different writers into the one essay. Since the quotations are never written in quite the same style as those of the writer of the essay, there may be a problem of continuity. Instead of reading like a logically ordered, carefully researched piece of work, the essay may start to sound like a series of disconnected statements.

Paraphrasing is expressing someone else's ideas in your own words. It can be a more effective technique than the overuse of direct quotations. It enables the writing to flow more smoothly without the disruption caused by other authors' styles. Paraphrasing does, however, change the original wording. Hence, it may not be as useful as direct quotation in situations where the exact meanings of words are being scrutinised for their connotations, or the expression of a particular phrase is being quoted for its pertinence.

Each technique—summary, direct quotation or paraphrase— must be documented to acknowledge the contribution of the original author and to enable other readers to find the same source. Failure to do this may result in charges of **plagiarism**. Plagiarism is using someone else's words or ideas and presenting them without reference. It occurs when directly quoted passages from another author's work are incorporated either without quotation marks or acknowledgement (or both), or when summarised or paraphrased passages are used without acknowledgement. Plagiarism is regarded as a serious offence in tertiary institutions, where the penalties may range from the deduction of marks to exclusion from the institution.

Exercise
Retrieve two or three of the references from the previous exercise. How do the authors quote other research (summary, quotation or paraphrase)? Find a direct quotation and re-write it as a paraphrase. What effect do the changes have?

Documenting sources
There are several ways to document sources, which will vary across disciplines. Each will be defined in a style manual. Two

examples of commonly used manuals for our purposes are the *MLA Handbook for Writers of Research Papers* (published by the Modern Language Association of America) and the *Style Manual for Authors, Editors and Printers of Australian Government Publications* (published by the Australian Government Publishing Service). There are others, each with their traditions of use and idiosyncrasies of style. Some styles use a system of **footnotes** (which may include bibliographical information) to acknowledge sources; some use **parenthetical documentation** for acknowledging sources, together with a full bibliographical listing at the end. Even the contents of the brackets in parenthetical documentation may vary. In **MLA** style, the brackets usually contain the author's name and the page number of the source material, but in the **Harvard** system, the bracketed information usually consists of the author's name and the year of publication.

Rather than learn the rules of a particular style, we need to remain flexible and adopt whichever is appropriate for writing in a particular discipline.

Exercises

1 Read the articles reprinted on the following pages on:

The Republican Debate in Australia, and
Affirmative Action.

Choose one topic and make a 150–200 word summary of each article, noting the main points.
2 Write a short critical response to each article in the chosen set (150 words).
3 Using your summaries and critical responses, prepare a thesis statement in accordance with the principles discussed in Chapter 6. On the basis of your thesis statement, construct an outline for an academic essay (1,500 words) which argues your case.
4 Using the articles provided (supplemented by other research if possible) write the essay, paying close attention to the incorporation of other people's findings (use quotations and paraphrases as appropriate), and the documentation of these (use the style of referencing recommended by the teaching staff in your area).

Topic 1: The Republican Debate in Australia
Removing the crown with light fingers

George Winterton

A republic is a State in which sovereignty is derived from the people and in which all offices are filled by persons ultimately deriving their authority from the people

The *Macquarie Dictionary* defines a republic as 'a State in which the supreme power rests in the body of citizens entitled to vote and is exercised by representatives chosen directly or indirectly by them . . . a State, especially a democratic State, in which the head of the government is an elected or nominated president, not a hereditary monarch'.

Since the Commonwealth Constitution can be amended only by the people in a referendum, ultimate sovereignty in Australia resides in the Australian people. Moreover, the provisions of the Constitution were approved by the Australian electors before its enactment in London.

Australia is therefore, already a State in which sovereignty derives from its people, and in which all offices, except that at the very apex of the system, are filled by persons deriving authority directly or indirectly from the people. The only Australian office incompatible with a republic is the monarchy, so that it is not inaccurate to regard Australia as a 'crowned republic', a view favoured by some monarchists. Accordingly, all that is required to make Australia completely republican is to remove the monarchy: no other constitutional change is required.

'Republican' government is a concept of Western political science with a long history, during which it has acquired constitutional and moral connotations, including fidelity to the rule of law, protection of personal liberty, and the checking of governmental power through the separation of powers. In this respect also, Australia is already republican.

Accordingly, all that is required to convert Australia into a republic is to remove the monarchy and implement consequential constitutional amendments. This is the so-called 'minimalist' position embodied in the Terms of Reference of the Republic Advisory Committee, which require it to describe the 'minimum constitutional changes necessary' to achieve a viable federal republic of Australia which maintains intact 'the effect of our current conventions and principles of government'.

Such a republic would substitute an Australian head of State for the monarch and the governor-general, and make consequential provision for the president's appointment, removal and powers.

Under such a model of republican government, the present relationship between the political executive and the governor-general would be maintained essentially unaltered. All other institutions of Australian government—the States, the Senate, the High Court—and our fundamental constitutional principles—federalism, responsible parliamentary government, the separation of powers, judicial review—would remain completely unaltered.

The concept of a 'minimalist' republic has been criticised from both ends of the republican spectrum: for ironically, the one issue that unites radical republicans with monarchists is opposition to the 'minimalist' model of republican government.

Some republicans claim that constitutional change should not be confined to the head of State: for them, the proposed changes are too minimal. However, many of these critics do not really advocate more substantial republican changes; rather, they advocate wider constitutional reform or, even more generally, wider governmental reform. Many of their proposals, such as greater governmental accountability to parliament or Aboriginal land rights, do not necessarily involve any constitutional change, and even those proposals that do, such as the enactment of a constitutional Bill of Rights, are not particularly 'republican' in nature.

Of course, 'republicanism' as a concept of political science has a certain ethos, which emphasises the rights and obligations of citizenship and stresses individual and communitarian concepts of civic virtue. But this ethos is more psychological than constitutional and does not entail specific constitutional consequences.

This is demonstrated by two recent critiques of 'minimalism'. Peter Cochrane advocated the scrapping of 'the tinsel obeisances in our culture that amount to a giant colonial hangover', such as royal prefixes, the Constitution's 'arcane language', and mayoral and judicial regalia (*The Sydney Morning Herald* 2/8/93), while Wayne

Hudson and David Carter suggested a combination of 'minimalist constitutional change and maximalist political, social and cultural reform' (*The Australian* 28/7/93).

Indeed advocates of wider 'republican' principles are often hard-pressed to cite concrete constitutional change which ought to result from 'republicanism', except perhaps recognition in the constitutional preamble of civic principles enjoying virtually universal support, such as commitment to democracy, the rule of law and protection of fundamental rights and freedoms.

Comparative government demonstrates that many of the constitutional reform proposals of republican opponents of 'minimalism' are not specifically 'republican'. Constitutional Bills of Rights, for example, are found in most constitutional monarchies as they are in virtually all republics. Some 'maximalists' seek to 'piggyback' their personal reform agendas on the republic but they will inevitably sink both. The proposal to convert Australia into a republic must be examined on its own merits and not become enmeshed with wider unrelated constitutional issues.

Monarchists oppose even a 'minimalist' republic on two related, supposedly non-sentimental grounds.

First, they adopt an *in terrorem* argument, maintaining that the monarchy is so central to our constitutional system that its removal would undermine the entire system and cause its collapse. As D.P. O'Connell wrote in 1977: 'The monarchy is the keystone of the system. Remove it and the system must collapse.' This is difficult to reconcile with monarchists' oft-repeated assertion that we are a republic already—a 'crowned republic'—and is belied by the experience of successful 'Westminster-style' republics such as Germany and Ireland.

Moreover, their assertion is ultimately based on sentiment, not constitutionalism. Having noted that 'what is important about the monarchy is that it embodies the principle of continuity without which there is no political security', O'Connell conceded that 'the principle of continuity is nourished by myth and enshrined in mystery'. If the monarchy is revered as a living symbol of links with British tradition, this should be admitted openly, not concealed beneath a veneer of constitutionalism.

The monarchists' specific attack on 'minimalism' rests on the argument that it is inherently self-contradictory because a president would inevitably be 'political', radically changing the political system. As their convenor Lloyd Waddy recently argued: 'Any change means giving more or less power to the executive (and prime minister) and either change is wholly undesirable.'

While it is true that the existing balance between prime minister and head of State may not be duplicated exactly, why should it be? Is it so perfect that improvement is impossible? Would not a president with more secure tenure than the governor-general be a more effective constitutional guardian?

But in any event, the present balance of power between head of State and prime minister could be maintained essentially intact. Monarchist claims that a republican head of State would inevitably be politically partisan are unfounded. A president elected by two-thirds majorities in parliament would be at least as bipartisan and non-political as a prime ministerial appointee like the governor-general.

The experience of successful parliamentary republics with a largely ceremonial head of State, such as Germany, Australia, Ireland and India, demonstrates the feasibility of the 'minimalist' model.

Comparisons between governmental systems are useful only if like is compared with like. Comparisons are too often drawn between constitutional monarchies and undemocratic republics. But it is just as misleading to compare Denmark or The Netherlands (both monarchies) with Iraq or Uganda (both supposedly 'republics'), as it would be to compare pre-1945 Japan or Mussolini's Italy (both monarchies) with contemporary Germany or Ireland (both republics). Constitutional monarchy must be compared with constitutional republic for the comparison to have any point at all.

Even so, such comparisons prove little unless a causal link can be established between the method of selecting the head of State and a country's political stability or economic success. Politically stable monarchies like Britain and Sweden are matched by politically stable republics like the United States and Switzerland and economically republican Germany is matched by monarchical Japan. But can any of this be linked to the head of State? Does Germany's better economic performance than Britain's tell us anything regarding the head of State that is not negated by comparing Japan's economic record with that of (republican) Argentina?

The only lesson, surely, is that Australia's political stability reflects a combination of political, social, economic and cultural factors, including the moderation, good sense and democratic instincts of the people. A relatively minor change to the largely ceremonial office at the apex of the constitutional system is hardly likely to change any of that. In assessing the risks or dangers of various republican options, let us be realistic and address real issues, not phantasms.

Source: The Australian, 11 August 1993

Breaking up is hard to do

Robin Hill

Prime Minister Paul Keating says our national identity will blossom. Sections of the British press believe it is inevitable. Opinion polls claim we want it. But how close are we to becoming a republic? Some believe it will happen only when the National Party starts to advocate change. And no one can tell when that will be.

Some academics and lawyers say there is one essential prerequisite to Australia becoming a republic: unity. In theory, that means the national political parties, six states and the community must unite before there is a referendum on the matter.

Any hint of division probably would mean the referendum will fail and history suggests it would not succeed were it presented to voters a second, third or fourth time. Referendums to increase federal powers have failed repeatedly over the years.

Tug-of-war

So far, we have been led to believe that becoming a republic would be straightforward. Until now, the political tug-of-war has dominated the debate but our constitution also is looming as a stumbling block on the road to a republic. Dr Greg Craven, a reader in law at Melbourne University, has publicly spoken about the difficulties involved.

'It is terribly unfashionable to say that there are problems with changing the constitution,' he says. 'So far there has been a conspiracy of silence. We are in for an absolute bunfight, it is going to be huge.

'There has never been a fundamental amendment to the Australian constitution. All we have ever done is tinker around the edges. As with any constitution, as soon as you start tinkering with the bits that are at the absolute core of the structure, for instance, federalism or the traditional independence of parliament or the monarchy, it becomes much harder.'

Others agree with Craven. Shadow Treasurer Alexander Downer says 'it is massively difficult to change the constitution' and pro-monarchist Dame Leonie Kramer agrees 'it is a very complicated question'.

To amend the constitution, a number of steps are required, as set out in section 128 of the constitution. First, a bill setting out the necessary changes would have to be passed either by both houses with an absolute majority or by one house passing it twice with a gap of three months.

Second, the matter would then have to be put to a referendum

between two and six months after
the bill had been passed. The question put to voters may be something like: 'Do you approve of the
Constitution Alteration Republic
Bill?'

Third, for the referendum to be
carried, more than three states would
have to pass it and there would need
to be a national majority of more
than 50%.

Chequered

Australia's referendum history is
chequered. Since 1906, only seven
of the 18 referendums put to voters
have been carried unanimously by
all six states. A total of eight proposals for amendments have been
passed. In 1988, not one state
voted in favour of the four referendum questions. If the plan, as
suggested by the republican movement and hinted at by the prime
minister, is to change from constitutional monarchy to constitutional
republic by January 1, 2001—to
mark the anniversary of federation—
we have only a few years to
examine important questions and
work out the mechanics of change.

So far, the public push for a
republic seems to be growing,
especially among the young, but a
combined political approach is still
a thing of the future. And although
the polls may indicate a national
majority is possible, it is still by no
means certain that four or more
states would vote in favour of a
referendum.

Exactly what form of republic
we will choose is yet to be determined. The Australian Republican
Movement (ARM), headed by author
Thomas Keneally and lawyer
Malcolm Turnbull, argues that
changes to the constitution and our
system of democracy should be
minimal. In particular, it has been

suggested that the governor general's
powers be 'transferred' to a president,
elected not by the people (as in the
United States) but by both houses
of parliament.

Severing our ties with the
Commonwealth is not favoured by
the ARM. Opinion polls have shown
we are generally not in favour of
adopting the American or French
system. Some suggest an Irish-style
republic, involving a directly elected,
high-profile president with only
limited powers, might work here.

The debate on what kind of a
republic we should adopt is still
embryonic, despite the fact that
Australians from the days of Henry
Lawson have been advocating a
pro-republic stance.

Michael Lavarch, attorney general designate, has indicated he has
an 'open mind' on the question. 'I
have no opinion,' he says. 'We need
to define this debate more than we
have done. If possible, we need to
get it out of the party political atmosphere and look at the mechanics
of how we facilitate the debate.'
Lavarch adds that there is a risk the
public will switch off if the debate
gets too technical.

On the other side of the
political fence, Liberal leader John
Hewson dismissed the republican
issue during the election campaign
as a diversion. The Liberal Party is
yet to make it part of its policy
platform despite being implored to
do so by the Young Liberals. John
Brogden, president of the New
South Wales Young Liberals, says
he believes the mood for a
republic 'is very strong', especially
among 18 to 24-year-olds. The
NSW Young Liberals are about to
do some street polling of young
people across Sydney to confirm
just how strong the mood is.

Open discussion

'Our view is that the party should start talking about the issue very openly . . . You will find a lot more Liberals, both in parliament and out of parliament, identifying them-selves with the issue in the next 12 months,' he says. Brogden, 23, believes that even if the Liberal Party went to a referendum opposing a republic, the referendum would 'still get up and the Liberal Party would be found to be right out of touch with Australia'.

Gerard Henderson, executive director of the Sydney Institute, agrees that the Liberal Party should start to address the issue more vigorously. He says the Labor Party tends to have a far greater under-standing of 'symbolic politics' than the Liberals. He believes momen-tum for a republic will probably increase in the next three years. 'It may well be the national issue in that election,' he says. However, Downer, 40, a failed contender for the deputy leadership of the Liberal Party, argues we have little idea of what is involved. 'There is a low level of public understanding on the matter,' he says. 'People who think this is simple are mad. This is massively difficult. It won't happen in my lifetime because people will give up when they realise how complicated it is. The debate needs to be taken a lot further than the simple proposition as to why we have a British queen as our head of state.'

Hurdles

He argues that among the major hurdles will be how we define the powers that would be given a president. Our constitution does not, for example, define the gover-nor general's reserve powers because it assumes they are basically the same as those of the Queen. If our ties with the Queen are cut, these powers probably would need to be re-examined. Do we make them larger or smaller? Would we give the president more powers than the prime minister?

Once these questions start being debated publicly, Downer says, voters will begin to have second thoughts. 'Australia is a conservative country,' he claims. 'The people will not accept radical change like this. It really is hard to believe that it would be possible to get a wide consensus on the nature of the republic, the powers of the president, the nature of the reserve powers.'

No one really knows how con-stitutional change would occur. It is widely believed, for example, that Keating is yet to fully familiar-ise himself with the intricacies of the matter. Constitutional lawyers who have examined the question generally agree it is possible but the nuts and bolts are still to be worked out. Do we keep the constitution similar to the one we now have, apart from a few 'cosmetic' changes, or do we put a red pen through the whole docu-ment and rewrite it to suit more modern times?

The Centenary Constitution Foundation, formed in 1991 and headed by Sir Ninian Stephen, is examining this very question. The foundation believes our consti-tution can be amended to form a republic but it has not issued any absolutes on what form that entity should take. Paul Keating says that becoming a republic will make us a more confident nation and believes he has a mandate for that change. It is understood that the government soon may be setting up a constitutional committee to examine the nature of the question to be asked in the referendum.

How might the constitution be changed? Professor George Winterton, professor of law at the University of New South Wales, says it is not a difficult exercise—if some simple rules are followed. 'Most lawyers say the actual changes themselves are not major, that lots of sections would have to be changed because the Queen and governor general are mentioned, but that's mostly cosmetic,' he says. 'The substantive changes are few but the major problem is political.' He adds that unless the political divisions can be ironed out, a referendum would have little chance of success. Winterton agrees that a vital point would be determining the powers and method of election of the president. According to Melbourne constitutional lawyer S.E.K. Hulme, QC, the minute we begin to define these powers, we land in hot water.

Trouble

'You either have to say that person has the same powers as the governor general used to have or you have to define the powers the president has and that is going to cause a lot of trouble,' he says. 'It is not easy to define exactly what those precise powers are because the minute you define them with any closeness, someone will invent a political situation that you have not coped with yet.' Hulme believes a referendum would need to be put when about 80 per cent of the population is found to be in favour of a republic. However, previous referendums show that although there may be enormous public support for them, they can still fail.

According to Winterton, our history shows great public support does not mean all the states will vote for it. 'A very early substantial majority can greatly dissipate during a campaign,' he says. 'Some of the Hawke government proposals in' 1988 had very large majorities in favour reflected in the opinion polls but it dissipated once the campaign got going. And in the Communist Party one in 1951, there was a huge majority of around 80 per cent in favour but, in the end, it lost. It is relevant to the republic question, which shows a high number of people in favour of it.'

One thing the republican movement privately fears is a GST-style scare campaign against the republic because few understand exactly how it would work. The pro-monarchists have raised the question of what would happen if four states voted for a republic but two vehemently opposed it. Could we exist in a divided country (half republic and half monarchist) and would it create constitutional chaos? Winterton says it would be possible to exist in a divided country—but not for long. He believes there is no great difficulty in changing our constitution—it would require altering about 30 sections—but how the states vote in the referendum may cause a major hiccup.

'There are two questions,' he says. 'Can you amend the state constitutions under section 128 of the federal constitution and secondly, if you can, and most people think you can, then you have the political problem that since you only need a majority of four states you could, in effect, be thrusting a republic upon two states who might vote by a large majority to stay as they are. Should we thrust a republic on a state that didn't want it?'

NSW opposition leader Bob Carr has written to Premier John Fahey, asking him to look at the state's constitution to determine how it would need to be changed to embrace a republic. A few days after Fahey dismissed the request as a publicity stunt, he told the NSW Liberal state council that a republic was inevitable. This led other state premiers, including Tasmania's Ray Groom, to agree with Fahey's push for a republic.

Pro-monarchists have, however, seized upon an article written by Greg Craven last year in which he explains that changing the constitution may not be possible. Dame Leonie Kramer and the pro-monarchy group, Australians for a Constitutional Monarch (whose members include Justice Michael Kirby and Sir Harry Gibbs), have asked Craven whether they can use his article in their own publications. (Craven has allowed this, although he is not aligned with either the monarchist or republican camps.) Craven's article, entitled *The Constitutional Minefield of Australian Republicanism*, which was published in *Policy* last year, points to several problems. First, he says the constitution contains several 'covering clauses' which have several references to the monarch and are not covered by section 128. Therefore, Craven suggests there is a problem in amending them.

Growth industry

'This very real difficulty with the covering clauses has produced a serious growth industry among constitutional academics (especially those of a republican opinion) directed towards finding a

plausible ground for arguing that these inconvenient provisions can indeed be amended under section 128,' Craven writes.

Second, Craven suggests that if the constitution is changed federally, there is no real indication that it can be altered at state level.

Craven goes on to say that during a referendum campaign, 'monarchists would have abundant opportunities to impugn the legality of the proposed constitutional amendment. Such charges of unconstitutionality would only secondarily and as a matter of last resort be addressed to a court of law. Their main purpose would be to frighten the electorate away from a positive vote by the allegation of illegality and illegitimacy and as such they would be potent weapons.' He concludes: 'It is abundantly clear that the line espoused by some republicans—that there are no conceivable constitutional difficulties in the way of an Australian republic—is far from accurate.'

However, Winterton (who describes himself as a 'moderate' republican) and other constitutional academics (including Geoff Lindell, a reader in law at the Australian National University) dismiss Craven's arguments. 'Is he really saying we can never change the constitution to become a republic?' Winterton asks. Thomas Keneally believes Australians will be voting in a referendum on the republic in 1998. 'If you believe the latest Quadrant poll [which found that 65 per cent of Australians favour a republic], our attachment to the monarchy is even less popular than the GST,' he says.

Indirect election

Keneally says the president should be indirectly elected by the people. 'What we think will probably happen—and most constitutional experts think this—is that we will have a head of state who is elected indirectly by the people. That is, elected by members of the two houses of parliament by either a simple or two-thirds majority. Now, because the two houses of parliament are of different composition, it will be very hard for anyone to appoint a Bill Hayden or anyone who has been politically rewarded or politically sidelined. We feel that there are a couple of problems with a direct election like we have for the Senate, because then the political parties will inevitably get involved and it will become a political race.'

Keneally stresses that the plan would be to continue as part of the Commonwealth and our British heritage would still be important. It should not be assumed that voting for a republic means a rejection of our past. 'It is true, nonetheless, that there are plenty of people who do not know what it implies constitutionally,' he says. 'What they are more concerned about is the tenor of Australian society the day after we become a republic. Will the Brits be prejudiced against us, will the war dead be spat upon as naïve idiots for dying for Britain, will jackbooted republicans go rampaging through RSL clubs and schools pulling down pictures of the monarch, will we try to rewrite history? If there was any risk of that happening, then we should not vote for it.'

Status quo

Keneally points out that the ARM's approach is to maintain the status quo—while changing the constitution to delete references to the monarch and governor general—but keeping our Westminster system of government.

Keneally says the ARM promotes four main points on how the republic would work. They are:

- We would have an Australian head of state with powers similar to those currently held by the governor general. The prime minister would retain executive powers but the president would have reserve powers (similar to the governor general) which would allow him or her to sack the prime minister if he/she had lost the confidence of parliament.
- We would still operate under the system of parliamentary democracy.
- The head of state would be either directly or indirectly elected by the people of Australia.
- Australia would remain a member of the British Commonwealth, with the Queen as titular head.

More practical changes, such as changes to our currency, would be very gradual, Keneally says. He admits that if the referendum fails, it would put back the republican cause by 10 or 15 years.

Opinion polls so far show the community still has mixed feelings about becoming a republic. A Saulwick survey conducted in May 1992 and published in *The Sydney Morning Herald* shows 56 per cent of Australians say we should become a republic, while 42 per cent believe we should remain a constitutional monarchy and 2 per cent are not sure. A Saulwick survey published earlier this month found that 70 per cent of NSW and Victorian voters favour a republic. However, the AGB McNair poll published in *The Bulletin* in March last year found that 41 per cent favoured a republic and 45 per cent did not. AGB McNair says research it conducted in November last year found the figure has increased to 47 per cent of Australians who feel we should not become a republic.

Skate
Keneally says that it is mainly the 55-plus age group who still favour a monarchy. If they were suddenly to disappear, he argues, 'the referendum would skate it in'. ■

Source: The Bulletin, 26 April 1993

A defence of the constitutional monarchy

Michael Kirby

The Australian Constitution is one of the six oldest constitutions continuously operating in the world. Those who feel that this is a matter for proper pride and who consider that we should stick with the Commonwealth which the Constitution establishes should not feel afraid to express their views. What a sad day it will be for us if diversity of opinion is discouraged and fear replaces reason.

I support reform of society and its laws. But reform means more than change. It means change for the better. My proposition is that it has not been shown that the establishment of a 'Federal Republic of Australia' would be a change for the better. We should not forget that, for the whole modern history of Australia, we have been a monarchy. This indisputable historical fact of our sovereignty is part of what it is to be an Australian. For more than 200 years Australians have had a King or Queen. It has become, and is, part of our society's very nature.

I acknowledge that the debate about our Australian polity is a legitimate one. We may have it, unimpeded by guns or the opprobrium of official orthodoxy, precisely because of our constitutional history,

conventions and instrument. I can, of course, understand some of the criticisms of our constitutional monarchy. For example, I acknowledge that in some parts of Asia the concept of Queen Elizabeth II, as Queen of Australia, may be difficult for some to grasp. Yet I have no doubt that there are niceties of the constitutions of the monarchies of Japan, Thailand and Malaysia—not to say of the republics of the region—that we do not fully understand. No self-respecting country should abandon its history and institutions out of deference for the misunderstandings of its neighbours. No country should alter its constitutional arrangements, if they work well, simply because neighbouring countries do not fully appreciate its history or understand its independence. Regional comity has not, nor should it, come to this.

I can appreciate that there are difficulties, even in some Australian minds, in seeing Queen Elizabeth II as the Queen of this country. But that, undoubtedly, by law she is. I admit that there has been a failure to educate our young people concerning our Constitution. It is a failure which I deplore. It should be rectified. But change this as we may it must be accepted that, generally in the world, the Queen is seen as the Queen of the United Kingdom. Indeed, it is by that sovereignty that she becomes the Queen of this country, under our Constitution, made by us. This was something which the Australian people themselves accepted by referenda at Federation. They did so despite arguments advanced most powerfully then in favour of a republic. Of course, when the Queen goes to Europe or to the United States, she will normally be seen as Queen of the United Kingdom. But when she is in Australia, she is undoubtedly our Head of State just as in Canada she is their Head of State, or in New Zealand theirs. At other times in Australia, her functions are carried on, on her behalf, and in her name, by an otherwise completely independent Governor-General appointed under our Constitution and, in the States, by State Governors. For a long time, Governors-General and Governors in Australia have been Australians. The true measure of the independence of the office was fully seen in 1975. The Queen herself declined to intervene in our Australian constitutional crisis. It arose, and had to be solved, exclusively within Australia. That was as the Constitution required and as befits an independent country. The Queen respected this.

Yet these matters being said, I accept that there are sincere advocates of various forms of republican governments. They will remember that no system of government is perfect or unchangeable. In Australia, we should certainly continue our search for the least imperfect form of government. There are various models. But we should not dismiss constitutional monarchy, as it works in our independent country, simply because it is seen as unfashionable by some or because the popular media are going through a phase

of disaffection with some members of the Royal Family who, earlier, they covered with fawning attention.

Those who would change the Australian Constitution must, if they are sensitive to their fellow citizens, reflect upon the feelings of those who would keep certain fundamentals unchanged. And they must reckon with the strength of those feelings. To be indifferent to such feelings—in an intolerant pursuit of one's own conception of society— runs the risk of the worst kind of majoritarianism.   Paradoxically, democracy works best when it respects the opinion of diverse groups in all parts of the population, not just the majority.

I am willing to concede that in the long run some changes to our constitutional monarchy may occur in Australia. The moves from colonies to dominion and from Commonwealth to a fully independent country continue apace. Our country, like every nation, is on a journey. If Europe is any guide, the journey will probably take us to an enhancement of regional relationships rather than to a retreat into the isolation of the nation-state. And our region, in the coming century of the Pacific, offers us the opportunities of a special relationship with our neighbours if we can harmonise our national role with our geography.

In our relationship with our sovereigns, Australians have been fortunate for most of the modern history of Australia in the high sense of service and duty which those sovereigns have displayed. I concede at once that the recent controversies about some members of the Royal Family—and particularly Prince Charles as heir to our sovereignty— have damaged in some people's minds the cause of constitutional monarchy. In the modern age, it seems, it is necessary for the monarch to be admired at all times. I think all would concede this virtue to Queen Elizabeth II. Some people—based upon taped eaves-dropping of private conversations and snooping photographers—have formed a different view about the Prince and Princess of Wales and other members of the Royal Family. I pass over how such intrusions came about; how they passed into the hands of a voracious media; how suddenly elements in the media turned upon members of the Family; and how intercontinental media interests played off each other like modern brigands. The role of the modern media in manipulating public opinion—even in constitutional fundamentals—must be a source of grave concern to all serious observers. It is virtually impossible to get published in Australia serious opinions in defence of our constitutional system. This is in itself astonishing and disturbing.

But all that is as it may be. We must see recent events in their proper context. Of the Royal Family, only the Queen has any part in Australia's constitutional arrangements. She enjoys good health. Her mother still happily prospers. The Queen will probably be around for a very long time—well into the next century. The crises of the last year will inevitably fade in public memory. In considering republicanism, Australians will see—in increasingly stark relief—the continuity of the service of their Queen. And they will increasingly begin to ask about the arguments which suggest that this stable constitutional system should be preserved or overthrown.

In my estimation those arguments are of two kinds; arguments

from *Realpolitik* and arguments of principle.

Arguments from *Realpolitik*

Before we change our Constitution, it is essential that we make very sure that the change is undoubtedly for the better. The following considerations must therefore be kept in mind.

First, there is the great practical difficulty of securing constitutional change in Australia, given the provisions of section 128 of the Constitution. In the whole history of our federation there have been sixty-three proposals to change the Constitution. Only twelve have succeeded. We started well enough with the first referendum in 1906 which concerned Senate elections. Six states voted in favour of the change; the popular vote in favour was nearly 83 per cent. In 1910 two proposals were put forward. Only one succeeded and that by a whisker. By 1911 the course of our constitutional history was becoming clearer. Two questions were put. Both were rejected; the favourable vote was less than 40 per cent and only one State favoured the change. Thereafter the history of formal constitutional change in Australia has been one of intense conservatism.

Unless there is concurrence between the major political parties, it would seem that the people will reject proposals for constitutional change. And even the existence of such concurrence is certainly no guarantee of success. In 1977, the proposal of the Fraser Government for simultaneous elections had the strongest bipartisan support. Indeed it won 62.2 per cent of the popular vote nationally. It even accompanied three proposals which were indeed accepted (casual vacancies;

territorial representation; and retirement of Federal judges). But the electorate discriminated. The proposal carried in only three States. It was therefore rejected in accordance with the Constitution, as no affirmative majority of the states was secured.

Not all of the rejections of constitutional change have been an exercise of unwisdom. I think it would now be generally accepted that the rejection of the Menzies Government's referendum in 1951 to dissolve the Australian Communist Party was an important protection of civil liberties in Australia. At the beginning of the campaign which was waged by Dr H.V. Evatt against that referendum, polls showed that 80 per cent of the people favoured the proposal. But when it came to the vote, only three States could be gathered in; only 49.44 per cent of the popular vote was won. Sometimes section 128 of our Constitution has been a wonderful guardian of our freedoms.[1]

Nor are we alone in constitutional caution. In Canada recently, a proposal, settled by the politicians, for constitutional changes to meet the demands of the people of Quebec was rejected by the people. The people of Canada affirmed the status quo. One commentator has observed that 'the Canadians ended their constitutional odyssey by constituting themselves a people through an affirmation of the constitutional status quo'.[2]

There is an added complication in the Australian case. The States of Australia are also constitutional monarchies. Their separate polities cannot be ignored. The notion that a future Federal Republic of Australia could dragoon a number of States which preferred to remain

constitutional monarchies is, as it seems to me, unthinkable. Containing continuing monarchies within a Federal Republic might be theoretically conceivable but it would certainly be extremely odd. Effectively, this means that a republican form of government could not easily be adopted in Australia without unanimity within all parts of the Australian polity.

The last experiment in constitutional change should also not be forgotten by the proponents of a referendum about becoming a republic. It will be recalled that in 1988, for the bicentenary of European settlement in this country, we were told that we had to accept certain changes and to do so by our two hundredth birthday. The changes concerned parliamentary terms, fair elections, the recognition of local government in our Constitution and the extension of the protection of certain rights and freedoms to the States. Again, at the opening of the campaign, the polls showed overwhelming support for the referendum proposals. But when it came to the vote, not a single one of the proposals passed. Indeed, not a single one gained a majority in a single State. One only gained a majority in one jurisdiction. The proposal for fair and democratic parliamentary elections throughout Australia—so seemingly rational and just—was accepted in the Australian Capital Territory alone. The dismal showing of the voting of the people of Australia reflected their great caution in altering our constitutional instrument. The average vote for the four proposals was approximately 33 per cent in favour and 66 per cent against. If this record of constitutional change does not have lessons for the republicans in Australia, nothing will teach them the realities of Australia's basic constitutional conservatism.

Secondly, as I hope I have already shown, the proposal for a republic, at least at this stage, would not go by the nod. There would be many people who for reasons of principle or other priorities, would fight the referendum. Any referendum that promises more real or apparent power to any politician—even a single one as President—faces an especially rough passage. This can be shown clearly enough by the rejection of the proposals relating to the terms of Senators. These had bipartisan support of the political parties in 1977 and 1984. On each occasion a majority of the people was secured; but not a majority of the States. Every other proposal for constitutional change by referendum in the last fifteen years has failed dismally.

In these circumstances, many would consider that our national energies should be devoted to priorities which would not be so divisive and which would seem to some to be rather more urgent. Priorities such as the reconciliation and proper provision for the Aboriginal people of Australia. The extension of an accessible legal system to our people. The improvement of the operations of Parliament. The provision of new initiatives to reduce unemployment amongst the young and not so young. The assurance of equal opportunity to Australian women and to other groups who suffer discrimination. The provision of proper educational opportunities and fair access to health care and services. The building of a truly multicultural society. The improvement of local government, roads,

sewerage and other necessities of government. These are aspects of Australia's national life where things are undoubtedly wrong. They represent areas in which we stand a real chance of forging the national resolve that is necessary to secure positive action. And we need no constitutional changes to gain success in them. To inflict upon our country the wound of a divisive debate about a republican form of government—in a form not yet identified in its particularity— would be grievously damaging to the spirit of the country, at least at this time.

Thirdly, it is important to emphasise that in every legal and real respect Australia is a completely independent country. Its independence of the legislative power of the Westminster Parliament began long ago. It passed through the Statute of Westminster in 1931. It was finally affirmed when the Queen of Australia personally assented to the *Australia Act* 1986 in Canberra. The United Kingdom Parliament now has no legislative authority whatsoever in respect of Australia. An attempt, even indirectly, to extend the United Kingdom's official secrets legislation to Australia in the celebrated *Spycatcher* litigation failed both in my court and in the High Court of Australia. A similar result ensued in New Zealand. The legislative link—except to the extent that we have retained, by our own decision, great English constitutional and other statutes (such as *Magna Carta*)—is completely and finally severed.

So is the executive link, as the events of 1975 demonstrated. Those events have had their counterparts in Fiji and Grenada where the

Queen, being absent, declined in any way to interfere in the independence of action of the local Governor-General. The idea of the United Kingdom or its Ministers advising the Queen of Australia in respect of Australian matters, or in any way interfering in the executive government of Australia, is now unthinkable.

The judicial link with the United Kingdom has also been totally and finally severed. Severing the mental links of some Australian lawyers to the laws pronounced in London is a rather more difficult task. But the High Court of Australia has made it plain that English law is now but one of many sources of comparative law assistance available to Australian courts. It has no special legal authority whatsoever in this country. The common law throughout the world is a great treasure-house upon which we can draw in Australia's independent courts. But we are completely free of legislative, executive, judicial, administrative or any other formal links to the United Kingdom. Suggestions that we are in some way still tied to mother's apron strings are completely false. If such links exist, they reside in history and spirit. Legal links reside only in the minds of the wilfully ignorant or paranoid. It is therefore important to realise that republicans in Australia are not dealing with practical realities of constitutional independence. Their concern is only with a symbolic link in the person of the Queen. It is symbols, not realities, that they want to eradicate—at least that is the position of those of the minimalist persuasion.

Fourthly, republicans do not speak with a single voice. The standard proposal is for a minimalist change to the Australian Constitution—virtually substituting nothing more than a President for the Governor-General. But this does not satisfy the true republicans amongst us. For example, Associate Professor Andrew Fraser has described the Australian Republican Movement as the 'Australian closet monarchist movement'.[3] According to Professor Fraser they are merely tinkering with names. Their system of government remains fundamentally that of a constitutional monarchy. Nothing much at all changes. For Professor Fraser and his supporters nothing less will do than to root out the notions and approaches of constitutional monarchy and replace them with a thoroughgoing change of the basic form and nature of our Constitution. This must start with securing a completely separate constitutional convention to bypass (or at least complement) the procedures provided under section 128 of the Constitution.[4]

So far, the vocal republicans appear, for the most part, to have rallied around the minimalist approach. Perhaps that simply shows how abiding and congenial our system of constitutional symbols is. According to Professor Fraser it demonstrates the mind-lock of most Australian republicans into constitutional monarchy. The vocal republicans want a constitutional monarchy—with symbols above politics—but without a monarch. Is this all that we are to achieve at the price of dividing our country, diverting our national endeavour from achievable gains and hauling ourselves to the brink of a referendum on a political question where sharp divisions are very likely to result in the continuance of the status quo?

Fifthly, we should keep in mind that our present constitutional arrangement is remarkably inexpensive. It is true that the Queen and members of the Royal Family, when invited, make visits to Australia. That costs Australians something. But we do not pay for their upkeep at other times. We avoid the expensive trappings that typically surround a national Head of State today. Or at least we contain them within decent and very Australian bounds.

Sixthly, there is the personality of the present monarch. Although it is the *system* which is basically in issue, it is difficult to disentangle, in the proposed debate, the system from the current incumbent. Queen Elizabeth II is a person whose life symbolises duty and service. These are symbolic values of great importance in fast-changing times. They constitute a special impediment to those who would change our system and who need a positive, even overwhelming constitutional affirmation to do so. They reinforce an instinctive view that the citizens of Australia, asked to reject this dutiful woman and enhance the powers of local politicans, will decline to do so.

The arguments of principle
There are three arguments of principle for sticking—at least for the foreseeable future—with our present Constitution.

The first is the argument against nationalism. Much of the rhetoric of republicanism smacks of nineteenth-century nationalism. This rhetoric is completely outdated and unsuitable and we should grow beyond it. Since Hiroshima, it behoves intelligent people to abhor nationalism and to seek after international harmony. Our present Head of State is an international one. The idea that we must have a local Head of State,

always resident in our midst, is one which derives from an orthodoxy set firm before the age of telecommunications, the jumbo jet and a globalising economy.

Against narrow nationalism Australia's constitutional monarchy presents a tempering force. It is no coincidence that the most temperate of the states of the developed world, in the Organisation for Economic Co-operation and Development, are constitutional monarchies, just as it is no coincidence that more than half of the members of that club of democracy are constitutional monarchies.

Those who harbour a hope of closer relations with New Zealand must also keep in mind the utility of sharing a constitutional monarch with that close neighbour. It seems unlikely, at least in the foreseeable future, that New Zealand will change its basic constitutional arrangements. We should pause before severing such a special link with the country closest to us in history and identity.

The second argument of principle relates to the dangers of ill-judged constitutional change. There is a danger that an elected republican President would conceive that he or she had the separate legitimacy which came from such election or appointment. At the moment there is—and can be—no such legitimacy in the Queen's representatives apart from the popular will. One of the reasons why the events of November 1975 shocked many Australians was precisely because of the perceived lack of popular legitimacy for the Governor-General's actions. It is this perception which puts a severe brake upon the use by the Governor-General of the prerogative powers. It is a brake I strongly favour. But

130   Structures and Strategies

there is little doubt that, without specific and detailed constitutional amendment, the prerogative powers of the Queen would pass to an elected or appointed President. That this is so has been demonstrated in Pakistan (including recently) and in other countries where a Governor-General has merely been replaced by a President.

In short, there is a risk that a local Head of State—especially one enjoying the legitimacy of a vote into office—would assert and exercise reserve powers which would be most unlikely to be used by an appointed Governor-General or State Governor. We have only to watch the spectacle of the contemporary conflict between President Yeltsin and the Congress of People's Deputies in Russia to understand the instability of a political system with two potential heads. Under our present system our Head of State can aspire to no such political role or power. Nor should—or do—her representatives. The same may not be true if we alter the incumbent and the method of determining the incumbency. This is as true of the State Governors as of the Governor-General.

The third reason of principle concerns the utility of our present constitutional compromise. What we have in Australia is a *crowned* republic. We have the historical symbols of a constitutional system of a thousand years without the trappings of the aristocracy and other features that would be inimical to Australian public life. At the same time we avoid the pretensions to which a home-grown republic could easily succumb: the fleet of stretch limousines, motorcycle escorts, streets blocked off as they pass, a 'First Lady'. In fact, we have developed in Australia to a mature system in which we are mercifully free of the pomposities that elsewhere accompany local Heads of State. To the complaint that we have no Head of State to travel overseas for us, I would say: we have our Head of Government. It is he or she who should ordinarily do the travelling. I can live quite peacefully with the sombre fact that our Head of Government attracts only a nineteen-gun salute. A mature democracy can easily miss those extra two guns, and a lot more arrogant pretension besides.

Like so many features of British constitutional history (the jury being the prime example) our constitutional arrangements function well, even though originating in a quite different purpose. They have evolved to a point where they are fairly well understood. The Queen and her representatives have extremely limited constitutional functions: to be consulted and to caution and warn. Because they are psychologically or even physically removed from political strife, or political dependence, their advice can sometimes be useful. Occasionally they can give the lead to the community where politicians are cautious. It is no accident that the elected President of the republic of the United States of America (Mr Reagan, the Great Communicator) could not bring his lips to mention AIDS in the first four years of his Presidency. During that time our Governor-General founded the AIDS Trust of Australia. Our Governors repeatedly supported AIDS benefits. They went to hospitals and hospices. They spoke amongst citizens about this matter of concern. And so in England did the Queen and members of the Royal Family. Occasionally it is important to have courageous but non-political leadership on matters of sensitivity which politicians—answerable to the ballot box—feel unable to give.

And then there is the element of ceremony and history. In my role as a judge and formerly as a university chancellor I can see the deep well-springs of human need for the ceremonies that mark important occasions in life. This does not mean that we should sanction pomposity or resurrect the idea of a bunyip aristocracy. I deplore that notion. Many may laugh at the investitures; at the openings of school fêtes; at the Vice-Regal presence in the country agricultural shows and for community groups. But these are places where our fellow citizens gather, where they seem to feel a need for ceremony and personal recognition.

The need for open-mindedness
The only criterion for deciding upon Australia's constitutional arrangements is what best advantages Australia and its people. We must avoid rejecting something that is old simply because it is old and seems to some to be unfashionable. We must beware the changing winds of fashion—especially in constitutional fundamentals and particularly when whipped up by self-interested and one-sided media campaigns. We must be clear-sighted about the great difficulties of securing a change to our Constitution. We must be sensitive to the divisiveness and sharp differences that any such proposal would bring. In our multi-cultural society even the majority ethnicity has a place to be proud of its culture and history. As a mature people, we should be specially cautious about invocations of nationalism more apt to centuries past than to the century yet to come. We should not be too proud to stay—at least for the present—with a system of government which has served us well. We should measure carefully the advantages of our crowned republic—of our modest ideas about a Head of State. It is a mature country that basically gets by with a Head of State who is usually absent and which refuses to submit to the calls of those who feel the need for a more constant, ever-present symbolic leader. In the words of the poet laureate of a practical people: 'If it ain't broke, don't fix it.'

Notes

1 M.D. Kirby (1991) 'H.V. Evatt, the Anti-Communist Referendum and Liberty in Australia' *Aust. Bar Rev.* 1993

2 P.H. Russell (1992) 'The Canadian Referendum: Canadians Affirm the Status Quo' in *Constitutional Centenary* 3.5

3 A. Fraser (1992) 'What's in a Constitutional Name? Disarming the Australian Republican Movement', *Cross Examiner* 2.22; cf W. Hudson (1992) 'An Australian Federal Republic?', *Aust. Quarterly* 64

4 See generally A.W. Fraser (1990) *The Spirit of the Laws: Republicanism and the Unfinished Project of Modernity,* University of Toronto; note review by B. Edgeworth (1991) *UNSWLJ* 14

Source: Quadrant, September 1993. Justice Kirby AC CMG is a member of the Council of Australians for a Constitutional Monarchy

Topic 2: Affirmative Action

Discriminating—for women

Bronwyn McNaughton

The Human Rights and Equal Opportunity Commission (HREOC) recently considered a complaint (made by three men) that a national women's health program, funded jointly by State and Federal Governments, was in breach of the *Sex Discrimination Act* 1984 (Cth).[1] Although HREOC dismissed the complaint, it is far from certain that the proceedings have brought the complaint to a satisfactory conclusion.[2] This may simply be the first step in a protracted series of events that run the gamut from constitutional challenge to proposing amendments to the Act. It is also entirely possible that the success of such claims ultimately could result in the collapse of the health program and subsequent threat to other women-only programs.

Such complaints are not unique to Australia. For example, in July 1991, a complaint alleging unlawful discrimination against a female family law specialist was filed (by a male) with the Massachusetts Commission Against Discrimination. While resolution of that complaint will necessarily take place against the backdrop of the local law, in substance it bears a strong resemblance to the recent Australian complaints.

The complaint

The Massachusetts complaint raised for the first time the question of whether a lawyer was covered by the Massachusetts State law prohibiting 'discrimination in admission to, or treatment in, a place of public accommodation'. That law provides as follows:

> Whoever makes any distinction, discrimination or restriction on account of race, color, religious creed, national origin, sex, sexual orientation . . . deafness, blindness or any physical or mental disability or ancestry relative to the admission of any person to, or his treatment in any place of public accommodation, resort or amusement . . . shall be punished by a fine of not more than twenty-five hundred dollars or by imprisonment for not more than one year, or both, and shall be liable to any person aggrieved thereby for . . . damages . . . All persons shall have the right to the full and equal accommodations, advantages, facilities and privileges of any place of public accommodation, resort or amusement subject only tọ the conditions and limitations established by law and applicable to all persons. This right is recognized and declared to be a civil right.[3]

The complaint was laid by a man who had been refused the assistance he had requested from the woman lawyer, J. The man had been in the process of mediating his divorce. The mediation had resulted in a draft separation agreement which the mediator had recommended each party have reviewed by his or her own counsel. To assist the parties in finding suitable counsel, the mediator had provided them with a list of lawyers well qualified in family law. J was named on the list.

J's background includes founding and leading a local women's resource centre, participation in a task force on domestic violence and a lawyer's group monitoring implementation of the *Abuse Prevention Act*, and lecturing from time to time on family law and on the legal rights of women for continuing legal education programs, the bar association and at a community college. She is managing partner at a three partner firm in the small town of Lawrence, just outside Boston, Massachusetts. The firm handles a range of work, including social security, workers compensation, lead paint litigation, personal injury for plaintiffs, consumer protection for consumers and landlord and tenant work for tenants. J specialises in family law and related matters (i.e. divorce, custody, adoption, wills and estates) and works almost exclusively in the Probate and Family Court. When it comes to matters related to divorce, she represents women only, although in other kinds of matters, such as guardianship, medical emergencies or conservatorships that are dealt with in the Probate Court, she represents both men and women. The other partners in her firm act for both men and women.

When the complainant called her office asking for representation and assistance, J explained her position and offered to recommend other lawyers who could assist. Her offer was refused and shortly afterwards the complaint was filed with the Commission Against Discrimination.

The Commission's policy is to encourage parties to resolve complaints rather than to investigate them formally and to litigate. Thus J was asked to respond to the complaint that had been made against her. In response, she argued, among other things, that the *Public Accommodations Act* (under which the complaint had been made) did not apply to lawyers; that ethically a lawyer could not represent a client when she or he believed that because of a clash of interests she or he was not able to do so zealously; and that limiting one's professional practice to representing traditionally disadvantaged groups was not unlawful discrimination.[4]

Public accommodation
A 'place of public accommodation, resort or amusement' is defined to include 'any place, whether licensed or unlicensed, which is open to and accepts or solicits the patronage of the general public'. A lengthy list of examples follows, examples which are obviously intended to be illustrative as they are expressly not intended to limit the generality of the definition (which refers to, for example, hotels, resorts, elevators, gas stations, restaurants, beauty parlours, public libraries, hospitals and public highways).[5]

The essence of the definition is the solicitation and acceptance of patronage from the general public[6] and J pointed to the absence of mention of lawyers, law firms, the practice of law or indeed any comparable type of service in the definition. In contrast to the expectation to be treated or served on paying the asking price that was the focus of the definition, there was no such expectation in relation to a lawyer. Not only was there no obligation on a lawyer to accept every client who walked through the door, there were various ethical reasons that could *compel* a lawyer to turn a case away. Accordingly there was no entitlement or expectation on the part of potential clients that a lawyer would automatically accept any particular case. If legislation dealing with public accommodations had been intended to do away with the unfettered discretion of a lawyer in regard to the acceptance of cases, it was argued, surely the legislature would have done so expressly.

Ethics

The second part of the response dealt with the ethical obligations of the lawyer to represent a client zealously.[7] Ethical rules require a lawyer to decline a case when 'the exercise of his [sic] professional judgment on behalf of his [sic] client will or reasonably may be affected by his own financial, business, property or personal interest' or when the potential client's case 'would be likely to involve him [sic] in representing differing interests'. The definition of 'differing interests' is extremely broad and includes 'every interest that will adversely affect either the judgment or the loyalty of a lawyer to his client, whether it be conflicting, inconsistent, diverse or other interest'.[8]

The particular argument was that, given J's dedication of her divorce practice to advocacy, development of domestic relations law and education of judges and family law mediators in relation to the special interests of women, she would be presented with an 'issue conflict' if she were to represent a man in such proceedings. This was particularly so as she practised almost exclusively in a single court and did not want to be 'talking out of both sides of her mouth' on the host of issues that divided husbands and wives in divorce proceedings. Zealous advocacy of a husband in these circumstances would be impossible and, moreover, unethical.

It was also pointed out that issue conflict commonly led lawyers to limit their practice to one side or the other of various legal fields. Thus a lawyer working in labour law might represent labour but not management, or in the field of personal injury plaintiffs but not insurance companies.

A further argument was made that forcing a lawyer to represent a client or take a case that the lawyer disagreed with would constitute a violation of the lawyer's own civil rights. Reference was made to a Massachusetts decision that requiring a school teacher to lead a class in the pledge of allegiance would violate the teacher's right of freedom of speech.[9] It was asserted that lawyers did not lose their rights of free speech when they became members of the bar.

Positive dicrimination

J also argued that rather than discriminating against men she was helping women. She pointed out that the law is commonly seen as a means of promoting social justice for various groups who may have been denied their rights at law and that if the act of discrimination in this case were to be found illegal, then the anti-discrimination law itself would only serve to punish a range of public spirited and public interest lawyers and organisations acting in the interests of particular disadvantaged minority groups. Ironically, what it would not be effectively preventing would be truly sexist refusals to represent clients as these could potentially retain their cloak of other, spurious, reasons.

At the time of writing, the complaint and response lie in an in-tray somewhere in the Massachusetts Commission Against Discrimination. It is possible that there they will remain for some considerable time, perhaps in someone's too-hard basket, especially if the heat that animated this particular complainant has died. The issue will not be hidden so readily, however; whatever the fate of this complaint, it will remain to be dealt with.

Notes

1 Note, e.g. the reports 'Legal threat to women's programs' and 'A test case on women's programs' by Margo Kingston, *The Age*, 25.11.91, pp. 1, 6, 13
2 See 'Landmark sex discrimination ruling fails to clear the air', *Financial Review*, 19.3.92, p. 5
3 Massachusetts General Laws, chapter 272, s.98
4 It is interesting to note that it was this latter point that was the basis on which HREOC dismissed the complaint referred to above
5 See Massachusetts General Laws, chapter 272, s.92A. See also *Local Finance Co of Rockland v Massachusetts Commission Against Discrimination* (1968) 242 N E 2d 536, 355 Mass 10: enumerated specific examples do not restrict the general statutory language or provide for applying the principle of *ejusdem generis*, and no prior Massachusetts case is conclusive as to the meaning of 'place of public accommodation'
6 See Opinion of the Attorney-General, 28 April 1964, p. 224
7 Expressly set out in the Canon of Ethics and reinforced in the case law e.g. see Commonwealth v Tabor 376 Mass 811, 817 n 10(1978)
8 Disciplinary Rules 5–101(A), 5–105(A); Canon of Ethics, rule 3:07, definitions (1)
9 Opinion of the Justices 372 Mass 874 (1977)

Source: Alternative Law Journal, 17(2), 1992
Bronwyn McNaughton is an Australian
lawyer currently studying at Harvard.

Argyle Diamonds sets shining example

Jill Rowbotham

Behind the legislation, the programs and the ideology of affirmative action, there sometimes lies a genuine commitment to equality in the workplace. Argyle Diamonds has been striving for it for almost 10 years, and is the overall winner of the *BRW* Affirmative Action Awards this year. It has also won the employment practices section for encouraging women to move into non-traditional fields.

There were 42 entrants in four sections of the awards. Their initiatives ranged from making language in the workplace less discriminatory to including lectures on affirmative action, equal opportunity and anti-discrimination in university undergraduate courses. The biotechnology company Biotech Australia won the work and family section for its organisational flexibility, a program that includes variable working hours and special leave for employees whose immediate family is sick.

The Queensland University of Technology won the higher education section for a strategy aimed at enhancing women's career advancement, and the telecommunications company NorTel Australia won the achievement category for its program supporting female participation within the company and in the broader engineering industry.

Recognition was given to Caltex and Unisys Australia in the work and family section; the universities of Western Australia, Canberra and New South Wales in the higher education category; Unisys Australia and the NRMA in the employment practices category and the AMP Society in the achievement category.

The awards, sponsored by *BRW*, were presented by the federal Minister for Consumer Affairs, Jeannette McHugh, at a lunch at the Park Lane Hotel in Sydney last week. She said some of the most productive workplaces in the world promoted equity. 'These companies know fairness issues are efficiency issues,' she said. However, there was still a long way to go in improving the lot of women in the workplace.

The editor of *BRW*, David Uren, said affirmative action meant companies pursuing affirmative action with the same vigor they would display in the pursuit of any other corporate objective. 'The management of human resources is an increasingly vital and central part of management,' he said. Affirmative action was important 'in order simply to exploit the talent available in your company'.

The director of the Affirmative Action Agency, Valerie Pratt, congratulated Argyle Diamonds on its award and praised it for following up the affirmative action program when required. 'They do not shy away from problems,' she said.

One quality the Western Australian company shared with the other section winners was its youth. All the organisations introduced their progressive policies when they were greenfield operations or soon after they were founded. The Queensland University of Technology was the product of the 1990 merger of the Queensland Institute of Technology and the Brisbane College of Advanced Education. 'It is a different starting point, but they are not hidebound by conservative culture,' Pratt said.

Some entrants were still working on formal plans. The oil company Caltex Australia and the New South Wales motoring and insurance organisation NRMA have been in consultation with employees about appropriate initiatives. Caltex Australia began consulting in 1990 and appointed an equal employment opportunity officer in 1991 to develop a plan for the company. The co-ordinator, who was hired for two years, discovered that staff were having difficulty balancing work and family commitments, and conducted a comprehensive survey to gauge the extent of the problem. The co-ordinator's tenure has since been extended by two years to develop a plan to implement recommendations from the survey.

The NRMA also researched and analysed the position of women in its workforce. The big issues discovered were lack of flexible work practices and childcare assistance, few incentives to return from parental leave and a lack of women in senior positions. Recommendations implemented included the appointment of a full-time equal employment opportunity officer, an improved childcare referral service, the development of a career workshop to assist staff in career development and advertising all job vacancies internally.

Although companies such as Caltex Australia and the NRMA are pioneering their programs, others are well down the track. However, none are as advanced as Argyle Diamonds, the joint venture between CRA and Ashton Mining. Argyle was deemed noteworthy in the awards two years ago for its video and training program called Groundwork, which was about accepting workplace diversity.

The video was one part of a drive to produce equity in the workplace that started soon after the discovery of the kimberlite pipe, which was to support the world's most productive diamond mine.

In the late 1970s a team, including mostly female diamond sorters, went to prospect the Smoke Creek area near Lake Argyle in the far north of Western Australia. When the diamonds were taken from the first alluvial mine, it was again a mostly female team that sorted the diamonds. Women were hired because they were regarded as having a good eye for detail and an ability to apply themselves to a repetitious task. (Today, 66 per cent of the company's diamond sorters are women.) Their presence in the early camps was a civilising influence.

The management seized upon a unique opportunity to build a mining culture that did not have the usual characteristics of all-male workforces: stress and hard living. Instead, it created a highly mobile community 'normalised' by the presence of women. Staff commute daily between the mine and the farming and tourism centre of Kununurra, 25 minutes away by air. Some also travel from Perth on a two-weeks-on, two-weeks-off roster. It avoids the risk of being cooped up in a traditional mining town and is a reason women have been able to move into a male-dominated sector and prosper.

The time was ripe for taking the risk because affirmative action was high on the Australian political agenda. A time of big recruitment in 1985 coincided with Argyle Diamonds becoming part of a set of affirmative action pilot projects.

There were 11,000 phone inquiries, 8,000 written applications and 2,000 interviews for 400 jobs. 'Each supervisor had a crew and each had a four-day workshop on how to interview, and there was particular attention to gender neutrality,' the principal consultant on organisation effectiveness, Joanne Farrell, said.

Pratt, then part of the new Affirmative Action Resource Unit within the federal Office of the Status of Women, remembered last week when CRA committed Argyle Diamonds to the pilot. 'CRA are usually in the forefront of ideas about management,' she said. 'They went out of their way to make it a women-friendly site.'

Women were encouraged to apply from the first intake and made up 15% of the original workforce. That figure is now 28 per cent of a 1000-strong workforce, a success rate achieved in part because there are no jobs on the site for which physical strength is a prerequisite. Further, work has gone into designing jobs and structural training so that experience is not necessary. Women are now scattered through the workforce in positions as electricians, truck drivers, mine plant operators and overseers of the processing plant.

Senior support staff commute daily from Kununurra, but most staff fly from Perth for a fortnight of 12-hour shifts before returning to the state capital for two weeks' recreation. Job sharing has been introduced, so some employees are working two weeks in eight, using the rest of the time to be with their families or pursue other interests and study. In the Perth office, women with family commitments can work between nine and 30 hours, some on weekly contracts.

There are Tafe-accredited skills extension program modules at the mine, which can also be used as credit for engineering-related tertiary courses.

Argyle Diamonds' willingness to face up to problems that arose in trying to achieve equality was exemplified by efforts to make further improvements in the late 1980s. A discussion paper produced by a student at Murdoch University, Perth, in 1988 was a catalyst for the Groundwork program, aimed at promoting better relations among people who worked together. 'It was getting people to confront how they were treating other people and how that affected the team,' Farrell said.

The company still aimed to boost the number of female workers but was restrained by a lack of supply and tough economic times. 'It's been hampered by the recession in business,' Farrell said. 'One of the things we have found is a very low turnover rate (of staff), so recruitment is low and finding opportunities to increase the profile of women is hard.'

The company was continuing to seek new ways of promoting the policy. Farrell admitted that the media coverage accompanying the awards was a reason Argyle Diamonds entered. 'It is difficult to employ women if they do not apply to you; we want them to know we are female-friendly,' she said.

It was a sentiment shared by the telecommunications company NorTel Australia, winner of the achievement section, which has put a lot of energy into attracting women into engineering, another field dominated by men. At the start of last year, NorTel devised a strategy to boost female participation within the company and to encourage women to become engineers. Company representatives went into schools to talk to female students about the profession and give profiles of the company's female professionals and managers. Female engineers from NorTel also held seminars for female students on tertiary campuses and the company gave money to Women in Engineering groups.

NorTel was established as a subsidiary of the Canada-based telecommunications giant Northern Telecom in 1986 with five employees. By the end of this year there are expected to be almost 300. Last year there were 200, of whom 28 per cent were women and 13 per cent at manager level. The company has aimed at creating the most productive workforce it can manage, with the ultimate aim of becoming a leader in the telecommunications industry in Australia.

'Women are a subset for us— we see diversity as a real plus for us,' the company's human resources director, Adele Thomson, said. Apart from programs in schools and tertiary institutions, the company set itself targets for recruiting women graduates and senior managers and also made strong efforts to support the participation of women at professional and senior levels in the company.

Managing this kind of workforce 'feminisation' is a complex task, as the University of Canberra discovered recently. After five years of affirmative action, it found the number of women in senior academic ranks was decreasing—from 21 per cent in 1986 to 16 per cent in 1991. According to the university this was because many new staff, often women, were appointed on

temporary contracts. That disqualified them from promotion.

Although women were a greater proportion of staff (up from 29 per cent to 40 per cent), that was in lower and middle academic positions. The university has since improved conditions for its temporary academic staff, of which 66 per cent are women, to include them in big staff development programs and give them superannuation, eligibility for promotion and consideration for permanence.

Accommodating women workers who have children is a target of affirmative action policy, and childcare has emerged as a crucial ingredient in women's careers. The University of Canberra recognised that for its temporary female staff to progress, not only would they have to be allowed to apply for the outside studies program, but the dependants of staff who travelled would have to be catered for.

The Queensland University of Technology, the winner of the higher education category, came to the same conclusion. Apart from planning more child care centres at its Brisbane campuses, it has provided funds through its professional development program for young children to accompany a parent going overseas or interstate when they have no other means of child care. The move was in response to statistics that showed women were applying for less funding, and used the program to complete tertiary qualifications rather than for international study tours and overseas conferences.

Women represented 46 per cent of the 6,259 staff last year, up 2 per cent since the merger, and filled 54 per cent of the 437 new positions created in that time. The most obvious increase in their number has been at the associate professor and professor level, where they represent 11 per cent, a 4 per cent increase last year.

Nina Shatifan, the university's equality co-ordinator, said her job has been to pick up the threads of various initiatives and provide more of an equitable framework for the way they were being done. Shatifan said: 'For example, I was looking at policies and seeing where they were not necessarily meeting the needs of women, especially regarding women with family responsibilities.'

Upgrading qualifications and gaining promotion and career development for secretaries have been areas of endeavour, as well as a professional development program and award restructuring. Shatifan said the process required talking about women's interrupted careers and the impact that has on career opportunities.

Affirmative action was more than removing obstacles that prevented women gaining advancement. 'We were very concerned about the women once they get there, and providing them with support and career opportunities,' Shatifan said. She wanted a commitment to equal opportunity at the highest level in the university. 'I would be one of the few equal employment opportunity people actually involved in award restructuring.'

The AMP Society also pushed affirmative action further into the mainstream of company concerns by including it in the present enterprise bargaining. Its affirmative action consultative committee met union representatives, produced a document about enterprise bargaining and sent it to all staff, who then met in groups to discuss enterprise bargaining and constraints on productivity at AMP. The draft agreement that resulted has not yet won final approval from senior management. Apart from five days' emergency leave, it included removal of restrictions on job sharing and work from home, and increased flexibility in working hours.

Flexibility was a strong suit of Biotech Australia, the winner of the work and family section, as shown by its parental leave policy, flexible working hours arranged around a core of 10am to 4pm and the introduction of special leave of up to five days for staff whose immediate family fall ill. Of 100 Biotech Australia staff, 75 per cent were scientists and 47 per cent women. (The company was recently acquired by the German pharmaceutical giant Hoechst.) 'As the company has grown we have managed to maintain the small-company atmosphere and have seen the need to keep some of the employees who are extremely well qualified and talented,' the company's superintendent of personnel and training, Menaka Cooke, said.

The parental leave policy was adopted in 1991, and although women were regarded as the main beneficiaries, because they were traditionally the carers, a significant push for the leave policy came from senior male management.

Pratt found Biotech Australia a particularly interesting entrant in the awards because it was a small organisation with a high proportion of scientists and women. She judged the entries alongside *BRW's* Uren; the director of the Labor Management Studies Foundation at Macquarie University's Graduate School of Management, Ed Davis; the executive director of the Council for Equal Opportunity in Employment, Heather Carmody; the assistant secretary of the ACTU, Jennie George; the president of the New South Wales Equal Employment Opportunities Practitioners Association, Jacqueline Gillespie; and the manager of human resources, Toyota Motor Corporation Australia, Peter Holland.

Biotech's approach was a good example of a growing understanding of the purpose of affirmative action in Australia, according to Pratt.'It has picked up the need

in the community that if you want to have the best people you have to have flexible working hours.' She said there was a general and logical trend towards realising that getting the best meant accommodating their needs. One of the greatest trends was an intelligent approach to the work and family issues that can hold back women. 'Women still have the major responsibility for family life.'

Source: Business Review Weekly,
12 March 1993

Why women don't make it

Sheryle Bagwell

Ingrid Hestelow thought she would make it big as an architect. She had the skills, the talent and certainly the drive needed to get to the top. Or so her employer, a middle-sized commercial architectural firm in Sydney, told her when she was taken on board in the early 1980s.

Things started well. Within a year, she was promoted to associate director, the only woman among five men.

But like all upwardly mobile executives, she soon had her eye on the next rung of the ladder—director. She worked long hours. She brought in new clients, managed staff and even agreed to do media interviews that promoted the firm as a progressive operation.

Nothing happened. Year after year she asked her superiors what it took to become a director and share in the firm's profits. Each time she was told to try harder.

After nine years, 44-year-old Hestelow finally gave up. She left the firm—and the profession.

'They kept moving the goalposts to the point where I got completely disheartened,' she said.

'At the time I didn't know that I had hit the glass ceiling. I just knew I had hit something.'

No doubt, Hestelow's employer would tell a different story. The firm might say it had been mistaken about her abilities for the top job. Maybe her style did not fit the firm's culture. Perhaps it was nothing more than wanting to hold back on promotions during the recession.

Yet, whatever the reason, one argument that cannot be refuted is that Ingrid Hestelow—as a woman who has failed to reach the very top of her chosen field—is not alone.

Nearly a decade after Australia introduced landmark sex discrimination laws—and seven years after affirmative action legislation aimed at redressing the gender imbalance in the workforce—women are still virtually absent from the top layers of management in the public and private sector.

Women in the 1990s are better-educated, better-trained and now make up no less than 42 per cent of the workforce.

But industry surveys show that they still occupy less than 3 per cent of senior management jobs and directorships—a proportion that has remained virtually unchanged over the past five years.

Despite the years of rhetoric about the emerging army of highly skilled corporate women, none has managed to climb to chief executive at any of Australia's top 200 companies. Only a handful have won board posts.

Even the encouraging signs from Australia's leading MBA schools about the growing number of female students undertaking post-graduate business courses—still the fast-track route to senior management—has turned sour. Academics believe that the growth of the 1980s has now stopped.

Meanwhile in the public sector, which is proud of its affirmative action record, still less than 10 per cent of the prized senior executive service positions are held by women.

Even the Prime Minister, Paul Keating, did not increase the number of women in his Cabinet from one (Ros Kelly) after an election where he had thanked the women of Australia for their unprecedented support.

'It is one of life's real enigmas,' says Valeria Pratt, the director of the Federal Government's Affirmative Action Agency whose job since 1988 has been to ensure business, the public sector and universities regularly report on their progress in the promotion of women.

'There has been great change over the decade on such issues as child care and sexual harassment. There has been a tightening up of the recruitment and selection process in the workplace. But when it comes to the senior levels, it is still very much a boys' club.'

So what has gone wrong? Why is it that a woman can successfully sue an employer who sacks her merely because she has fallen pregnant, but for the most part still fails to move beyond traditional female jobs such as a secretary or clerk?

Why is it that executive head-hunters can report that corporations are today gender-blind when it comes to the promotion of senior staff, but then fail to come up with the name of one woman they have recommended for a senior job in recent times?

Are men unwilling to share power with women in their last bastion, the workplace? Or are women using the glass ceiling as a shield to hide their own short-comings, such has a lack of will and tenacity to climb the corporate ladder?

It used to be that the simple excuse for women's poor performance in the workplace was their lack of education. But that no longer holds true.

Today, 55 per cent of all students studying for an undergraduate degree are women. And although women are still under-represented in such important industry disciplines as engineering, in professional areas such as law they have been graduating in equal numbers with men for the past five years.

So why are the numbers of women being made partners in major law firms now reportedly in decline?

It's the same story across the industries—from the media to advertising, computing to manufacturing, there is hardly a woman to be found in the managing director's chair.

There are, of course, many women who have carved out successful careers as lawyers, financial experts, human resource managers and marketing directors.

But the fact that they are still considered pioneers decades after the advent of the women's movement suggests not only that women's career paths have stalled, but that they are at least another generation away from attaining real success.

Even the top men in business agree. Although there have been no surveys of their attitudes in Australia, a recent *Fortune* magazine poll of 201 chief executives of America's largest companies found that only 16 per cent believed it was 'very likely', or 'somewhat likely' that they could be succeeded by a female CEO within the next decade.

Heather Carmody, a Melbourne-based business consultant on equal opportunity issues, says: 'I'm an active non-subscriber to the "pipeline" theory . . . that there are talented women coming through and that it's only a matter of time. People have been saying that for 20 years in the US and for the past 10 years in Australia. Yet there has been no evidence of significant progress [on the work front] over that time.'

During the past two weeks, *The Australian Financial Review* has conducted a wide range of interviews with executive recruiters, consultants, academics and executive women. All point to a complex set of reasons behind women's relative lack of progress'—and no simple solution.

But equal opportunity consultants like Carmody believe that the root of the problem remains the workplace itself—they say it is still an unfriendly, inflexible environment for the working woman, particularly if she has children.

Whether they are hitting the so-called glass ceiling because of the discriminatory promotional decisions of their bosses or whether they are finding it too stressful to balance the demands of work and family as a full-time worker, highly competent women are falling—indeed jumping—off the career track in growing numbers.

In the present 'downsizing' climate, companies, even those with good records in the promotion of women such as IBM and Esso, are reporting that it is largely their female staff, including those who are highly trained, who are predominantly electing to take voluntary redundancy, according to Rohan Squirchuk, executive director of the Business Council of Australia's Council for Equal Opportunity.

Although many are using the cash to take a break for child-care reasons, a significant proportion of women in search of more flexible hours and better career—and salary—prospects are using it to fund a venture into small business.

According to the National Small Business Centre, the number of women with their own small business is increasing at three times the rate of men. If the trend continues, women are expected to out-number men, both as small business owners and employees by the mid-1990s.

'It's not a question of whether women can make it [in the corporate sector] following the male rules, it's just that they are electing not to' says Squirchuk.

But the majority of women end up staying in the system. Some try to work their way up the ladder. For many it is a battle—even before they decide to take a break to have a baby.

The Lavarch Report on the status-of-woman last year, called *Halfway to Equal*, noted that in law firms, for example, male partners were reluctant to appoint women because of the perception that they would leave and have children—even if they had no plans to—and thus waste the firm's investment in their training.

If the woman did go off and have children, she was seen as lacking commitment to her career. Although the corporate sector in general has been forced to embrace the notions of maternity leave, part-time work, job-sharing and child care, few have been willing to take seriously the notion of the upwardly mobile mother.

Heather Carmody says the message from business is still: 'Yes, you can work part-time but don't expect the same opportunity for promotion. Yes, you can have some flexibility to pick up your kid before the creche closes, but don't expect to be taken as a serious career person.'

And while business still honours the traditional model of the executive as someone who works long hours and always puts work before family, the second-class status of the working mother is likely to remain unchanged.

The statistics tell the story. Sheila Rimmer, a labour market economist at La Trobe University, says the average working woman will take at least one career break, often returning to a different job altogether, because of pregnancy or relocation (most often to follow her partner).

But unlike men who change jobs, women tend to move downwards in terms of status and pay rather than up the ladder. Rimmer says this is because they may have spent an extended time away from the workplace, thus allowing their skills to erode. Mostly it is because they return as part-time workers. 'And there are few good jobs that are part-time,' she says.

It's not surprising then to find that women who have achieved success often don't have children, or even a partner.

Kate Ramsay, a consultant who 'coaches' women in senior management and has just done a survey of their attitudes for the NSW Department of Industrial Relations, found two-thirds of the women she spoke to were not in a serious relationship, let alone contemplating children.

While men in high-powered jobs complain in later years of missing out on their children growing up, high-powered women are opting out altogether. 'There are still corporate wives, but corporate husbands are less likely to accept their role in the game,' says Ramsay.

Ramsay says female business executives, as 'pioneers' in a male-dominated environment, also felt 'isolated, lonely and exhausted' by the role they were forced to play. They were forced to walk a 'fine line' between not being seen as too hard, or male, or too soft, or female.

'I feel quite pessimistic about the future of women in corporations,' says Ramsay 'The price they pay is very high. While the salary and perks might be good, they are asking some very deep questions about what it is all about.'

Indeed, several senior women executives who spoke to the *Financial Review* said they did not expect to remain in the corporate sector for much longer, nor did they aspire to, or expect to get the top job in their corporation.

One 31-year-old woman without children, who recently became general manager of the human resources division in a major blue-collar organisation, says she plans to leave her job in about a year and go into business for herself. Although the company was paying her tuition at a leading management school, she saw no long-term future there.

She believed she had hit, not a glass ceiling, but a glass wall. As the head of a service division, she was unlikely to be given the opportunity to transfer to an operational division, still the only way to the top in most industrial companies.

'I'm seen as the soft option,' she says. 'I am often excluded from general manager meetings because they don't think I have anything to offer.' She had to work hard to get information that the men found out informally. 'A lot of stuff gets done on the golf course and I don't play golf.'

Yet who should change? Those men with their hands on the levers of power who expect new entrants to play the game as it has always been played? Or women who want it all on their own terms?

Professor Leonie Stills, the Dean of Commerce at the University of Western Sydney, believes that unless the overwhelmingly male culture in business changes—the language, the code of conduct, even the role models—to encourage women and the feminine way of doing things, big corporations will continue to lose talented women to smaller, more flexible workplaces.

Stills, whose book on the lack of progress of women in management will be published later this year, charted the progress of women in 262 organisations from 1984 to 1992 and found the companies offered fewer opportunities for women now than nine years ago. She believes it will be some time before women managers move 'in any great numbers into the mainstream of commercial life'.

'While some progress has been made in a few areas such as exposure to training, it is felt that this has been brought about more by compliance with equal opportunity laws than a recognition of women's worth,' argues Stills.

'It is no wonder then that scores of women are voting with their feet and leaving corporate life altogether.' But not all women share the view that the onus should be necessarily just on men to change.

Linda Bardo Nicholls, an executive director of investment banker County NatWest and a member of the advisory board of BP Australia, believes it is women who should be more flexible.

They should be more prepared to move to a workplace that suits their skills and attributes, rather than stay put in a company where they do not, just as career-minded men have to do.

Nicholls, a mother of three whose longest break from the workplace was six weeks and who has crossed continents for new job opportunities, says that women have to be prepared to accept 'trade-offs,' if they choose a career.

'This will not make me very popular among the sisterhood,' says Nicholls. 'I hear a lot of people who haven't made it whining about the glass ceiling. But I don't hear people complaining about it who have managed to crash through it.'

Others may not share Nicholls' harsh view. But they agree the glass ceiling has become a negative, disempowering concept for women.

Management consultants like Attracta Lagan in Sydney believe that women should not so much lament their lack of progress doing it the male way, but capitalise on their 'female' management skills such as a preference to manage co-operatively and in teams.

'Most successful women in business have adopted the male model and not changed the culture,' she says. 'The more innovative ones are out there on their own, doing it for themselves.'

Yet not all believe the only course is to jump ship. Some women are doing it their own way within the system. And according to these women, the system is responding.

The most senior woman at Westpac Bank and a former Business Woman of the Year, Helen Lynch, says the bank's US-born managing director Bob Joss had helped bring about a rethink in management ranks that should see more senior jobs for women in the 1990s.

(Joss was apparently surprised to find that only 2 per cent of Westpac's branch managers were women.)

Yet Lynch who, in her new job as chief general manager, corporate affairs, reports directly to Joss, also believes that women need to more confidently state their goals in the workplace. Although she benefited from 'forward thinking mentors' during her steady rise to the top, she says she has also tried to be 'open and forthright' about her ambitions.

She learnt that lesson 12 years ago, she says, when she was passed over for a training programme in the bank because, according to the selectors, she had failed in the interview 'to aspire for the top job' as the male candidates had done.

'Since then I have not left things to chance,' she says.

Other organisations have strived to encourage women through mentoring. MBA schools like Melbourne University's Business School have developed programmes to encourage and support women who may lack the necessary confidence to undergo a gruelling management course, or have been passed over by their company for selection.

The Sydney-based Women Chief Executives group, which has as members Janet Holmes à Court and Ita Buttrose, sponsors a scholarship for women at the Macquarie University Graduate School of Management to help 'expand the imagination of what is possible', says vice-president Wendy McCarthy, who is also executive director of the National Trust of NSW.

Another, the international group, Women Chiefs of Enterprise, has sent out résumés of all its 200 members to government and private sector companies around the country 'in case they are having difficulties finding suitably qualified women for their boards', says Queensland businesswoman Lorraine Martin who is the group's Australian president.

All the women own, run or manage companies with turnovers of more than $3 million a year.

'We are always hearing that experienced women who have run companies and are thus well-qualified to sit on a board are in short supply,' says Martin, who is the only woman on the board of Austrade. 'Yet we are here. Perhaps we have to go out and market ourselves better.'

For their part, executive recruiters remain doggedly optimistic. 'More and more women candidates are being put up for senior jobs and I see no resistance to that from business,' says Gary Reidy of international search firm, AMROP.

'I believe the glass ceiling is slowly going to fracture but it won't go bang,' says Paul Murnane of Russell Reynolds. 'But it will happen because you can't afford to ignore a big chunk of the workforce.'

Yet after decades of such promises, that big chunk of the workforce remains largely sceptical. Approaching the next millennium, they are demanding action, not words.

'In my mind, we will have equal opportunity when a woman is considered for the position of managing director of BHP,' says Professor Leonie Stills. 'She doesn't have to get the job. She just has to be considered for it.'

Until then, highly talented women will continue to be lost to industry as they vote with their feet and leave to set up their own businesses.

Ingrid Hestelow, after spending two years helping her husband set up his management consultancy business, has just returned to her profession of architecture—but in a smaller firm in association with another woman.

Another, Roseanna Donovan, who spent 25 years trying to beat the statistics and become one of the few women to be promoted to creative director in Australia of a major multinational advertising agency, finally gave up four years ago to set up her own agency, Donovan McAlpine. It is Australia's only all-female ad agency.

'The glass ceiling teaches you to take the knocks,' says Donovan.

'If you spend 25 years getting doors slammed in your face, you are not going to take "no" for an answer any more in your own business.' ■

Source: The Financial Review,
27 August 1993

Works cited

Bagwell, Sheryle (1993) 'Why women don't make it', *Financial Review*, 27 August

Hill, Robin (1993) 'Breaking up is hard to do', *The Bulletin*, 20 April

Kirby, Michael (1993) 'A defence of the constitutional monarchy', *Quadrant*, September

McNaughton, Bronwyn (1992) 'Discriminating—for women', *Alternative Law Journal* 17 (2): 89–90

Rowbotham, Jill (1993) 'Argyle Diamonds sets shining example', *Business Review Weekly*, 12 March

Winterton, George (1993) 'Removing the crown with light fingers', *The Australian*, 11 August

Section 3

Writing Strategies and Representation

8 Analysing texts

In the previous section, we discussed the processes of organising an argument essay and using research findings to support a case. We now need to stand back and consider some of the implications of the choices academic writers make when constructing these texts. By considering such choices, we can arrive at a clearer understanding of both how academic texts work in themselves, and how they relate to various kinds of non-academic writing that people read and produce professionally and socially.

This third section of the book will accordingly examine the conventions and strategies used in academic texts in more detail. It aims to arrive at a clearer understanding of the structures and strategies of academic texts by comparing and contrasting them with other kinds of writing. In particular, it will study the roles of **function, perspective** and **structure** in relation to academic writing. The effects of argument and persuasion, objectivity and logic will also be shown to be crucial features of academic texts.

Through closely analysing a number of academic texts, and then comparing them with non-academic ones, we will suggest that these various features—argument, persuasion, logic, and so on— aren't simply the basic ingredients of academic discourse. Rather, they are its **conventional strategies of representation**, used to convey information and viewpoints with particular effects (perhaps the main one being to try to get readers to *agree* with the viewpoint that is being offered). As we will see, in this sense, academic writing works like all other forms of writing—through using conventions that are recognised and frequently accepted by authors and readers.

Before we start, however, to analyse examples of academic writing, we need to say a little about the process of textual analysis itself.

Textual analysis

Analysis, the *Macquarie Dictionary* explains, is the 'separation of a whole, whether a material substance or any matter of thought, into its constituent elements... this process is a method of studying the nature of a thing or determining its essential features'. Hence, in analysing something we separate it into parts which we examine. We are not necessarily looking for answers or solutions, but are seeking knowledge about these constituent parts and the relationships that hold them together.

While it generally adopts this approach, analysis will vary according to the purpose and particular interests of the analyst. For example, the abstract concept, 'Australia', could be studied, but the results would depend on who is doing the analysis and why. The type of analysis of 'Australia' a demographer would come up with would differ from that of, say, a constitutional lawyer. Whereas a demographer would focus on statistics that would show the relationship between population and wealth or resource distribution, a constitutional lawyer would be more interested in the constituent states or territories and their relationship with the federal government. Historians, geologists, manufacturers and primary producers would all analyse 'Australia' differently because they would each have a different purpose in doing this work and a different interest in the results.

When we undertake **textual analysis**, our general purpose is to find out something about how the text is structured and what its key features and elements are. Our specific interest lies in the way that it produces meaning. We fulfil this interest by looking at particular elements of the text and the relationships set up between them to construct meaning. Since the focus of this book is academic writing, we will examine examples of this type of writing, but to recognise academic conventions more clearly, we will also make comparisons with other kinds of texts.

The chapters on description, narration, exposition and argument have already used textual analysis to explain how writers construct meaning and how readers understand it. We did this by a *critical reading* of the texts, in which we noted the organisation and many of the distinguishing features of each mode of writing. Regardless of the type of text we discussed, we found three aspects especially useful in understanding the social meaning created in the text: **function**, **perspective** and **structure**.

Function, **perspective** and **structure** create social meaning in texts.

Let's take up these notions again and use them to analyse academic texts.

Function in academic texts

As we have already seen, writing transforms ideas into textual form. Academic writing is a particular type which transforms complex and often innovative ideas into a certain form for a specialised audience within various fields or disciplines. The resulting text with its well-defined readership conforms to certain conventions and uses appropriate strategies in the same way that other types of social writing do.

Academic writers aim to convince their readers of the **truth** of their assertions through a number of strategies. These include:

> **precision** and **attention to detail**,
> meticulous **research**, and
> **evaluation** of findings through **logical** reasoning.

These strategies are used as much in a paper on literary criticism as in a study on space research. They are equally applicable to academic writing that appears in scholarly journals, papers or books. The use of precise language and scrupulous detail along with solid research and logical evaluation remains the basis of all academic writing.

In the chapters on causal logic and argument, we saw that academic argument differs from persuasion. This, we can recall, tries to motivate the reader to agree with the writer by appealing to emotions. Argument tries to establish truth by appealing to the intellect of the reader. In practice, these distinctions are often less clear. As we will see, the conventions and strategies used by academic writers can also be persuasive. The rationality they construct has a powerful effect on their readers, so much so that argument is often referred to as the **rational mode of persuasion.**

Perspective in academic texts

Perspective as both physical place and mental attitude has been stressed in this book as an important component of many types of writing. Perspective denotes the position of the writer in relation to the text. We have seen how the use of personal pronouns construct particular relationships between writer and reader. By using 'I', the writer is expressing personal thoughts and ideas and so becomes written into the text. 'We' can be used in the same way, or can be used to imply both writer and reader and hence construct collaboration and suggest agreement (in many ways, this is the aim of the authors' use of 'we' throughout this book).

Either way, the use of a personal point of view builds a link between the writer and the topic. This kind of link suggests **subjectivity**. Subjective representations are personal ones and carry their persuasive weight by the authority and experience of the writer.

In the following extract from a chapter entitled, 'What's in a Frame? Surface Evidence for Underlying Expectations', Deborah Tannen uses a strong personal point of view to set up her argument that people use expectations to make sense of the world:

> I have been struck lately by the recurrence of a single theme in a wide variety of contexts: the power of expectation. For example, the self-fulfilling prophecy has been proven to operate in education as well as in individual psychology. I happened to leaf through a how-to-succeed book; its thesis was that the way to succeed is to expect to do so. Two months ago at a conference for teachers of English as a second language, the keynote speaker explained that effective reading is a process of anticipating what the author is going to say and expecting it as one reads. Moreover, there are general platitudes heard every day, as for example the observation that what is wrong with marriage today is that partners expect too much of each other and of marriage.
>
> The emphasis on expectation seems to corroborate a nearly self-evident truth: in order to function in the world, people cannot treat each new person, object, or event as unique and separate. The only way we can make sense of the world is to see the connections between things, and between present things and things we have experienced before or heard about. These vital connections are learned as we grow up and live in a given culture. As soon as we measure a new perception against what we know of the world from prior experience, we are dealing with expectations.

Tannen's examples are taken from her personal experience. The how-to-succeed book she read, the keynote address she heard and the general observations she relates, are all very specific instances of the power of expectations to create meaning. As readers, we find the examples compelling because they seem just like our own experience. Personalised treatment of the topic seems, however, to be the exception rather than the rule in academic writing.

Academic texts which do not use personal perspective and instead use the force of supporting facts as evidence are attempting to connect that evidence directly to the subject matter, rather than through the writer's experience or beliefs. These texts do not link the writer overtly to the topic. They construct their meaning using **objectivity**. In other words, the impersonal point of view suggests (but does not ensure) an objective treatment of the topic. We see this sense of objectivity every day in the way the news is constructed for us on radio, on television and in the newspapers. The news represents material to its audience as factual, and an important part of that representation is the absence of the reporter's or newsreader's personal opinion.

The construction of objectivity is an important part of academic writing as well. Since such writing aims for truthfulness, and since truth in our culture is closely related to notions of objective fact rather than subjective opinion, writers of academic texts tend to distance themselves from their topic. By removing themselves from the text, academic writers play down their role as creators of meaning (along with any hint of subjectivity), and instead emphasise a sense of objectivity.

In the next extract, the abstract from Vincent Price's paper, 'On the Public Aspects of Opinion: Linking Levels of Analysis in Public Opinion Research', the author has been removed entirely from the text and the topic is constructed objectively:

A new information-processing paradigm, drawing heavily upon concepts generated by the cognitive sciences, has emerged in research on mass communication and public opinion. To make significant contributions to public opinion theory, however, this new cognitive paradigm must properly incorporate the 'public' aspects of opinion formation—finding suitable ways to link individual-level information processing to the higher-level processes of public communication and social organization. Fundamental to public opinion theory is the notion that members of a public organize collectively through communication over a point of conflict. Researching this communicative process requires the analysis of cognition and opinion formation as individual-level phenomena that operate within, and that are thus largely dependent upon, the wider social context of public debate and collective organisation. It is suggested that current developments in social identification theory may be particularly important in helping us to understand better how a mass of individuals can become a structured public through communication.

The function of an abstract is to summarise the paper. Abstracts frequently use the impersonal point of view to emphasise the importance of the work by focusing on the topic rather than the writer.

While academic writers do not usually write themselves into the topic, they do sometimes write themselves into the process of the argument. Vincent Price does this in his paper. He inserts himself into the text wherever he is laying out his argument, as this example shows:

> My outline is twofold. I begin with the general proposition that communication research—and especially research into mass communication—is absolutely central to advancing public opinion theory. Unlike purely individual-level or group-level analysis, the investigation of communication necessitates the analysis of *co-operative* cognition and expression undertaken by individuals attempting to chart a course of collective action. As I will illustrate, the notion that members of a public organize collectively through communication is fundamental to public opinion theory, having been with the field virtually since its inception. Researching this communicative process, I submit, requires us to analyze (a) cognition and opinion formation as individual phenomena that (b) operate within, and are thus largely dependent upon, the wider social context of public debate and collective organization. How might this multilevel theoretical task be accomplished in opinion research? That is the question to which I turn on the second part of this article, taking as my starting point some possible applications of current social psychological theory.

Even from such short extracts, it is possible to see that academic writers can manipulate point of view for particular purposes. In Price's abstract all attention is on the topic so the writer seems absent. In the second extract, the writer is very much in evidence to guide the reader through a complex argument. In other types of writing we expect the point of view to be consistent. Why might the writer of this text have chosen to change from an impersonal to a personal approach? What effect may the change have on the meaning of the text for its readers?

Tone and objectivity

Another technique academic writers use to distance themselves from the topic is through the **tone** they use. The choice of tone is also tied up with ideas about objectivity. Since the tone of a text suggests something of the attitude the writer holds towards the topic, academic writers tend to use a serious and formal tone to imply that that is the way they are treating the topic. In turn, this tone has an effect on the writer-reader relationship. By adopting a serious and formal tone, the writer is treating the reader as knowledgeable and able to follow a complex argument. Accordingly, the manipulation of tone is an additional strategy writers can use to suggest objectivity.

Passive voice and objectivity

Sometimes, academic writers use passive constructions to emphasise objectivity. Normally, when we write, we use the **active voice** to emphasise the subject of a sentence as the agent of the action. The use of the **passive voice** tends to de-emphasise the agent. In the next extract, from *The Madwoman in the Attic*, Sandra Gilbert and Susan Gubar are discussing older critical evaluations of Jane Austen's writing:

> Repeatedly, in other words, Austen was placed in the double bind she would so convincingly dramatize in her novels, for when not rejected as artificial and convention-bound, she was condemned as natural and therefore a writer almost in spite of herself.

In this passage, the passive voice avoids reference to whomever was criticising Austen, and emphasises the criticism itself and its effects, rather than the critics involved. It creates a sense of disinterested evaluation rather than personal attack.

The relationship between writer and reader of academic texts is a complex one. On the one hand, the reader is not often directly addressed, but on the other, the reader is assumed to be part of an academic audience with the specialised knowledge and interest to understand the text. The following example, from an article entitled 'The Escalation and Maintenance of Spouse Abuse: A Cybernetic Model', by Gerald M. Erchak demonstrates the complexities of perspective in the writer-reader relationship:

> Scholars and the general public alike have in recent years been bombarded by scores of volumes, articles, papers, television programs, films, newspapers stories, and public lectures—often factual, sometimes wildly inaccurate and misleading, but always disturbing—on the subject of intrafamilial violence, particularly child and spouse abuse. Americans

seem to believe that family violence is a 'growing problem', although there are no data to demonstrate whether this is or is not the case, simply because of the lack of reliable historical data and the nearly insurmountable problems involved in collecting accurate information at the present time. Nevertheless, there is much that can be done to improve our knowledge of the phenomenon in both the areas of theory and research. There are clearly significant gaps in the theoretical understanding of family violence. While major advances have been made in the construction of models of spouse and child abuse, especially by sociologists, the area of microprocess, of escalation and pattern maintenance, is still poorly understood. This interactional dynamic, especially as it applies to wife-beating, is the primary focus of this essay.

Once again, the writer seems absent from the text and yet, there is a subtle relationship constructed between writer and reader. This relationship relies not just on the use of pronouns (note the use of 'our knowledge'), but on the use of particular technical words. The terms 'intrafamilial violence', 'the lack of reliable historical data', 'the theoretical understanding of family violence', 'models of spouse and child abuse', 'microprocess' and 'interactional dynamic' all suggest that the text has been written with a particular reader in mind.

This reader will have knowledge of the field and the technical jargon that accompanies it and will expect to be treated as a peer. The tone in this extract is serious and formal as befitting the subject matter and the function of the paper. This again constructs the reader as a peer. The reader, then, becomes part of a wider audience sharing the intellectual insights and findings of academic writing but not sharing the experience in a personal or emotional way as when reading other types of texts.

Structure and academic writing

We have already stressed the importance of structure in writing. Structure helps organise the writer's ideas and aids the reader's expectations. The previous section of the book examined the use of structure and logical organisation in argument. We saw how an argument was organised around a thesis statement which was expressed in the introduction and defended through the body of the argument. We also noted that the construction of the thesis statement determines the direction of the argument. The use of evidence to support the points was emphasised, and we stressed the need to make the points link together. Finally, we saw that a conclusion is used to round off the argument and return to and reinforce the thesis statement.

We can consider that each of these structural features works strategically to convey meaning and can analyse them accordingly—that is, the structural elements of academic texts all have strategic functions and effects for readers.

Thesis statements

The thesis statement sets up the argument. The use of a vague thesis statement leads to a vague argument. Tighter thesis statements give more focus. A statement like 'This paper argues that the effects of economic rationalism are still being felt in this country' gives the writer the opportunity to provide a list of effects to be supported with evidence, and to be hierarchised and evaluated. However, a more sharply defined position could be gained by using a statement like 'Increased levels of unemployment can be attributed to policies of economic rationalism.' This thesis shifts the emphasis of the argument and makes it more specific. The identification of the thesis statement in academic papers is an important part of understanding how an argument constructs its meaning. It provides the reader with the chance to focus on the case that is being put forward.

Links and transitions

Since this type of writing consists of points supported with evidence, it is important that these be connected in a purposeful way. Academic texts stress relationships between points, placing them in hierarchies. To do this, academic writers rely on patterns of logical development such as those we discussed in the chapters on cause and effect and argument. The use of a definite structure and clear logic suggests that the writer has thought about the points and is presenting them in a rational way. This organisation can have a powerful effect on the reader as if the very rationality of the text's structure guarantees the truth of the argument.

Evidence

Providing evidence is at the heart of argument. Quoting the published findings of others helps establish the validity of points in

academic writing. A bibliography and the use of citations distinguish academic texts from most other forms of writing. The
incorporation of the research of others suggests to the reader that
the writer has researched the topic thoroughly and is representing
it fairly, giving credit to those who have already contributed to the
field of the debate. Once again, this helps to reinforce the idea of
objectivity that is so important in academic writing.

Conclusions in academic writing

Academic writing is *directed* writing. By that we mean it conveys a
strong sense of purpose. To be directed or purposeful implies an
endpoint in any academic argument. This is why conclusions play
such an important role. To set up a thesis and provide evidence
aimed at convincing the reader of the truth of the writer's claims is
to imply that the thesis can be defended, the point can be proved
and the writer is correct. Academic writing always finishes on a
note that supports the original thesis statement and rounds off the
argument.

Not all academic writing, of course, takes the form of an
argument essay. Some disciplines, especially the sciences, have
particular ways of representing research findings. While the principles and strategies are similar to those we have listed above,
there may be strict categories into which certain aspects of the
work must be fitted. A common arrangement in the sciences
consists of:

> Abstract
> Introduction
> Method
> Results
> Discussion
> Bibliography

Such an arrangement constructs meaning according to the
conventions of scientific disciplines. Like other writing structures,
it affects the way in which writers can represent their findings and
influences the relationship between writer and reader.

Exercises

1 Find a research paper which uses a set of conventions similar to
  the ones listed above. Analyse it carefully, noting the constraints
  the structure imposes on the meaning. How is the relationship

between writer and reader constructed? (You will gain further insight into this process of meaning construction if you refer to the style manual that relates to the particular discipline of your paper.)

2 Analyse the following texts, Text A from a newspaper and Text B from an academic journal, using the notions of function, perspective and structure we have been developing in this chapter. Although each text relates to the topic 'New Technologies', they approach the subject matter differently and use different forms of representation to construct their meanings.

Text A

25 October 2010

You could have cut the atmosphere in Beijing with a laser beam last night when the European President, Charles Windsor, began disparaging the local architecture. It was the signing of the latest trade deal between Europe and Greater America, brokered by China, which had again averted a bloody trade war. I was virtually there, of course, via new programs compiled by my personal tele-computer according to my tastes from news agencies and played on my wall-mounted, life-sized, three-dimensional, high-definition screen.

Over breakfast I read, hear, see and (if I'm really interested) personally experience the news. My PTC has already checked my pulse, temperature and blood pressure—before and after my 15-kilometre cycle along the virtual Great Ocean Road—and notified me of any irregularities. It has also paid any bills due today.

My PTC reminds me that I have a teleconference this morning with a client about a new entertainment centre my firm is designing, and that tomorrow is our wedding anniversary. Knowing what my interests are, it also alerts me to some quaint old theatre (with human actors) playing in town, for which I book some tickets, and the latest European multimedia theatrical production (based on the European conflicts of the late 1990s), which is available through channel 1495 from tonight and said to be enlivened by brilliant synthespian and human acting, stunning virtual sets and hundreds of optional plots. My PTC records these things on CD if I am not around.

My son, who lives in Tokyo and only ever sends me electronic mail when he needs money, has e-mailed for one million, which I credit to his account. A friend reports her husband's abdominal operation went smoothly after surgeons dealt with a complication anticipated by the customary virtual reality rehearsal—he'll be up to a videophone conversation later in the day. She's also wondering whether her teenage son is really learning about the universe as he zooms about in virtual space or just getting kicks zapping aliens.

And a colleague in Chicago responds to my inquiry about the latest entertainment centre designs, offering to show me through one he has just completed.

Text B

In common with other new technologies, computer-mediated communication (CMC) has opened up new social and organizational horizons, so that individuals who use it are increasingly freed from the strictures of time and place in their dealings with others. As with earlier technological advances such as printing and the telephone, CMC introduces the possibility of revolutionary social and structural changes in the ways people communicate and relate to each other (Hiltz and Turoff 1978–92, Marvin 1988, Sproull and Kiesler 1991). This article explores how the medium of text-based electronic communication can affect the relations between people, and perhaps even more fundamentally, how CMC helps to constitute people in ways that affect such relations. Our basic point of departure is the emerging view that CMC facilitates forms of communication, interaction, and organization that apparently undermine unequal status and power relations. This view can be characterized as the liberation or 'equalization' model of CMC. It has been argued that CMC extends and equalizes information exchange, that it releases the individual from the proximal power of others and from the influence of the group, and that consequently it cultivates diversity and democracy in collective activities and decision making. In support of this view, a steadily accumulating body of empirical evidence from social psychological studies in particular, suggests that CMC can serve to reduce the social barriers to communication, and thus the impact of status differentials, resulting in greater equality of participation (eg. Dubrovsky, Kiesler and Sethna 1991, Kiesler and Sproull 1992, Sproull and Kiesler 1991, Weisband 1992).

Editing and textual analysis

The above forms of attention to detail are part of all kinds of textual analysis. They are particularly important in evaluating and intepreting research material that we may have to consult and in deciding whether to integrate it into our own ideas, either paraphrasing or quoting it. Textual analysis is a crucial part of responding thoughtfully to the work of others.

At the same time, it's also important that this kind of analytical viewpoint, along with the same level of textual scrutiny, be applied to our own writing. The features of academic writing we have discussed are available for use in our own writing, but rather than adopt them as a set of fixed rules, we should think of them as a range of **strategic options** or **conventions**. Even within the terms and topics of academic writing, we will find ourselves writing on a range of topics, for a variety of purposes and for different audiences. An essay written in an English seminar will differ from a paper presented to a Sociology class. There will be some stylistic conventions that must comply with the practices of the discipline and the writing task at hand. Once the first draft is completed, we can *edit it critically* by thinking about how it constructs its meaning according to its function, perspective and structure.

We should make sure its **function** is clear; that is, that it addresses the set task appropriately, that it presents the case clearly and precisely, that it supports the points with the published findings of others, and that it evaluates those findings and its own conclusions critically.

The **perspective** adopted deserves attention too. We should check to see that the text has the appropriate degree of objectivity. Do we need to strengthen the feeling of objectivity by removing personal pronouns or by making the tone more formal? Are we treating the reader respectfully, as an intellectual equal? If the passive voice has been adopted, have we thought about the change of emphasis it creates?

Finally, we should assess the **structure** that has been used. The writing should have a clear introduction which contains the thesis statement. The middle paragraphs should show the logical development of ideas. We should make sure the quoted evidence is both appropriate and sufficient to demonstrate our point. We should check that adequate transitions have been used to guide readers from one point to the next. The conclusion should round off the text and link back to the thesis statement.

Editing our own work is not a chore or an afterthought. Instead, it is an *application of textual analysis* which both improves our awareness of the techniques writers use to construct meaning, and provides the opportunity to improve our standing as academic writers.

Function, perspective and structure are key concepts in under-standing how texts create meaning for their readers. Con-centrating on these factors is important not only when analysing academic texts written by others but also when critically evaluating and editing our own.

While we may often tend to think of academic writing as a special category, academic writers are similar to most writers in that they, too, use a variety of conventions and strategies to convey information, point of view and meaning. In the rest of this final section of the book, we will be looking at other conventions and strategies which also help establish textual meanings, including figurative language and style, genre and context. These features operate across all categories of texts, from academic to many other social and professional types.

Exercises

1 Find two texts about multiculturalism in Australia, one from an academic journal and one from a daily newspaper. Using the notions of function, perspective and structure, analyse and discuss the conventions and strategies used in each text.

2 Choose a particular medical issue such as one of the following: ageing, exercise, nutrition, weight loss or a specific disease state. Compare its representation in a medical journal or textbook with that in a popular magazine. Is the information presented objectively or subjectively? Write a short essay explaining and supporting your interpretation.

Works cited

Erchak, Gerald, M. (1984) 'The Escalation and Maintenance of Spouse Abuse: A Cybernetic Model', *Victimology* 9.2: 247–53

Gilbert, Sandra M., and Susan Gubar (1979) *The Madwoman in the Attic: The Woman Writer and the Nineteenth-Century Literary Imagination*, Yale University Press, New Haven

Potter, Ben, and Virginia Trioli (1993) 'Our Virtual Future', *The Age*, 25 October

Price, Vincent (1988) 'On the Public Aspects of Opinion: Linking Levels of Analysis in Public Opinion Research', *Communication Research* 15.6: 659–79

Spears, Russell, and Martin Lea (1994) 'Panacea or Panopticon? The Hidden Power in Computer-Mediated Communication', *Communication Research* 21.4: 427–59

Tannen, Deborah (1979) 'What's in a Frame? Surface Evidence for underlying Expectations', in *New Directions in Discourse Processing*, editor, Roy O. Freedle, Ablex, Norwood

9 Figurative language

Conventions and style

Textual analysis enables us to see that all texts, including those written for different academic disciplines, operate through various types of **conventions** which are recognised and interpreted by authors and audiences. Conventions operate like **codes of meanings** that help writers group together their ideas and present them in a text. For instance, there are many kinds of conventional openings we can use when writing a letter, ranging from a casual 'Hi', to a formal 'Dear Sir/Madam', to an emotional 'My Dearest...'. Depending on the social situation, by using one of these greetings we set a certain tone for the letter as well as expressing our feelings to the reader.

In turn, we expect the reader to pick up on the tone and respond appropriately. A reader's knowledge of textual conventions is an important part of his or her ability to understand and decipher texts. Hence, for authors and readers, conventions are a central aspect of social communication.

By analysing textual conventions we can often get beneath first impressions and start to see what kinds of effects and meanings a text is seeking to establish. Thus, as discussed in the previous chapter, the tendency to avoid the first person pronouns 'I' and 'me' in academic writing is not done merely out of shyness or restraint. It aims for an effect of objectivity, to suggest that the research and opinions being presented are not too closely bound to the author's personal perspective or preferences.

In this and the following chapters, we are going to continue analysing conventions and language style. We are also going to expand our focus by looking at a number of specific issues and concepts—such as figurative language, genre and textual strategies—that affect conventions and styles used in a wide range of texts, from poetry to magazine advertisements to academic essays. Throughout these chapters we will continue our dual concern of examining how other writers use stylistic and conventional features in their work and how we can employ them in our own.

165

Figures of speech

As the title suggests, this chapter will examine the roles that **figurative language** plays in texts. After giving some initial definitions and examples of what figurative language might be, we will consider in more detail the various ways in which figurative language generates different meanings in different contexts. By introducing the idea of **context** we can start to see that figurative language involves much more than simple stylistic effects, and instead participates in personal and social, as well as academic processes of meaning. We will come back to these functions of context later in the chapter.

Our first step is to recognise that the stylistic and conventional features which we read and analyse do not simply make up the surface finish of texts. Instead, style and convention are markers of the ways that texts represent ideas and material. They reveal attitudes and evaluations of these ideas, and therefore influence and affect readers' understandings of them. As we have seen, for example, in the case of an essay in an academic journal, the use of notes and a bibliography doesn't merely show that the essay is serious or clever. Instead, it relates the ideas in the article to studies on similar subjects in two ways:

1 by locating the essay in a context of academic work in the area;
2 by introducing ideas and research of other people that will help to clarify and support the author's case.

These conventional elements of an academic paper help to reinforce its argument and point of view for readers.

Figurative language works in a similar way. While at first it may appear to provide a text's finish or gloss, in most if not all cases, the kind of figurative language used is a key marker of the *viewpoints* which the text is trying to get across. Accordingly, by studying a text's figurative language we don't just get a feel for its 'artistic' qualities; we are actually engaging with its ideas and attitudes in a very close way.

> The key function of **figurative language** is to represent the ideas, attitudes and point of view of a text.

Before expanding our analysis of figurative language's key function, we need to develop a working definition of it. Obviously, such language uses **figures of speech**. The *Macquarie Dictionary* defines these as:

> a literary mode of expression, as a metaphor, simile, personification, antithesis, etc., in which words are used out of their literal sense, or out of ordinary locutions, to suggest a picture or image, or for other special effect.

This definition offers a starting point. It reminds us of some of the basic figures of speech and what their general effect is. It does not, however, go on to consider the ways in which such figures affect readers' understandings of texts, or influence writers' motives for expressing ideas in certain terms. (We wouldn't really expect a dictionary definition to go into this amount of detail.) Yet it is these kinds of questions and effects that make figurative language and figures of speech complex aspects of many kinds of writing.

Exercise

Look up the following figures of speech in a dictionary (a dictionary of literary terms should give more detailed definitions):

metaphor	simile
synecdoche	metonymy
antithesis	irony
hyperbole	personification
allegory	pun
understatement	imagery

Try to find or make up an example for each one. Are any of the examples similar to each other? Do any of your examples seem to differ from the definitions? In what ways?

Imagery

We can start to unravel the complications around figurative language by examining a number of cases and trying to judge their effects. Let's begin by considering a famous poetic example, from John Donne's early seventeenth century poem, 'A Valediction: Forbidding Mourning':

> Our two souls therefore, which are one,
> Though I must go, endure not yet
> A breach, but an expansion,
> Like gold to airy thinness beat.

If they be two, they are two so
As stiff twin compasses are two,
Thy soul the fixed foot, makes no show
To move, but doth, if th' other do.

And though it in the centre sit,
Yet when the other far doth roam,
It leans, and hearkens after it,
And grows erect, as that comes home.

Such wilt thou be to me, who must
Like th' other foot, obliquely run;
Thy firmness makes my circle just,
And makes me end, where I begun.

The poet uses two **images** to talk about his and his lover's souls: thinly beaten gold and a compass. The exaggeration of these images strikes us pretty strongly, the compass more so because it continues for three stanzas. They both seem out of the ordinary, as if a real effort has been made to translate feelings of unhappiness, because the two lovers must separate, into a certain sort of language.

If we focus more closely on the two images we can see that they are interestingly relevant to what is going on. First, the image of thinly beaten gold suggests that the lovers' affair continues rather than breaks down, and also hints at the quality or value of their relationship—it gets finer even when they are apart. Next, the compass image suggests that any separation will ultimately lead back to reunion. The lover is the part of the compass that stays still and the poet becomes the other part, that moves or travels around. If she stays still he will come back to where he started, and the circle they have drawn together will represent their perfect union.

Clearly, Donne's image is exaggerated. On the one hand, we might think what is the point? Why doesn't the poet just say what he means? On the other, we wouldn't think that the poet has not meant what he has written or that he has made a mistake. The effort he has put into developing the two images suggests that what is being said in the poem is what is meant.

Figurative language thus appears to have an ambiguous effect of seeming both *to say and not to say what it means*. Let's consider this ambiguity in some more detail. Why is this type of language called *figurative*? What do we mean by a *figure of speech*? The terms figurative, figure and image connect processes of visual representation to language. Just as we might draw an image or a figure of a landscape or a person, so a verbal figure or image depicts something else in language—the compass is used as an image of the poet's relationship with the lover because it depicts separation and connection, departure and return.

An image can thus create a verbal picture of a scene, event, relationship or even an emotion, or it may evoke a number of senses in implying its meanings. Consider the momentary feelings of optimism that the narrator in Coral Lansbury's *The Grotto* experiences:

> I walked out to the back and down into the orchard ... I reached up and picked an apricot, rubbing off the soft down against my breast. It was tart, but I could taste the promise of sweetness. For so long I had lived in the forest of death. Now as I walked through the orchard I felt as if all the strength of summer were rushing through my veins.

Here the language works through vision, taste and touch to suggest the pleasure of the speaker's emotions. The details of the apricot, forest and orchard trigger notions of the future's sweet taste, the past's darkness and danger, and the present's energy and strength. Each of these natural images works to consolidate the meanings of the others. We might note that authors frequently use a series of related images in this way—to reinforce the main, underlying image for the reader's understanding.

Alternatively, authors often mix together a number of different images to make a kind of mosaic of meaning. The images add up to create a combination of ideas that produce the whole meaning. The following wine reviews illustrate this approach:

> The word exotic is the most obvious description of the nose: spice, black cherry, liquorice, earth and raisin are all to be found here. Super ripe flavours of blackberries and pepper are bound by some small tannins.

> Fresh and clean, there are some apricot and peach characters on the nose. The palate is an explosion of fruit and the acid keeps all in fine balance.

Different fruits are listed to try to capture for readers the taste and smell ('nose') of the two wines. 'Explosion' is used metaphorically to capture the sudden burst of flavour we would taste if we drank the wine.

As we saw in Chapter 2, using imagery in these kinds of cumulative ways can be effective in *describing* things to readers. However, if the chosen images seem to contradict each other the effect may be unclear. In the previous example, at first it seems a little hard to imagine that blackberries and pepper can go together; presumably the author is pointing to the subtle variations in flavour. Variation in imagery can have striking effects, but it may also be a little confusing at times for readers. Hence a text's imagery should be linked to its function. In expository and academic writing, images should relate to each other in a way that readers can interpret.

Exercises

1 In one or two paragraphs, describe a close relationship you have with someone by using nature imagery. What aspects of the relationship do these images seem to emphasise?
2 In the news media, sporting metaphors and images are often used to report on political events. Try to find a newspaper story on politics that uses sporting imagery, and rewrite the article using theatrical, family or another set of images.

Vehicle and tenor

Much figurative language works similarly to the above examples. It develops one extended image, or it builds up a sequence of related images and metaphors to suggest the visual or other sensory features of what is being described or depicted. We can now draw two conclusions about this figurative process:

1 Figurative language is **condensed**; it may pack a number of meanings into the one image (for example, the nature imagery in the Coral Lansbury extract describes her sensations and also grants them a positive naturalness).
2 Any image or figure has two main parts: what you are talking about (the lovers' separation and contact, the wines) and the images you are using to talk about it (the compass, the combination of different fruits).

We will consider the condensed meanings that imagery has later in the chapter. Let's now examine the two components of an image. These two parts are often called the **tenor** and the **vehicle**, where the tenor is what you are talking about and the vehicle is the image which 'carries' the meaning.

If you are trying to analyse how a text is working it can be helpful to use these two terms to name the different parts of the figurative language process. In a way, however, vehicle and tenor always go together in an image. There cannot be one without the other: you can't talk about something without having something to talk about and without using something to talk about it. Vehicle and tenor imply each other. So while we might distinguish between them when analysing a text they are always linked together in a process of **meaning transfer**—that is, the meaning of the vehicle (the compass, nature or fruit) is transferred to the tenor (the lovers, the character or the wine).

Meaning transfer

Figurative language is based on a process of **meaning transfer**. Although there are different types of figurative language, they all involve this process. In the examples we have looked at so far, the meaning transfer has taken place rather obviously. In some cases, it has been marked by the words 'like': 'Such wilt thou be to me, who must/Like th' other foot, obliquely run'; and 'as': 'I felt as if all the strength of summer were rushing through my veins.' This type of meaning transfer is called a **simile**—a comparison between two objects, feelings, actions, and so on, which uses 'like' or 'as'. There is no necessary limit to what can be compared to what, or which vehicle can be linked to which tenor. In an unusual simile, the narrator of 'Streetcorner Man', a short story by Jorge Luis Borges, compares guitars with people: 'the pair of guitars sat straight up on the seat like men'. As with all similes, here the use of 'like' or 'as' serves to signpost that a transfer of meaning is taking place. The signposting prepares the readers to look for the connection between the tenor and vehicle.

Another dominant process of meaning transfer is **metaphor** ('metaphor' is the ancient Greek word for transfer). The difference between metaphor and simile is that metaphor does not formally mark its transfer with 'like' or 'as'. It tends to move straight into the meaning transfer, without first signalling it to the reader. Janet Frame's short story 'The Reservoir' uses a number of metaphors to detail a landscape:

> We passed huge trees that lived with their heads in the sky, with their great arms and joints creaking with age and the burden of being trees . . . The damp smell of the pine needles caught in our breath. There were no birds, only the constant sighing of the trees . . . The fringe of young pines on the edge, like toy trees, subjected to the wind, sighed and told us their sad secrets.

In this excerpt, the main effect of Frame's metaphors is to personify the landscape. The trees have heads and arms, and they sigh and talk to the narrator and her friends. We could generalise that the tenor is the landscape and the vehicle is human life: the meanings of human life are transferred to the land. However, unlike the similes we considered earlier, the transfer process is not marked or introduced by 'like' or 'as'. There are no verbal signposts.

There are some significant differences in the effects for readers of this contrast between simile and metaphor, the signposting of meaning transfer. In a way, the simile alerts us to the fact that a transfer of meaning from vehicle to tenor is going to occur. This can have three consequences:

1 In the case of an extreme or exaggerated transfer, the simile prepares us to accept the transfer by revealing that a possibly unusual or unconventional image is about to be used.
2 The transfer of meaning is slowed down in a simile; there is a deliberate pause in the train of thought followed by the reference to another idea.
3 Due to this signposting and slowing down of the meaning transfer, the reader has an opportunity to evaluate the figurative language, to weigh up the relevance or validity of the transfer of meaning. A simile seems to invite the reader to read and interpret the text *actively*.

By contrast, the unmarked meaning transfer of the metaphor seems to take place more quickly. The transfer occurs implicitly and can hurry the reader's thinking along with it. In the example from Janet Frame's story, a reader might not immediately pick up on the humanising of the landscape, yet the figurative language might still predispose him or her to accept the personification. Metaphor may induce a type of passive reading, where the text insinuates its meanings less obviously, making it harder for readers to evaluate what is being implied in the transfers of meaning.

Hence the contrast between metaphor and simile as two processes of meaning transfer is important not simply in terms of being able to identify what is a tenor and what is a vehicle. We don't want to play 'spot the simile or metaphor'. Rather, the significance of this contrast is to reveal that **figurative language involves thinking and conceptual processes**. Like textual style and conventions, figurative language isn't simply a surface process, where the meaning of the tenor gets 'dressed up' in terms of the vehicle. Instead, the vehicle opens up the meanings and the ideas that are written about to the *evaluating viewpoint* of the reader's active understanding of the text.

Figurative language and point of view

Figurative language influences the ways a reader deals with and responds to a text—agreeing with the transfers and equations of meaning that are being represented, or questioning and disagreeing with them. These meaning transfers and responses to them suggest that reading and writing are an *ongoing dialogue of points of view*, where ideas and opinions on topics get worked through. Figurative language isn't simply a fancy effect of imagery; rather, it's a conceptual process where authors' and readers' *viewpoints* come into contact with each other.

Therefore we shouldn't think of figurative language as a feature just of poetry or fiction. Although most of the examples considered above are from those genres, the fact is that many ordinary types of texts and expressions are based on metaphorical transfers of meaning which go unnoticed or remain implicit. The metaphors and similes of poetry and fiction are the marked case of a more general process of figurative imagery that runs through all kinds of texts, from everyday expressions to academic and scientific papers. As readers, we tend to expect literary genres to display imagery, but this anticipation often serves to block our awareness of the metaphorical processes of figurative meaning in other sorts of texts.

Up to this point we have used poetry and fiction to bring the process and effects of figurative language out into the open. Now we need to try to track this idea back to non-literary texts in order to see how they also use imagery to influence the responses, thoughts and viewpoints of readers.

We noted earlier that figures of speech tend to condense a number of meanings and that metaphor often seems to hide the process of meaning transfer, or at least not to foreground it with 'like' or 'as'. This metaphorical process of condensing and concealing transfers of meanings and the exchange of concepts exemplifies what goes on in non-fictional texts. They often seem to compress, hide or disguise their own use of figurative language and imagery.

Often a non-fictional text is crucially constructed on a **dominant metaphor** which shapes and determines its point of view while concealing its operation beneath the text's surface meaning. This kind of dominant metaphor regularly works in two steps:

1 It will structure the ideas and values represented in a text; and
2 It will conceal its own influence under the seemingly natural surface and meaning of the text's ideas.

Therefore it is important for us, as analytical readers of texts, to be alert to the structuring effects of figurative language upon textual meanings.

Let's consider some examples. One of the main forms of academic writing we consider in the second section of this book is the argument essay. As an academic convention, argument seems an objective way of putting a case. Yet underlying its supposed objectivity is a metaphor of *accusation* ('argue' can be traced to a Latin verb meaning, among other things, 'to accuse'). In putting forward a viewpoint, argument frequently requires that we confront, oppose and refute other ideas; it participates in an adversarial process rather than a co-operative one.

A written academic argument assumes that it puts its case effectively. Yet in doing so, it may lose insights that other viewpoints have to offer. Because it is set up in terms of accusation and refutation, argument cannot easily compromise or borrow good ideas from an opposing view. Its conception of correct or appropriate thinking and writing is based on a metaphor of one side gaining victory over another.

In this example, we see a type of academic writing which is structured on the basis of a metaphor that is not openly acknowledged. Everyone who writes academic arguments, from students to professors, tries to adhere to the implications of the argument-accusation metaphor. In this way the underlying metaphor becomes the key concept which guides what people do. Figurative language can affect social thought, actions and writing.

Two linguists, George Lakoff and Mark Johnson, have studied how **metaphorical concepts** often determine the ways that people think, write and act in everyday situations as well as in more specialised ones like academic work. Some of the examples they discuss clearly show how such metaphors influence people's points of view:

> **Ideas are plants**: That idea has come to fruition. It is a budding theory. That idea is an offshoot of another theory. Engineering has many branches. Her mind is fertile but his is barren.

> **Ideas are commodities and products**: It's important how you package your ideas. That idea won't sell. He is a source of valuable ideas. That idea is worthless. This idea needs to be refined.

> **Love is madness**: He's crazy about her. She drives me out of my mind. He is mad about her. I'm wild about him.

Life is a container: You have led a full life. His life is empty. Live life to the fullest. Her life is crammed with excitement.

Many of these expressions are part of everyday language. When someone uses them we don't necessarily think that they are speaking metaphorically. However, Lakoff and Johnson contend that people are in fact talking about, understanding and even experiencing their situations in terms of these metaphors. They structure our thoughts and actions.

A striking example of the ways that such metaphorical concepts can affect texts, ideas and actions about a certain topic can be seen in Susan Sontag's discussion of how the metaphor of *plague* has been applied to the disease AIDS, and then how both plague and AIDS are used metaphorically by authors to criticise social or political groups which they oppose. A chain of metaphor effects is set in motion:

> Plagues are invariably regarded as judgments on society, and the metaphoric inflation of AIDS into such a judgment also accustoms people to the inevitability of global spread. This is a traditional use of sexually transmitted diseases: to be described as punishments not just of individuals but of a group. Not only venereal diseases have been used in this way, to identify transgressing or vicious populations. Interpreting any catastrophic epidemic as a sign of moral laxity or political decline was as common until the later part of the last century as associating dreaded diseases with foreignness (or with despised and feared minorities) ... The AIDS epidemic serves as an ideal projection for First World political paranoia. Not only is the so-called AIDS virus the quintessential invader from the Third World. It can stand for any mythological menace ... AIDS is a favorite concern of those who translate their political agenda into questions of group psychology: of national self-esteem and self-confidence.

Sontag is analysing the way people use 'plague' and 'disease' as metaphors to understand AIDS and then connect it to a range of social conditions. We can note two points about her discussion: 1. The metaphors she is considering are taken from non-fictional texts (scientific reports, newspaper columns and editorials, political statements). 2. The impact of these metaphors on readers and audiences is related to the *social values* that they invoke.

This second point is the more important one. The effects of figurative language in a text depend on the social weight that the images carry and the cultural attitudes that they refer to. The texts that Sontag evaluates use images of politics, race, morals and sexuality that strike and involve their readers powerfully. The social concerns in these images make the connections between them and AIDS all the more significant. In some texts, AIDS can start to operate as a metaphor for immorality, sexual deviance or even national and political decay.

We can call the social references that images and figurative language take on for readers their **connotations**. A connotation is **the network of social meanings that an image can have**. We might also note that since all words can have connotations, all words can have figurative social meanings—AIDS, a scientific term invented in the early 1980s, may name a medical disease or a society out of control. The distinction between figurative and non-figurative language starts to break down. It seems there is no absolute difference, because in a certain **context** any word might start to have a range of social connotations. It may start to work like figurative language.

Exercises

1 Think of a metaphorical concept similar to the ones that Lakoff and Johnson raise, and then write a 500-word essay in which you examine the cultural attitudes that underlie the concept. Try to provide extra examples to support your analysis.
2 Find a newspaper article that uses disease or another strong metaphor to represent a controversial social issue. Write a 600-word essay in which you analyse the metaphors that have been used. Consider their conceptual structure for the author and their possible influence on readers.

Context and meaning conflict

The key factor that determines the range of figurative effects and connotations that words may have is the **context** in which they are used. In language studies context has three main meanings—the social situation in which a text is produced (e.g., a university essay, a job application letter in a business context); the social situation in which a text is read (as for John Donne's poem, it might be hundreds of years after it was written); and the social situation that the text refers to, is about, or is influenced by. In each of these three ways, context influences which connotative meanings will be emphasised. Often, if there is a clash among the three types of context there will be a clash among the connotations that a reader emphasises as opposed to the text or author.

For example, a student's academic argument about industrial reform and enterprise bargaining may represent a thesis which differs from her opinion about pay rates and conditions for a part-time job. It's also likely that her boss might respond to the argument in ways different from her tutor. Clearly, for all concerned the context and textual meanings have shifted in important ways, and a term like 'enterprise bargaining' assumes different connotations. As the social contexts and connotations of figurative language change, reading can become a process not just of meaning transfer but of **meaning conflict.**

We can see this kind of meaning conflict in the following essay by Stephen Jay Gould, called 'Racist Arguments and IQ'. There is a collision of contexts and connotations in scientific writing and thought:

Racist arguments and IQ

Stephen Jay Gould

Louis Agassiz, the greatest biologist of mid-nineteenth-century America, argued that God had created blacks and whites as separate species. The defenders of slavery took much comfort from this assertion, for biblical proscriptions of charity and equality did not have to extend across a species boundary. What could an abolitionist say? Science had shone its cold and dispassionate light upon the subject; Christian hope and sentimentality could not refute it.

Similar arguments, carrying the apparent sanction of science, have been continually invoked in attempts to equate egalitarianism with sentimental hope and emotional blindness. People who are unaware of this historical pattern tend to accept each recurrence at face value: that is, they assume that each statement arises from the 'data' actually presented, rather than from the social conditions that truly inspire it.

The racist arguments of the nineteenth century were based primarily on craniometry, the measurement of human skulls. Today, these contentions stand totally discredited. What craniometry was to the nineteenth century, intelligence testing has been to the twentieth. The victory of the eugenics movement in the Immigration Restriction Act of 1924 signaled its first unfortunate effect—for the severe restrictions upon non-Europeans and upon southern and eastern Europeans gained much support from results of the first extensive and uniform application of intelligence tests in America—the Army Mental Tests of World War I. These tests were engineered and administered by psychologist Robert M. Yerkes, who concluded that 'education alone will not place the negro [*sic*] race on a par with its Caucasian competitors'. It is now clear that Yerkes and his colleagues knew no way to separate genetic from environmental components in postulating causes for different performances on the tests.

The latest episode of this recurring drama began in 1969, when

Arthur Jensen published an article entitled, 'How Much Can We Boost IQ and Scholastic Achievement?' in the *Harvard Educational Review*. Again, the claim went forward that new and uncomfortable information had come to light, and that science had to speak the 'truth' even if it refuted some cherished notions of a liberal philosophy. But again, I shall argue, Jensen had no new data; and what he did present was flawed beyond repair by inconsistencies and illogical claims.

Jensen assumes that IQ tests adequately measure something we may call 'intelligence'. He then attempts to tease apart the genetic and environmental factors causing differences in performance. He does this primarily by relying upon the one natural experiment we possess: identical twins reared apart—for differences in IQ between genetically identical people can only be environmental. The average difference in IQ for identical twins is less than the difference for two unrelated individuals raised in similarly varied environments. From the data on twins, Jensen obtains an estimate of environmental influence. He concludes that IQ has a heritability of about 0.8 (or 80 per cent) *within* the population of American and European whites. The average difference between American whites and blacks is 15 IQ points (one standard deviation). He asserts that this difference is too large to attribute to environment, given the high heritability of IQ. Lest anyone think that Jensen writes in the tradition of abstract scholarship, I merely quote the first line of his famous work: 'Compensatory education has been tried, and it apparently has failed.'

I believe that this argument can be refuted in a 'hierarchical' fashion—that is, we can discredit it at one level and then show that it fails at a more inclusive level even if we allow Jensen's argument for the first two levels:

Level 1: The equation of IQ with intelligence. Who knows what IQ measures? It is a good predictor of 'success' in school, but is such success a result of intelligence, apple polishing, or the assimilation of values that the leaders of society prefer? Some psychologists get around this argument by defining intelligence operationally as the scores attained on 'intelligence' tests. A neat trick. But at this point, the technical definition of intelligence has strayed so far from the vernacular that we can no longer define the issue. But let me allow (although I don't believe it), for the sake of argument, that IQ measures some meaningful aspect of intelligence in its vernacular sense.

Level 2: The heritability of IQ. Here again, we encounter a confusion between vernacular and technical meanings of the same word. 'Inherited', to a layman, means 'fixed', 'inexorable', or 'unchangeable'. To a geneticist, 'inherited' refers to an estimate of similarity between related individuals based on genes held in common. It carries no implications of inevitability or of immutable entities beyond the reach of environmental influence. Eyeglasses correct a variety of inherited problems in vision; insulin can check diabetes.

Jensen insists that IQ is 80 per cent heritable. Princeton psychologist Leon J. Kamin has done the dogwork of meticulously checking through details of the twin studies that form the basis of this estimate. He has found an astonishing number of inconsistencies and downright inaccuracies. For example, the late Sir Cyril Burt, who generated the largest body of data on identical twins reared apart, pursued his studies of intelligence for more than forty years. Although he increased his sample sizes in a variety of 'improved' versions, some of his correlation coefficients remain unchanged to the third decimal place—a statistically impossible situation.[1] IQ depends in part upon sex and age; and other studies did not standardize properly for them. An improper correction may produce higher values between twins not because they hold genes for intelligence in common, but simply because they share the same sex and age. The data are so flawed that no valid estimate for the heritability of IQ can be drawn at all. But let me assume (although no data support it), for the sake of argument, that the heritability of IQ is as high as 0.8.

Level 3: The confusion of within and between-group variation. Jensen draws a causal connection between his two major assertions—that the within-group heritability of IQ is 0.8 for American whites, and that the mean difference in IQ between American blacks and whites is 15 points. He assumes that the black 'deficit' is largely genetic in origin because IQ is so highly heritable. This is a *non sequitur* of the worst possible kind—for there is no necessary relationship between heritability within a group and differences in mean values of two separate groups.

A simple example will suffice to illustrate this flaw in Jensen's argument. Height has a much higher heritability within groups than anyone has ever claimed for IQ. Suppose that height has a mean value of five feet two inches and a heritability of 0.9 (a realistic value) within a group

of nutritionally deprived Indian farmers. High heritability simply means that short farmers will tend to have short offspring, and tall farmers tall offspring. It says nothing whatever against the possibility that proper nutrition could raise the mean height to six feet (taller than average white Americans). It only means that, in this improved status, farmers shorter than average (they may now be five feet ten inches) would still tend to have shorter than average children.

I do not claim that intelligence, however defined, has no genetic basis—I regard it as trivially true, uninteresting, and unimportant that it does. The expression of any trait represents a complex interaction of heredity and environment. Our job is simply to provide the best environmental situation for the realisation of valued potential in all individuals. I merely point out that a specific claim purporting to demonstrate a mean genetic deficiency in the intelligence of American blacks rests upon no new facts whatever and can cite no valid data in its support. It is just as likely that blacks have a genetic advantage over whites. And, either way, it doesn't matter a damn. An individual can't be judged by his group mean.

If current biological determinism in the study of human intelligence rests upon no new facts (actually, no facts at all), then why has it become so popular of late? The answer must be social and political. The 1960s were good years for liberalism; a fair amount of money was spent on poverty programs and relatively little happened. Enter new leaders and new priorities. Why didn't the earlier programs work? Two possibilities are open: (1) we didn't spend enough money, we didn't make sufficiently creative efforts, or (and this makes any established leader jittery) we cannot solve these problems without a fundamental social and economic transformation of society; or (2) the programs failed because their recipients are inherently what they are—blaming the victims. Now, which alternative will be chosen by men in power in an age of retrenchment?

I have shown, I hope, that biological determinism is not simply an amusing matter for clever cocktail party comments about the human animal. It is a general notion with important philosophical implications and major political consequences. As John Stuart Mill wrote, in a statement that should be the motto of the opposition: 'Of all the vulgar modes of escaping from the consideration of the effect of social and moral influences upon the human mind, the most vulgar is that of attributing the diversities of conduct and character to inherent natural differences.'

Note

1 I wrote this essay in 1974. Since then, the case against Sir Cyril has progressed from an inference of carelessness to a spectacular (and well-founded) suspicion of fraud. Reporters for the London *Times* have discovered, for example, that Sir Cyril's co-authors (for the infamous twin studies) apparently did not exist outside his imagination. In the light of Kamin's discoveries, one must suspect that the data have an equal claim to reality.

Gould's essay begins by alluding to nineteenth-century biological theories that God made blacks inferior to whites. There is a clash of contexts—nineteenth century America, science, religion, racism, and the late-twentieth century when Gould is writing—and so a conflict of connotations. Thus where nineteenth century biology uses the image of God to explain its theories, Gould uses the image of racism. In the twentieth century, there is a similar metaphorical process used to structure the racist theory of black people's inferiority. The vehicle for the tenor racism is no longer God; instead, it has become 'IQ'. IQ is, in turn, conceived metaphorically through the image of 'genetic inheritance' rather than in terms of environmental factors. Then Gould shows that inheritance is metaphorically conceived as unchangeable. These various meaning transfers and the connotations of key words like 'IQ' and 'inheritance' work to construct a supposedly scientific theory which we can see is based on certain social attitudes towards race and especially towards people who are not white.

In this essay, Gould exemplifies the process of critical, active reading which questions and evaluates the figurative language and metaphorical constructs that other authors have used to organise their texts. It does not make any difference that those texts are 'scientific' and not 'poetic'. Their ideas and terms are still determined by the contexts of when they were written, when they are read, and what social situation they refer to. Because Gould's reading context is different to the contexts where the other texts were written, he attacks their connotations. Basically, he is arguing that when these texts imply that their topic is science or that their connotative context is scientific, it really is racist. Gould *rewrites* the figurative language of these other texts, revealing racist connotations that had been concealed behind the metaphorical disguise of science.

As can be seen from this example, meaning conflict occurs when we read texts *actively*. It arises from differences in social and cultural attitudes which figurative language represents.

We noted earlier in the example of academic argument, that a whole style of writing can be structured through a metaphorical concept with its related connotations and attitudes. Gould's essay builds on this point. It shows us that different academic disciplines, or even the same discipline at different times and practised by different groups—biology in the nineteenth, early and late twentieth centuries—are based on different vocabularies of figurative language and their implicit social values.

The next essay, Greg Dening's 'Sharks that walk on the land: The death of Captain Cook' also reflects on the consequences of clashes between connotations within figurative language. The conflicts occur across Polynesian and English cultures as well as within the academic disciplines of history and anthropology:

Sharks that walk on the land: The death of Captain Cook

Greg Dening

The Polynesians are those people who some two or three thousand years ago spread to all the islands of the Pacific through the great triangle that reaches from Hawaii to New Zealand to Easter Island. That was their great cultural triumph. They had mastered the immense ocean. They had discovered all the islands of the Pacific and then in turn were discovered by European explorers from the sixteenth to the eighteenth centuries of the Christian era.

In their different island worlds the Polynesians developed separately, playing variations on their common cultural themes. They held in common, however, an understanding of themselves—call it an historical consciousness—expressed in the mythical opposition of 'native' and 'stranger'. This opposition of 'native' and 'stranger' was prior to and independent of the European intrusion. The Polynesians were native and stranger among themselves and to themselves. They saw themselves as made up of native, those born of the land of their islands, and stranger, those who had at some time come from a distant place. 'Tahiti' is, in its different forms, the Polynesian word for a distant place. Strangers came from Tahiti. Typically in their myths the first stranger, a chief, came many generations ago in a canoe from a distant place. He found the natives on their island and either overthrew the existing chiefly line by violence or married the highest born woman of the natives and established his strangers' line.

In myth and in ritual this opposition of native and stranger was a constant metaphor of Polynesian politics and social organisation. Political power was thought to come through usurpation by the stranger and was given legitimacy by the native. A reigning chief would trace in genealogy his line to a hero who would have come from a distant place and conquered the native inhabitants of the island and their chief. It was not just an event of the mythical past, however. The reigning chief, even if he had come to power by the natural death of his father, would have played out a usurping role in the rituals of his accession and would have married into that line which connected him most closely with the original natives of the land. So the opposition native and stranger was both history and cosmology. It offered an understanding both of the past and of the present: the conqueror, the stranger, came from the sea; the conquered, but founding force, the people, were of the land. So Land and Sea had the oppositions of Native and Stranger. And because Polynesian cosmology imaged the sky as a great dome reaching down all around the island to the circle of the horizon, those who came by sea came from 'beyond the sky'. They were *atua*, gods. Being called *atua*, gods, as they almost universally were, the European Strangers who came to Polynesian islands from beyond the sky, were both flattered and reinforced in their judgements of savage simplicities. We might hazard a guess that the Polynesians, just as they saw in their own Stranger Chiefs the incarnation of usurping power, so they expected the European Strangers from beyond the sky to play out their mythical usurping roles. Native: Stranger: :Land: Sea. There are other associations as well. Strangers from the Sea, from Beyond the Sky, Usurping Power, were chiefs; they were also man eaters, sacrificers. There was a Hawaiian proverb that caught it all: 'Chiefs are sharks that walk on the land.'

In Hawaii, as elsewhere in Polynesia, the structural opposition of Native and Stranger was played out in an annual cycle of rituals. Eight months of the year belonged to the Stranger Chiefs, and were the time of human sacrifice and war, the time of *kapu* (taboos), and of those protocols of the dominance of chiefly power. It was the time in which the chiefs walked on the land like sharks and the people of the land, the commoners, obeyed all the *kapu*, bowed their heads to the ground, removed themselves from the way of the chiefs: they obeyed all the *kapu* or suffered death as *kapu* breakers. These eight months of the year belonged to Ku, the god of war and sacrifice, the ancestral deity of the Strangers.

These were the ordinary months of the year. But there were four months beginning October-November that were a sort of carnival time, when the ordinary was overturned. These four months belonged to the people of the land, the commoners, the natives. It was a reversed world in which the chiefs ritually lost their power to the people, when *kapu* and protocols were put aside, in which there were no sacrifices or wars, in which the god of the land, Lono, returned to the islands. The chiefs went into seclusion, locked themselves away on their own individual lands. The time of Lono was called *makahiki* and it followed a strict calendar. It began with a procession of the priests of Lono right-handedly around the island. That is, the land was always on the right and the sea on the left. Right hand, life, land: left hand, death, sea. The procession of Lono was a symbolic act of his possession of the land. At the same time there were left-handed processions, counter-clockwise, around the lands of the chiefs, symbolic acts of dis-possession. In the time of their seclusion they lost that power which they had usurped from the people of the land. Lono's procession was led by Lono's symbol, a cross piece of wood from which hung banner-like pieces of white cloth made of bark. At all stages of the procession the common people came forward with abundant gifts. It was a time of feasting and games. There were great boxing matches, sledding, running races, javelin throwing and dancing. Like carnivals everywhere it was a time of freedom, sex roles were reversed, *kapu* were over-thrown and none were sacrificed for breaking them. When the island was encircled, the procession ended at Lono's temple. Then at the end of the four months of *makahiki*, the first or second week of February, the chiefs returned. They confronted Lono on the beach in front of his temple in an act of ceremonial

violence in which the chiefs re-enacted their usurping role. Lono's temple was dismantled, the new year of Ku was begun with a human sacrifice and the *kapu* were reimposed. Once again the sharks walked on the land.

In November of 1778 James Cook's *Resolution* and her consort the *Discovery* appeared off the north-west coast of the island of Hawaii. It was Cook's third voyage. He was a world famous man. His voyages of discovery had captured the imagination of Europe and America. He was also a tired man. It was his tenth year at sea on Pacific explorations. He was cranky. On this third voyage he had already flogged forty-five per cent of his crew and many of these more than once. Indeed as they approached Hawaii he was crankier than ever, because his crew, conservative as ever, would not drink the sugar-cane beer he had substituted for their grog for the sake of their health. And his crew were cranky at him, spoke mutinously as the phrase went, because instead of stopping at anchorage where they might enjoy the pleasures of the islands, he had, for the sake of manipulating the market on supplies, decided to keep at sea off Hawaii and to drop in only at selected bays. They had spent hard months mapping and surveying the north-west American coast in a vain effort to find a passage through to the Atlantic and had comforted themselves with dreams of wintering in the islands. Instead for nearly two full months in the winter seas of December and January off Hawaii, since made famous for their enormous surf and commented on by Cook as the largest he had ever seen, they made their slow clockwise voyage around Hawaii, beating constantly against the wind, tacking endlessly, the whole crew angry at Cook and he at them.

When they came close to land to do a little marketing, they noticed several things. There were only commoners and no chiefs to visit them. The offerings made were extraordinarily generous. The islanders all called Cook Lono. Finding none of the usual versions of Cook's name—Tuti or Kuki—would satisfy the Hawaiians, Cook's officers also began to refer to him as Lono when they spoke of him. The two vessels with their cross-pieced masts and sails proceeded on their right-handed procession around the island till on January 17 they anchored at Kealekekua Bay on the south coast of Hawaii. They received a welcome there the like of which they had never seen in the Pacific, a thousand canoes and ten thousand islanders in complete jubilation. Kealekekua is a large sweeping bay. High cliffs in the centre drop to the water's edge and divide the low-lying point on the western edge, where there were the many huts of a settlement, from a shallow valley in the south-east corner, where there was a large stone structure and a few huts. This last was a temple or *helau*. It happened to be Lono's temple at which the annual *makahiki* procession began and ended. It came as no surprise to the priests of Lono and all the people of Kealekekua that the two vessels with Lono's symbols displayed and seen off shore early in the *makahiki* season should have slowly made their way to where it all began and ended. There were no chiefs in all that welcoming crowd and the priest of Lono led Cook immediately to their temple where he let them do with him ritually what they wished. They took him to each of the images of lesser gods and he heard their denunciations of them. He let them hold his arms like the cross piece of Lono's symbol and offer him sacrificial food. He sat through the long litanies as they chanted 'Lono, Lono, Lono'. He then asked the priests whether or not the small enclosure beside the temple might not be his to erect a tent for astronomical observations. He needed to watch the stars. So the sailors erected a stranger little temple of a tent and talked stars and sun to the priests of Lono who knew all about stars and were watching them themselves because the *makahiki* feast was determined by the rising and setting of the Pleiades and the setting was nearly upon them.

The high chief of Hawaii, Kalaniopuu, did not appear for several days. When he did come on the twenty-fifth he came with a ceremony and majesty that the sailors had not seen before. He came in the great feather cloaks of Hawaii and invested Cook in one of them, still in the British museum. There is no evidence of the ceremonies of opposition, although Kalaniopuu would not meet Cook on the *Resolution*, only on the beach in front of Lono's temple. The Englishmen thought it curious that Kalaniopuu immediately and anxiously asked when they were going. The Englishmen left on 4 February. It was, as far as computers can calculate it, the last day of *makahiki* in that year. They did not go before two more unnerving coincidences. The Englishmen wanted firewood and asked for the fences, scaffolding and wooden images on Lono's temple and were surprised that the priests of Lono readily agreed. The priests demurred only at one statue. It was the image of Ku. That one stayed, the priests said, and busily helped the sailors dismantle Lono's temple at season's end.

Also a much loved gunner on the *Resolution*, William Watman, had a stroke and died. The chiefs asked that he be buried in the Temple. Old William Watman was buried with ceremony he could hardly have foreseen. 'As we were filling the grave', the *Resolution's* journal reads, 'and had finished reading the ceremony (during which they preserved the most profound silence and regard) they would throw in a dead pig and some coconuts, plantains etc.; and indeed were inclined to have shewed their respect for the dead by a great quantity of these articles, they also repeated some ceremonies, and although they were in some measure stopped from going through their funeral prayers, yet for three nights and in one it lasted the best part of it . . . [they] surrounded the grave, killed hogs, sing a great deal, in which acts of piety and good will they were left undisturbed: at the head of the grave a post was erected and a square piece of board nailed on it with the name of the decreased, his age and the date, this they promised should always remain and we have no doubt but it will as long as the post lasts and be a monument of our being the first discoverer's of this group of island.'

So the Hawaiians made the Englishmen's sacrifice their own. And while the season of Ku was thus begun, they had no qualms that it be marked with the cross and sign of Lono. As it happens William Watman's death is remembered there still with a sign that has lasted longer than his wooden cross. There is a plaque there now celebrating

this as the first Christian service on Hawaiian soil.

Makahiki was over and on those last days the people constantly asked when Lono was going. When Cook said his goodbyes and said he would be back next year in the winter from his search of the north-west passage, the priests said they expected him.

So Cook went and he would have been back next year, except that a few days out the foremast sprung on the *Resolution* and he was back in ten days. There was no welcome this time. 'It hurt our vanity,' the Englishmen said. The people were insolent and the chiefs sullen and questioning. There were immediately thefts and confrontations. The Englishmen could not believe that the atmosphere could change so rapidly and put it down to the strains that nearly three hundred extra mouths brought. Truth was they were out of season and out of role. They were not of the land: they were of the sea. They were not Native come to power for a season: they were Stranger, usurping power, sharks that walked on the land. The change in the Hawaiians brought changes in the English, and they say as much in their journals—that they displayed power and violence to get their way much more overtly. There were several incidents of violent clashes and on 13 February Cook himself was involved in a strange pursuit, alone except for a marine, running several miles, pistol in hand, after a thief. That night a cutter was stolen and on the morning of 14 February Cook closed the bay with armed men and went ashore looking for Kalaniopuu to take him hostage for the return of the cutter. Kalaniopuu was asleep and was obviously ignorant of the cutter's theft. He came willingly enough with

Cook down the pathway in his settlement till some of his relatives said something to him and he looked frightened and sat down. Then came news, first to the crowd and then indirectly to Cook, that another chief had been killed in a clash on the other side of the bay. The crowd around Kalaniopuu became threatening and Cook fired shot out of his double-barrelled gun at a man who was about to strike him. The shot was ineffectual against the warrior's protective matting, and when Cook fired a ball to kill another assailant it was too late. The crowd rushed forward and, with daggers that the Englishmen had given them, killed four marines and Cook at the water's edge. There was nothing that the waiting boats and the more distant ships could do. They saw their captain lying face down in the water with three or four Hawaiians beating him about the head with rocks. Then they carried off the body in triumph.

The English were enraged and dismayed, unbelieving that they could have shared in so awful a moment for a man of destiny like Cook. They looked for a reason for it all, and found it in the cowardice of Lieutenant Williamson who they thought had withdrawn the boats too early, or in the imprudence of Cook in carelessly exposing himself and being too precipitate, or in their own carelessness at not having demonstrated the power of their guns before it was too late. Clerke, Cook's successor, acted calmly enough and refused to allow wholesale retribution, but there was fighting and slaughter nonetheless. They do not describe in their journals acts which they say are better not described. But the sailors mutilated those they slaughtered, carried back their decapitated heads in the bottom of their boat, hung them around the necks of those they captured. It is difficult to know whether these actions were shocking to the Hawaiians or whether they fitted fairly exactly the expectancies of those who knew that in the time of Ku there would be sacrifice.

Certainly everything that the Hawaiians did was a mystery and a contradiction to the Englishmen. They could not reconcile the savagery they had seen with the nonchalance with which many of the Hawaiians now treated them. Cook's body had been carted up the cliffs to a temple of Ku where it had been ceremonially divided among the chiefs. It is something a conqueror would do to the defeated or the successor to his predecessor— bake or waste the flesh from the bones so that the bones could be distributed. 'Every chief acts as a conqueror when he comes to power,' the Hawaiians say. The priests of Lono who had been so friendly got their share of Cook's remains, and, mystified that the Englishmen should be so disturbed, brought a parcel of bones and flesh to the ships to placate them. When would Lono come again, they asked as they gave over Cook's bones. Return, of course, he did. *Makahiki* came every year and for forty years and more the right-handed procession of Lono at *makahiki* time was led by a reliquary bundle of Cook's bones. It did not mean that the annual coming of Lono was more real because of it: Lono's coming was always real. It did mean—it is Marshall Sahlins' point—that god was an Englishman.

E.H. Carr has scandalised his historian colleagues by enunciating the principle that an historical fact is not what happened but that small part of what has happened that has been used by historians to talk about.

History is not the past: it is a consciousness of the past used for present purposes. In that sense the death of Cook immediately became historical. Those on board his ship immediately began to write down what they thought had happened. An interpretation of what had happened mattered to them. They blamed one another for negligence or incompetence or cowardice. They examined the inconsistencies of their most consistent captain to excuse negligence, incompetence and cowardice on their part, to find a cause of his death in his weariness, his bad health, his crankiness. They searched their understanding of the uncivilised savage and of the treachery of natives. Clerke and King, at least, if not the rest of the crew who thirsted to be savage to the savages, sensed that what they had seen in their way the Hawaiians had seen in ways incomprehensible to them. None of them could comprehend why the Hawaiians seemed to presume that nothing had changed. The women still came to the ships at night even after the slaughters of the day. Old friends among the priests and chiefs and people came forward, and inquired for Lono as if he had never died.

There were two strange scenes in those confused days after the killings. One on the side of the mountain in the temple of Ku, Cook lying there dismembered but resurrected in those who possessed him. The other in the great cabin of the *Resolution*, the gentlemen of the two ships observing the proprieties of the navy in dividing up the clothes and possessions of their late commodore and buying them in a small auction.

We will never really enter the minds of those in the temple of Ku. It is hardly likely that they had killed

Cook in order to make actual the ritual death of Lono at the hands of the high chief Kalaniopuu. But when it was done they understood what had happened because their myths gave them a history and that history was necessary for the maintenance of all that they were. They were Native and Stranger to one another: Kalaniopuu was the greatest Stranger of them all, the usurper, shark that walked on the land. He was who he was because in the season of sacrifice and war, in the season of Ku, he was conqueror of the land, of the people, whose god was Lono and whose season was *makahiki*. All Cook's gestures and threats, done in his eyes for the sake of property and discipline, were gestures out of season. It was as if the right order had not been played out and Lono had not been conquered for the season. Cook was not Native now, but Stranger, a shark that walked on the land. In those circumstances the killing was easy and the death made everything come true again. So they kept asking when Lono would come again.

The gentlemen in the great cabin auctioning their captain's goods had their own proprieties. They had to find the correct balance between the pragmatism of navy men a year and more from home, making use of things their owner no longer needed and making sense of their own emotions. They had to cope with wearing the captain's shirt and britches and the growing realisation that they had lived with a hero. For if Captain Cook found resurrection among the Hawaiians in the spirit of Lono, he also found resurrection among his fellow countrymen in the spirit of hero, discoverer and humanitarian. It did not matter whether he was really Lono for the Hawaiians. It did not matter whether he was

truly hero, discoverer and humanitarian for his fellow countrymen.
When news got home to Britain,
the British, the continental Europeans
and the Americans made myth of it
in poetry, drama and paintings. And
the myth has had a sustained relevance in continually changing environments for two hundred years.
This has been not just in a prolifer-
ation of histories, but in continual
rounds of as many metric moments
of centenaries, sesquicentenaries and
bicentenaries as the birth and death
and all significant moments in
between can provide. There is an
Australian monument, and a Swedish
one, on the spot in Hawaii where
Cook was killed. A Victorian government, for no other reason than that
Cook probably saw a small eastern
promontory of New Holland and that
the Fitzroy Gardens in Melbourne
hold a reconstructed house which
is not his, sent an official delegation
to the bicentenary of his death in
Hawaii. If the myth of Lono sustained the realities of chieftainship
and power, the myth of hero, dis-

coverer and humanitarian expressed
in rituals, monuments and anniversaries, sustains our own image of
who we are and who we should
be.

One can walk from the water's
edge where Cook died, through the
tangle of undergrowth that covers
Kalaniopuu's village, along the path
they both walked 14 February 1779,
up to the temple of Ku. Here in 1826
Lord Byron set a monument when
he brought back the bodies of
Liholiho and his queen from Britain.
They had gone to secure the aid of
King George IV but had died of
measles. Liholiho was laying claims
on a special relationship that had
begun with Cook's death and resurrection. Lord Byron set a cross on a
cairn in Ku's temple. Its replacement
is there still, always the *double
entendre* that it ever was when
different eyes see the same symbol
as sign of the cross and sign of
makahiki. When the world is full
of sharks and gods as well as heroes
and discoverers, who can write the
history of them all?

The essay starts by discussing the different sets of metaphorical concepts which Polynesian and British people used to explain the arrival of Cook at Hawaii, his initially warm welcome, and then his death. These two sets are mutually exclusive. One cannot be used to understand the other, and apart from Captain Cook (who gets caught in the middle) they don't intersect. Dening goes on to show that the celebrated history of Cook in the Western world is built upon three images that figure his life and death and in so doing reinforce Western ideas about the world: 'the myth of hero, discoverer and humanitarian expressed in rituals, monuments and anniversaries, sustains our own image of who we are and who we should be'. The implication is that the subject matter of Western history is not simply the past but the present as well. Historical interpretations use cultural metaphors and connotations to explain, justify and elevate Western understandings of the past over other cultural understandings. History becomes a function of the power of figurative language.

As the Gould and Dening essays show, even academic disciplines may be based on certain metaphorical conceptions and constructions of things. Figurative language becomes an important factor which can disclose to us how all sorts of texts work. It reveals that:

1 Meaning is transferred between vehicle and tenor through imagery and other figures of speech.
2 Transfers of meaning often involve meaning conflicts among readers, texts and authors.
3 Differing social contexts are crucial in working out various connotations of meaning.
4 To understand the processes of meaning transfer, conflict and connotation we must read texts actively and critically.
5 Reading actively and critically means asking ourselves what are the social and disciplinary effects of the figurative language that texts use.

If we read figurative language actively and critically, it can become a way for us to examine and question the presumptions concealed in different styles and types of writing.

Exercise
Choose two academic essays from a subject you are studying. In a 750-word essay analyse their use of figurative language. In what ways do their imagery and metaphorical concepts contribute to the success or failure of the thesis they are trying to present?

Works cited

Borges, Jorge Luis (1981) 'Streetcorner Man', in *A Universal History of Infamy*, Penguin, Harmondsworth

Dening, Greg (1982) 'Sharks that Walk on the Land: The Death of Captain Cook', *Meanjin* 41: 427–37

Donne, John (1993) 'A Valediction: Forbidding Mourning', in *The Norton Anthology of English Literature*, 6th edition, Volume 1, Norton, New York

Frame, Janet (1991) 'The Reservoir', in *You Are Now Entering the Human Heart*, Women's Press, London

Gould, Stephen Jay (1977) 'Racist Arguments and IQ', in *Ever Since Darwin*, Norton, New York

Lakoff, George, and Mark Johnson (1980) *Metaphors We Live By*, University of Chicago Press, Chicago

Lansbury, Coral (1989) *The Grotto*, Knopf, New York

Shield, Mark, and Phill Meyer (1993) *The Penguin Good Australian Wine Guide*, Penguin, Ringwood

Sontag, Susan (1990) 'AIDS and Its Metaphors', in *Illness as Metaphor and AIDS and Its Metaphors*, Doubleday, New York

10 Style and genre

Style and strategy

Through much of this book, we have focused on the conventions and features of different types of writing. The first section looked at texts which deal with space and time as well as at those that seek to explain or analyse objects and ideas—description, narration and exposition. In the second section, we considered the ways that logic and persuasion operate in language to form a basis for certain kinds of analytical, argument and research writing. We concentrated on the academic essay, with its features of logic and research, quotations, documentation and bibliography.

In this third and final section of the book we have been reflecting on the effects of these numerous conventions and features for authors and readers. Textual analysis has emerged as an important technique we can practise and apply in order to sharpen the ways we interpret and respond to texts. By analysing the approaches that academic, fictional, journalistic and other texts use we become sensitive to the differences between them, and can also grow aware of techniques for realising aims and intentions in our own writing.

Textual analysis forms the basis for reading and responding to other writers' work, as well as for planning and structuring, and then revising, editing and proofreading our own writing.

Through the last two chapters we have seen that variations including changes to pronouns, verb tense or imagery can lead readers to understand a text's subject matter in diverse ways, and also lead them to differentiate between types of texts. The style of a text affects readers' perceptions of its contents and form—that is, its subject matter and the sort of text it is.

In this chapter we are going to develop these ideas of differences and similarities between texts in more detail. Basically, our opening questions are: How are we are able to distinguish some texts from one another, while judging others to be the 'same'? What enables writers and readers to make such distinctions?

In response to these questions, we can start by considering the functions of writing **style** in a slightly abstract way, analysing stylistic features of texts quite closely to note the varying effects of meaning they can produce. We will then take a less abstract, more socially based approach to these features, in order to study their effects on communication between authors and readers. Through taking this double analytical approach, stylistic and social, we will be able to see the ways that language styles work as **strategies for presenting social meanings and values**. Stylistic choices in a piece of writing do not simply change the way it reads or sounds. They influence the way readers think about and respond to topics and subject matter. Through its style a text can confirm or challenge what we think. Textual style is always full of social motives and strategies.

Comparing texts

A simple but important point to emphasise is that we never perceive a style of writing by focusing on a single text in isolation. No text is ever written or read by itself. The judgements we make on whether a text is description, narration, exposition or argument are always *comparative* ones. We are constantly surrounded by words, and we cope with this mass of language by grouping it into types. Even when we come across a text that seems unfamiliar and even confuses us, there is likely to be a sort of order in our confusion. We are confused because the new text does not fit into the various groups or species of writing with which we are familiar: we understand that we don't understand it. The text stands out because we cannot firmly place it among texts we have previously read, and which seem to form a more or less related group, based on their similarities.

The following excerpt from James Joyce's last novel *Finnegans Wake* is puzzling to follow. At first the style seems almost indecipherable:

> While that Mooksius with preprocession and with pro-
> precession, duplicitly and diplussedly, was promulgating
> ipsofacts and sadcontras this raskolly Gripos he had allbust

seceded in monophysicking his illsubordinates. But asawfulas he had caught his base semenoyous sarchnaktiers to combuccinate upon the silipses of his aspillouts and the acheporeoozers of his haggyown pneumax to synerethetise with the breadchestviousness of his sweeatovular ducose sofarfully the loggerthuds of his sakelaries were fond at variance with the synodals of his somepooliom and his babskissed nepogreasymost got the hoof from his philioquus.

However, when we look at the text more closely we can see that it bounces around between the unfamiliar and the known. It seems to contain and combine words (or parts of words) that aren't in the dictionary or don't usually go together. Nonetheless, we can make some sense of it even if we are a little uncertain. New words, like 'illsobordunates', 'asawfulas' and 'synerethetise' are made up from other words we seem to know. There are also other phrases we recognise immediately and that seem to give the passage a grammatical structure.

Perhaps after reading a lot of Joyce's text, we might think it forms a language style all to itself--that it is unique. Yet if we decide this we would also have to note that it's unique in an unusual sense. *Finnegans Wake* does not invent words out of nothing but combines different types and styles of language which we wouldn't imagine going together. This kind of writing seems unique because it is deeply *un-original*, a weird mixture of all the styles we could ever think of.

So even a piece of writing that seems strangely new is never read or written in isolation from other pieces. In the case of *Finnegans Wake*, what is striking is the way in which many styles are put together, in contrast with most texts, which stick more or less to one style. We can draw two conclusions from the example of Joyce's work:

1 No type of writing can be absolutely cut off from all other types; at the least it will be related to them through contrast and at the other extreme it might precisely copy or echo other texts.
2 Despite this overall scheme of relations, we generally do think of types of texts as separate and distinct from each other. Distinguishing between types of texts is a basic step in responding to them.

Logical argument appears to differ from emotive persuasion; description contrasts to narration; a newspaper article is distinct from a government report. Now there may be similarities or connections between these kinds of writing. As we have seen, narration and description frequently work together in fictional and expository writing, while the line between argument and persuasion is not absolute. Nonetheless, we base our use and understanding of these texts on being able to compare and differentiate between them.

Genre

Authors and readers conceive of texts as belonging to different types or categories. The word from language and literary studies used to designate the type is *genre*, from the Latin word *genus*, meaning 'race, stock, kind, sort, or gender'. Although we will see that the concept of genre can be quite complex, an initial definition could read as follows:

> **Genre**: a set of texts that share a number of common traits, features and effects which makes them distinguishable from texts with different features and effects.

The shared effects and features allow readers and writers to recognise that a text belongs to a certain genre, for example, the genre of academic essays. Each essay in this genre can be thought of as a member of a class or set that is held together by the similarity amongst all the essays in it, including such features as presenting a thesis, applying research, and so on. Once we recognise its genre we are prepared to read the text in a certain way. We look for certain features rather than others. Thus in an academic essay we would expect to find a thesis and some supporting information rather than a sequence of rib-tickling one-liners. Later in the chapter we will consider how genres set up readers' *expectations*.

The idea of similarity among texts may be applied in a number of ways to classify or group them into genres. By examining some of these variations, we can begin to observe the important functions of style and genre in texts.

Classifying texts

Two of the ways that libraries classify books are by author and subject matter. Now an author might write different types of books on different subjects. He or she might be the only link between these various works; we would not identify these works as belonging to the same genre just because they are written by one person.

The identity of the author is not relevant to the idea of genre. This identity can, however, be important for certain kinds of studies, such as biographies of authors. Nevertheless, it remains external to questions about the *type* of text we are reading. As we will see, questions of genre and style derive, in the first place, from textual features.

Instead, for our purposes, **subject matter** is a more important factor. Writing can be grouped into genres according to subject matter. Let's take some initial examples from traditional literature. Works in the genre of tragedy deal with the fall of great men and women, the death of kings and queens, for example, in a play such as *Hamlet*. By contrast, comedy deals with the ups and downs of ordinary folk, while works written about shepherds and their romantic affairs with dairy maids belong to the pastoral genre.

Turning to journalism, we can consider the way that different magazines focus on various kinds of subject matter. All these magazines contain a different type of writing, political and economic reporting in some, sport in others, fashion or entertainment in still more. Each magazine, with its own topics and styles, belongs to a different genre.

Subject matter is thus a way of making distinctions between different types of texts, and of grouping them into categories or genres. These distinctions can often be fairly broad. In fact under the heading of one of these genres and topics we might feel there are a number of smaller topics or sub-topics. Each of these would then have a corresponding **sub-genre**. For example, again in the genre of journalism, we see that a newspaper consists of a number of different sections, on varying topics. Each of these, politics, business, sport, fashion or entertainment, is part of a sub-genre based on that topic: political or sports reporting, fashion journalism, and so on.

Another example of the existence of topic-related sub-genres is within the wide genre of academic writing. There is a different type of writing for each of the disciplines within the university, each one having distinct subject matter and writing features. They include English, History, Sociology, Dentistry, Engineering, Biology, and so on. The texts in these areas come under the broad generic heading of academic writing, yet to register the important differences in them we could say that each forms a separate sub-genre.

A consideration of subject matter thus allows us to introduce the idea of genre into our thoughts about writing, and even to distinguish specific sub-topics and sub-genres within broader areas. Genres based on subject matter are an initial way of relating texts to one another and also differentiating between them. However, subject matter cannot be the central factor determining how we think of a text, its genre, and its relation to other texts. By itself, the topic may ultimately tell us little about the important stylistic features and conventions of the text and their effects for readers. We need to develop a more subtle way of thinking about how texts relate to one another in terms of genre.

Exercises

1 Select two articles from different sections of a daily newspaper (for example, from the business, arts and entertainment, or sport sections). How do the differences in subject matter affect the style in which the articles are written? Write a short analytical essay in which you contrast the two texts' subject matter, stylistic features and any apparent links between the subject and style in each one.

2 Now attempt to rewrite one of the articles as if it is to go in another section of the paper (e.g., a business article in the fashion section, a fashion article in the sports section). Pay close attention to the stylistic changes that you have to make. Can the same information be conveyed to readers in the new style that you use?

Evaluative attitudes

As examples of the limits of a topic-based notion of genre, consider a play about the death of a king which celebrates his death, or a news article on the opening of federal Parliament which sends up the various rituals and speeches. If we were to compare these texts to their serious counterparts only in terms of subject matter, we might say that they belong to the same genre or sub-genre—the two king stories to tragedy and the two articles to political journalism. Yet clearly there are significant differences in each of these pairs of texts, differences which the subject matter considered by itself cannot suggest. They are different types of texts; they belong to different genres.

This extra factor, of crucial importance in determining which genre a text belongs to, is the **tone** or **attitude**, the point of view the text takes towards its subject matter. Any piece of writing, any text, does *two* things with its topic:

1 It presents the subject matter; and
2 It adopts an **attitude towards** the subject matter.

It is through the combination of these two factors that we are able to identify the text's genre.

Genre is centrally related to the connections between subject matter and attitude or point of view that are set up in a text. The text's point of view towards its topic is a crucial marker of its genre, and a key factor in determining how readers will respond to and interpret the text.

Therefore the most useful way of thinking about genre is to view it not simply as a means of classifying texts, but as **a process that takes place whereby the subject matter and an attitude towards it intersect**. Every piece of writing takes an attitude towards the topic it presents. It *evaluates* the topic, sometimes seriously, comically, sarcastically, historically, politically, and so on. Whenever we read or write about something we are not just getting pure facts about that topic. We are receiving an **evaluative attitude** towards the topic. This attitude is just as influential as, and often more influential than, the 'facts' themselves.

In some examples below, we will look at how the evaluative attitude can affect our understanding of the 'facts' in texts. For the moment, however, the primary point to stress is that the text's evaluative attitude is generated through the style of the writing. **Style is the element which affects how we interpret what we read**.

Every text adopts an **evaluative attitude** towards its subject matter, which is shown through the text's **style**.

Analysing style

By analysing the stylistic features of a text we can establish its point of view towards its content—that is, the way it is evaluating its subject matter. The sorts of features we should look for include many of the aspects we have discussed in earlier chapters—descriptive and narrative features, logic, imagery, forms of argument and persuasion, and so on.

We can observe the shifts in style and evaluative attitudes by examining a number of texts on related topics. The similarity in issues makes the stylistic and evaluative shifts more noticeable. Let's consider a sequence of texts concerned with legal matters. As a key social area, law is written about in many different genres, from judicial reports to journalism to academic studies. All of these use specific stylistic features to convey distinct forms of information and viewpoints to their readers.

The first text we will analyse is an editorial on police powers from *The Australian* newspaper:

Forensic powers for the police

Law enforcement interest in acquiring stronger powers to obtain body samples from criminal suspects has largely been driven by advances in DNA research. The detection of crime is in itself a kind of science, and in the course of regulating police powers it is only commonsense for lawmakers to keep pace with potentially useful police applications of innovations in science and technology.

However, just as advances in medicine have compelled fresh ethical debate over such issues as euthanasia and *in vitro* fertilisation, there are also questions of privacy and civil liberties to be considered when assessing the merits of permitting intrusive forensic exploration against a person's consent. This debate is by no means new: it is many years since police first sought to examine the blood of suspected drunk drivers. But it is an issue that has steadily intruded into more walks of life.

Recently there has been debate over automatic AIDS testing of hospital patients, compulsory drugs testing of athletes, and random but just as compulsory drugs testing of employees in the workplace. The federal Model Forensic Procedures Bill takes the debate into new areas again. Its most controversial aspects are those that would, in practice, enable the police to forcibly obtain samples from a suspect. Those samples would then become an important factor in determining either the arrest or elimination of the person from further inquiry.

The federal and state officials responsible for drafting these proposals have, of course, been careful to promote safeguards. The most important would oblige police to obtain a magistrate's order before forcibly taking a body sample from a non-arrested suspect. The police would have to satisfy a court with evidence these procedures were warranted: which reasonably answers civil libertarian claims that the proposed new powers could enable police to go 'fishing' for evidence of a crime.

There is no question the new procedures would greatly assist the police in expediting inquiries, allow limited resources to be put to more efficient use and be an effective new tool in the fight against crime. But would they preserve an appropriate balance between society's interest in preventing and punishing crime, and the presumption of a person's innocence until proven guilty?

This will have to be settled by public debate preceding any law changes. But it is not the only ground for concern. After the Lindy Chamberlain case, where a miscarriage of justice occurred after a court accepted faulty forensic evidence, Australians have reason to regard this science warily. The scientific community has lifted its performance in response to criticisms arising out of the Chamberlain case. However, it is proper that our courts treat the presentation of forensic evidence, no matter how it is obtained, with the same caution they apply to all other evidence.

Probably the most notable aspect of this text is the attempt to offer a 'balanced' opinion on the issue of police powers to obtain forensic evidence. The editorial provides summaries of facts and situations rather than hard evidence. It also seeks to present all sides of the case. These include police, political, judicial, scientific and civil libertarian outlooks, as well as the viewpoint of possible suspects. Hence the use of words like 'however' and 'but' to mark a switch to a new perspective. The text does not speak for any one of these positions; instead it reviews them all.

In this way, the editorial's evaluative attitude tries to draw close to that of the paper's range of general readers. It acknowledges that this legal issue is a complex one, and that a 'commonsense' approach, balancing all the views against one another, will eventually sort it out. This kind of consensual social attitude to an issue is the distinctive trait of news editorials. They try to speak for all their readers. As a genre, editorials set themselves up as 'our' voice.

The next extract is taken from an academically oriented study of legal issues, Helena Kennedy's book, *Eve Was Framed: Women and British Justice*. As the title suggests, this text has a particular point to make: the unfair treatment of women under the British legal system. Unlike the editorial in *The Australian*, it is not trying to set up a point of view with which everyone will agree:

> Girls are referred to the Juvenile Courts for different reasons than are boys, and are dealt with differently. A son's overnight absence will earn him a knowing wink, and drunkenness will be seen as a natural part of his growing up—boys will be boys—but the same behaviour by girls calls down very different responses. There is a clear preoccupation with the sexuality of teenage girls and an over-emphatic concern with their moral welfare. If she fails to come home on time, hangs around the wrong part of town or adopts dubious friends, a girl is far more likely to be declared in moral danger, for which, at the instigation of her parents, school, social worker or the police, she may be taken into the care of the local authority. The same behaviour in boys does not evoke the same response from the courts. These young women often start off in the penal system having committed no crime at all, but once it is on their record that they have been locked up, a cycle of imprisonment begins, and offending often follows.

Rather than consensus, this text aims to make *difference* its key point. It contrasts both the treatment teenage girls and boys receive from the courts, and its own critical viewpoint of this situation with more conservative legal and social views. Various examples are given to support this thesis, and strong terms such as 'preoccupation' and 'over-emphatic' are used to disparage the opposing side. Details aren't included simply to illustrate the situation; they become part of the argument. The point of view attacks the present system and implicitly urges the need for reform. It draws near the perspective of the young women who are actually involved and distances itself from orthodox judicial, police, family, school and social work attitudes. The text's evaluative attitude towards the topic, along with the topic itself, marks the genre as a feminist critique of the law.

The final example of links between textual style and evaluative attitude is an administrative report. Here, the issue is whether people can appeal against non-judicial government decisions in the courts. It's a complicated legal subject, and the text is written for a specialist audience:

> Much of the problem arises because the common law powers of review have developed around particular procedures, and the remedies which result from those procedures, rather than substantive grounds of deficiency in the administrative decisions sought to be reviewed. There are technical rules of law which are associated with the procedures by which the common law remedies must be sought, so that too often the difficulty which a person seeking review and his or her legal advisers face, is not whether there is a substantial defect in the decision concerned which would justify review by the courts, but whether the situation can be brought within the scope of an existing procedure and the remedy available as a result of that procedure. The consequences are that even many practising lawyers are uncertain whether there is a remedy available for a person aggrieved by a government decision, the taking of proceedings is much more expensive that it ought to be, and it is fraught with peril of shipwreck on the reefs of technicality. The scales are weighted against those who seek review.

The text uses a relatively specialised language or *jargon* which its intended audience will recognise. The sentence structure is long and intricate, except for the last sentence. Its shortness contrasts with the others' length, with a direct statement of the situation, plus a slightly humorous allusion to the 'scales', a common symbol of the law. This complex style is linked to the description and

evaluation of the situation as complicated and difficult. In contrast
with Kennedy's text, this one does not seek to assign blame. It
aims to set up a consensual view that a problem exists, but also
that it can be rectified. It seeks agreement not so much among the
general public, whom an editorial on the topic would address, but
among people professionally involved in this aspect of the legal
system.

In these three texts, the style and tone are intertwined with
the evaluative attitude that is held towards the subject matter. In
each case, a different attitude could be taken to it. For instance, we
can imagine Kennedy adopting a more critical tone on administrative
appeals if she were to argue that they form part of the legal system
that works negatively against women. In that case, the stylistic and
generic features of the report would be *transformed* in order to
present a critique.

The 'same' content can always be represented in different
genres. When such transformations occur, however, the subject
matter assumes different meanings. Alternative viewpoints on the topic
emerge, and readers are asked to think about it in varying terms.
Transformations in genre involve shifts in both the style of language
used and the evaluative attitude towards the subject matter.

Exercises

1 Identify any figures of speech and imagery used in the three
extracts from legal texts. In what ways is their use of figurative
language tied to the genres of editorial, critique and report? How
is the figurative language linked to the three texts' consensual
and critical evaluative attitudes towards their topics?
2 Transform Kennedy's critical analysis into a consensus building
editorial for a daily newspaper. Pay close attention to any stylistic
changes you will have to make to fit the material to the new genre.
3 You are applying for a position on a committee which is
reviewing the way the legal system treats teenagers. As well as
recounting your qualifications and desire for the job, you need
to present your views on the committee's task. Write a two page
application presenting appropriate information and evaluative
attitude about the topic.

Facts and implicit viewpoints

In the above texts, the evaluative attitudes are quite clear. Readers
are able to identify the texts' genres and then consider where they
stand in relation to the viewpoints and topics. Some genres work
slightly differently from these ones. They tend to conceal their

particular evaluative attitudes, and instead present their account of
the subject matter as factual. The reader is left with little opportunity
to perceive the viewpoint, let alone question it. The text seems to
be entirely truthful.

By analysing such texts closely we can start to see that this
kind of truthfulness is not in itself absolute but a **function of the
genre and style that are being used.** As was noted at the end of
the last section, the 'same' material can be presented in different styles
and with different attitudes. Readers respond to these variations in
genre—that is, they understand the issue in different ways. No
response is superior to others, for each is influenced by the generic
version of the issue. In texts, **truth is always a generic effect.**

As an example of this truth-effect in texts, we can consider an
excerpt from Kate Grenville's short story, 'The Space Between'.
The passage is highly descriptive, a first person narrative with lots
of details about the backstreets of the Indian city Madras, seen
through the eyes of a single white woman:

> Not far from the hotel, there is a cluster of shacks that squat
> in the dust, lining a path of beaten earth. Hens scatter under
> my feet and skeletal dogs run along nosing the ground. Pieces
> of cardboard cover the walls of the huts. DETER UPER
> WASH. They *are* the walls, I see when I look more closely.
> Women sit in the shade, picking over the vegetables, while
> beside them their other sari hangs in the drying sun—
> tattered, dust-coloured with age, but washed. Is there another
> one in the dark interior of the hut? Is there, somewhere, the
> wedding sari, best quality cotton or maybe even silk, with the
> lucky elephant-border or the brocade border that reads
> GOOD LUCK GOOD LUCK GOOD LUCK all the way around
> the hem? As I pass, the women look up and stare, their lips
> drawn back to reveal stained teeth. They are not smiling, but
> only staring, and they look away when I smile.
>
> Out of doorways a few small children appear, staring
> shyly, their huge dark eyes full of astonishment as they look
> at me. They curl one foot behind the other in embarrassment
> when I look at them and twist their bodies as if fleeing, but
> their eyes never leave my face.
>
> As I pass the huts the children drift out after me and at
> each hut more emerge. I can hear their feet padding in the
> dust behind me. When I turn around to smile they all stop in
> mid-stride. They all stare, motionless except for a hand some-
> where, scratching a melon-belly, a foot rubbing the back of a
> ledge, a finger busy up a nostril.

The passage is notable for the amount of visual detail it includes. The narrator is highly attentive to the actions, expressions, dress and appearance of the local women and children, as well as their setting. She voices no opinion about what she sees: that is, the evaluative attitude towards the subject matter is not made explicit. Rather it is *implicit* in the sorts of details that are emphasised. These include cardboard walls, tattered clothes and stained teeth; the children's shyness and curiosity about the narrator; the narrator's own curiosity about the 'dark interior' of the huts and the wedding saris kept within.

The attitude here seems to underline the cultural distance between the Western narrator and the Indian people she observes. There is no direct judgement, and we read what seems an objective account of things. This attitude suggests a realistic genre, where the narrator seems to restrain her opinion or imagination from distorting or affecting what is seen. However, the narrator's *selection* of details reveals her interests in the economic, domestic and sexual situations of the women (also suggested by the large numbers of children).

Hence the evaluative attitude here is quite complex. On the one hand, we seem to be getting a straight account of the scene, and the text does not stand out stylistically. On the other, the choice of details does imply particular interests or concerns of the narrator, and her cultural separation from the Indian women. The 'truthfulness' of the account co-exists with certain social and personal attitudes.

Grenville's text is an interesting example of the genre of realist narrative. Although it does not highlight an overt attitude to its subject matter it still implies a cultural and social perspective. The text's 'facts' are seen from a particular slant, and this angle reminds us that even an apparently realistic or objective genre assumes a certain position or stance towards its topic.

This is an important point to note. **No text simply presents 'the facts' as they are.** A piece of writing always assumes a certain stance towards its subject matter, making changes to it by emphasising some aspects and ignoring others. This process of emphasis and selection is crucial to the way genres work in writing. Each is based on, and represents a certain understanding of the way things happen or the way they are. No single genre is better than others. Rather, each has a *motive*, a reason why it says what it says.

As readers, we should try to discover the motive in texts, whether it's consensual, critical, objective or realistic. And as authors, trying to fulfil the writing requirements of different disciplines, each having its preferred genre, we should try to be aware of the attitude towards the topic implicit in a particular genre, and then try to imitate that attitude in our own writing.

Exercise
Using Grenville's story as basis, transform the details the narrator observes into one of the following genres:

- a letter to a friend about your summer holiday in India;
- a letter to the editor of a newspaper on 'poverty in the Third World';
- a travel advertisement for 'Vacations in Mystical India';
- an academic essay on the breakdown of family structures in the late twentieth century.

Pay close attention to the stylistic and generic features you will have to use to ensure the 'truth' of your text.

Words and readers
The various texts analysed above are examples of all the points we have noted about genre:

1 We never simply consider one text in isolation from others (even if we think we are). Our readings are always *relative and comparative*. We get a sense of what texts are about and of the attitudes they express through contrasting them with other similar, or dissimilar texts.
2 Subject matter alone is not a clear enough guide to what a text is about or to what type of text it is. The *evaluative attitude* of the writing to the subject matter is all-important.
3 The evaluative attitude emerges through the *style* of the writing.

It is worth expanding this last point a little. At its most basic level, style is formed through the sorts of word choices that are made in a text. And every word choice can be highly significant for both the attitude and the genre of the text. When we write, we don't select words simply on account of their dictionary meaning. We choose certain words over others because, along with their meaning, they *reveal and reinforce the evaluative attitude that we hold towards the topic*.

Every word has an **evaluative sense** in addition to its dictionary meaning—that is, it evaluates or judges its meaning as well as signifying or denoting it. As readers and writers we must be alert to this sense, aware of the words' attitudes towards their own meaning. If we call a spade a spade or a digging implement, we are registering two quite different attitudes to its sophistication as a tool. The style of a text and its word choice goes deeper than its surface or finish. It's the key to the way the text provides the combination of subject matter and attitude, and takes its place within the genre of similar texts.

Another important point that emerges from the texts we have been analysing is that our awareness of a text's genre and style, subject matter and attitude, functions through a shared under-standing among the author, text and reader. The effectiveness of a text results from a *social connection* among it, the writer and audience, which is made through the genre and style. As a simple example, consider the following humorous fable for children:

When Little Lamb went out to play, he wandered off and lost his way. Little Lamb says, 'Please help me find my home.'

A squirrel called, 'Climb up with me. Perhaps your home's a leafy tree.' Little Lamb says, 'Thank you, but a leafy tree isn't home for me.'

'Perhaps your home is by this creek,' croaked Frog. 'Why don't you take a peek.' Little Lamb says, 'Thank you, but a home by a creek isn't home for me.'

'I want to help,' said small brown Mole. 'Come live with me. My home's a hole.' Little Lamb says, 'Thank you, but a hole isn't home for me.'

'My home's a cave,' said big brown Bear. 'It's warm and dry and cosy there.' Little Lamb says, 'Thank you, but a cave isn't home for me.'

'If home's a cocoon,' a caterpillar said, 'You'll find it right above your head.' Little Lamb says, 'Thank you, but a cocoon isn't home for me.'

Then Little Lamb looked up to see his Mum, who said, 'Come home with me.' Little Lamb says, 'Thank you, everyone—I'm going home.'

Home is with your family. And home is where you want to be. And Little Lamb says, 'I love my home!'

The humour and moral depend on child readers or audiences recognising, more or less clearly, that the animal images aren't just part of a story about animals. The text must give clues which they can pick up about its evaluation of Little Lamb's experiences. The references to 'Mum, home and family' orient the text away from the animal setting to children's domestic worlds, and allow them to identify Little Lamb with themselves. The style reproduces a kind of fable or fairy tale genre which lets them know how to read or hear the text. Through recalling this genre, the text sets up a code of interpretive behaviour, even for its young audience. It prepares them for the story and how to respond to it.

Expectations, surprises and inversions

Children's texts such as fairy tales and fables are a revealing example of the way that genres establish positions for reading and interpreting texts. Obviously, children aren't consciously aware of theories of genre. Yet from a young age they are highly skilled at understanding the social lessons and themes that much children's literature represents. Their responses indicate the evaluative effects of genre even if they don't know it.

Once a text's style communicates the genre to readers, letting them know the attitude and subject matter, we can see that a set of **expectations** is also established. When readers identify the type of text they are reading, they anticipate that the text will contain certain elements and proceed in a certain way. These expectations result from previous experience of texts in the same or a similar genre. Often they can make it easier to know what's going on in a text. Expectations can work as a kind of shorthand for readers and writers. Just as readers or viewers may be able to guess what is about to be written or shown, so authors can count on familiarity with the genre to help the audience follow the plot or argument.

Consider this extract from a textbook titled *Introductory Sociology*:

> Faced with the breakdown of the consensus politics of growth, European governments have increasingly attempted to erode the social security and union power of workers, while at the same time strengthening the capacity of agencies of law and order to resist 'internal subversion'.
>
> At the same time, Western economies have found themselves faced with an intractable combination of high inflation and recession in trade. Policies based on state intervention and spending come to seem ineffective in combating inflation.

The immediate response of governments has been to resort to harsh measures. Wage levels are squeezed through the pressure of unemployment, and state expenditure is curtailed; the goal of controlling the money supply replaces goals of growth and full employment—monetarism became the new cure-all in the mid-1970s. However, it is unlikely that these policies will be long-lasting, for they place intense pressure on industry and provoke hostility from trade unions, while achieving very little effect on inflation. Economic and political consequences will almost certainly force governments to return to economic intervention of a more positive kind.

Even though it is an introductory text, the authors rely on readers' awareness of fairly complex terms and concepts (taken from the jargon of academic sociology) and their ability to follow detailed exposition. Readers, on the other hand, will expect clear and specific explanations of the basic ideas and theories of sociology, with a number of illustrating examples.

Take another case. We are watching a romantic film, and just as the lovers are about to embrace, the camera focuses on waves tossing on a beach. We are not supposed to get restless and think that the story has taken a boring detour. We are expected to read the waves as a symbol of passionate love, and our experience and knowledge of the style of such movies allow us to do so.

We should therefore note that generic styles presume that there will be an **interpretive identity** between readers and the text—that is, readers will recognise the evaluative attitude to the subject matter that the text adopts. We mightn't agree with the attitude that is revealed through the genre. Some readers, for instance, may question the sociological account of union-government relations. The point remains, however, that to understand the text we need to be able to identify its evaluative attitude and style.

If we do accept a genre's attitude (that complicated social issues can be solved by everyone reaching consensus, as the editorial had it) then we are doing more that simply going along with the text. What is occurring is that the editorial genre is actually reinforcing a view that society works consensually. If we accept that evaluative attitude, we are, for the moment at least, taking one particular way of understanding society as being correct. It may even seem the only correct way to understand society.

We may then be less prepared to accept other genres' attitudes towards society, such as Kennedy's critical feminist view of the legal system, or the sociological account of economic and political struggle between governments and workers. At the same time, we might be quite happy to view Little Lamb's travels through a friendly world before returning to mother, home and family as ideal reading material for young children.

The evaluative attitudes of a genre thus have psychological and social effects on readers' ways of thinking. In accepting a genre, a reader joins the social group who uses that style to write, talk, and think about the particular subject matter. Genre and style can be a way of appealing to, and enlisting people in a particular social view of things. The genre and style of Winston Churchill's speeches during World War II, such as 'We will fight them on the beaches,' are a classic example. His words lifted the spirits of people in Britain and even as far away as Australia. They reinforced a national identity of shared destiny, powerful effects created in part through the deliberate stylistic use of the pronouns 'we' and 'them'.

Because language genres are so closely related to social attitudes, making fun of a genre or style can undermine the attitudes that the style presents. To **parody** or **invert** a genre is to question the serious viewpoints it represents. A simple example is a child who sarcastically repeats a request given to her by a parent, challenging the speech genre of the request and the system of family power that underlies it. In fact, the child may so weaken the request genre that the adult gives up, and resorts to a command genre.

The general point to note, therefore, is that if language genre and style can be used to impose certain social beliefs and ideas, then they can also be used to question or subvert them, through such means as parody, irony and mimicry.

Analytical readers and writers need to remain sharply conscious of textual genre and style. We have considered five main reasons:

1 This way of classifying and thinking about texts can allow us to get beyond the sometimes misleading impressions of subject matter on its own.
2 By carefully noting a text's style, we can perceive its evaluative attitude towards the subject matter, and compare it with other texts on similar topics.
3 It is the combination of attitude and subject matter which suggests the text's genre and guides our interpretation of it.
4 The function of this interpretation is not only to recognise the topic correctly, but to be able to evaluate the topic's background, whether that background is intellectually formed by the traditions

of a specific discipline or socially and politically formed. (In fact, each academic discipline can be thought of as a mini-society with its own rules, codes and genres.)

5 Genre and style can help us see that no text presents ideas or events totally truthfully. A text always re-presents them in terms of a specific genre, and by doing so influences the way we think about these events and ideas.

Exercises

1 Find two recent texts on the general topic of 'children and the family', one a newspaper article, and the other an essay in an academic journal in the areas of history, psychology or sociology. In a 600-word essay compare and analyse the evaluative attitudes towards the family displayed in both texts. Try to identify their main stylistic features and explain how they are related to these attitudes. Also consider if, and in what ways, the texts' attitudes contrast with one another.

2 Using the two essays that you find and the Little Lamb story as references, write a 1,000-word essay recommending and explaining the sorts of generic and stylistic features you think should be included in fiction for young children. If you wish, also refer to stories you recall from your childhood.

Works cited

Bilton, Tony, Kevin Bonnett, Philip Jones, Michelle Stanworth, Ken Sheard and Andrew Webster (1986) *Introductory Sociology*, Macmillan, Basingstoke

Editorial (1994) 'Forensic Powers for the Police', *The Australian*, 11 January

Electoral and Administrative Review Commission (Queensland) (1990) *Report on Judicial Review of Administrative Decisions and Actions*, Electoral and Administrative Review Commission, Brisbane

Grenville, Kate (1990) 'The Space Between', in *The Macmillan Anthology of Australian Literature*, editors, Ken Goodwin and Alan Lawson, Macmillan, Melbourne

Joyce, James (1964) *Finnegans Wake*, Faber, London

Kennedy, Helena (1992) *Eve Was Framed: Women and British Justice*, Chatto and Windus, London

Singer, Muff (1993) *Little Lost Lamb*, RD Press, Sydney

11 Language and society

In this final chapter we wish to review and develop the points we have been making about the ways in which language functions. As discussed in preceding chapters, a very important way that all texts work is by influencing readers' understanding of different topics through using **strategies of representation**. In addition to the structures of narration, description, exposition and argument, every text uses variations of style, figurative language and genre to **re-present** its subject matter. Texts do not, that is, make subject matter immediately present to readers, but re-present it in varying ways. These variations inevitably affect our comprehension of both the text itself and the 'world' which it depicts.

Let's now discuss these textual strategies more specifically in terms of their social functions and effects. We will then go on to consider these in greater detail by analysing a series of texts on fashion. One of the key points running through our discussion will be that **textual strategies are always social strategies**.

Strategy and meaning

The three strategies of representation that we have mostly been concerned with, style, figurative language and genre, all work *conceptually*. That is to say, they influence the way that readers think about the material that is being depicted. As we saw in the discussions of metaphor and genre, all texts, from highly specialised academic essays to everyday comments and remarks, work through **metaphorical concepts**. These metaphors set up certain patterns of response for readers. For example, the metaphor that argument is a kind of battle underlies many notions of debate and contention and leads us to think and act as if two sides of an issue are in conflict.

We drew two related conclusions from these observations. The first is that style, figurative language and genre do not simply affect the surface or finish of texts but influence possibilities for interpreting them. Second, these strategies are not only features of literary language. Once we tune in to the way they operate, we can

209

see that all sorts of texts—academic writing, journalism, memos, letters as well as literary and poetic works—use certain clusters of images and stick to particular generic conventions. In fact, these conventions often determine the way the texts can be written, from topic to structure to attitude.

A journalist, for example, cannot write a newspaper account of an event in any way he or she chooses. The conventional format is what is called the 'reverse pyramid'. A news article always starts with a statement of what is considered as the event's main fact, and then goes on to give extra details. Other notable features in this kind of text are one-sentence paragraphs and the absence of any reference to the author.

These features have *strategic effects* on our interpretation of the article. In its isolation and prominence, the main point may seem to assume an indisputable truthfulness, further reinforced by the apparent absence of the reporter's personal opinion. The use of an elementary paragraph structure may simplify the ideas that are being conveyed.

Now a letter to a friend would render the same reported occurrence very differently. After starting with a warm greeting, it might continue with a description of the event before giving a detailed account of the writer's personal opinions and feelings in longer, rambling sentences. The writer may pay little attention to grammar. Although these characteristics are quite dissimilar to those of a news article, in the genre of personal correspondence they may still have a high truth value. If a letter is too well written, it might seem to lack spontaneity or sincerity.

To understand the event or topic of the letter involves understanding what it means to the writer. Indeed, the main point of the letter may be to impart information about the author rather than the event itself. Obviously, these features would not have such effects if used on the front page of a newspaper. Unless the story were marked in some way as a special opinion or editorial, the personal tones would most likely be discredited as signs of bias.

The same event, then, can be written about in quite different ways, employing alternative textual features and strategies. Accordingly, the reader is being invited to respond in distinct ways, by focusing on and thinking about different factors.

We can summarise these distinctions as follows. An important element to note (which we will develop in the next sections of this chapter) is that each of these points relates as much to the possibilities of the reader's response as it does to the text's form and style, be it a news story or a personal letter. In both texts:

1 Different aspects of the event or idea will be highlighted or omitted. Each text will establish a distinct **point of view**—that is, the attitude to the topic and the selection of detail will alter depending on the writer's involvement, professional for a journalist, personal for a letter writer.

2 Contrasting stylistic techniques and kinds of **figurative language** will be used. Word choice and grammar in the letter may be unsuitable for a news article, while the news style will seem too impersonal for a letter.

3 In the two texts a distinct **evaluative attitude** will be adopted towards the event. It takes on different meanings for different texts: news seeks to describe a factual occurrence and its social value; a letter may reveal the event's personal relevance and interest.

4 Each text belongs to a different **genre**—that is, they represent ideas or events according to different motives and use different strategies.

Finally, we can add that the goals and effects of both texts are not totally dependent on the individual author's intentions. A news article has to fulfil certain requirements regardless of the journalist's feelings or opinions; an academic essay needs to satisfy certain criteria which are not chosen by the author; even a personal letter to a friend uses standard features and tokens of friendship in its greetings, commentary and farewell.

These points focus on the way the two texts are written. Just as we have been practising throughout this book, it is essential to examine these sorts of features closely if we are to understand the range of textual meanings and operations.

Exercises

1 Find a newspaper article and a letter to the editor on the same topic. Analyse and contrast the different stylistic and generic features of the two texts.

2 Transcribe a radio or television interview. Rewrite the transcript as a magazine article, paying close attention to the different stylistic conventions you have to use in the new version.

Introducing the audience: context

If the point of this kind of analysis is to establish the different ways in which texts can *mean*, it is now necessary to consider how texts relate to their audience and readers. For a text can only ever mean *something* to *someone*.

We must try therefore to expand the practice of textual analysis to include ideas of audience involvement. Texts do not operate abstractly, but are addressed to, and read by people. An important step in developing our analysis is thus to examine how texts function socially. A key concept that we can use here is that of **context**, the social setting or circumstances that surround a particular text.

The points detailed above implicitly raise the idea of context. The stylistic and generic contrasts between, say, a letter and a news article arise since each text is written in different social circumstances. In many ways, the context influences the functions a text is trying to fulfil. A factual news report occurs in a broad public setting, and a personal opinion and emotional response in a more private one. Contextual factors determine which strategies of representation are used.

There is also another side to context. Texts are not only *written* in particular settings, but are also *read* in specific contexts. By examining this second factor, we can start to consider the ways that texts may influence readers.

Context and social meaning

The setting in which a text is read may vary greatly from the one in which it was written. This variation can occur in many ways, but perhaps the most obvious becomes apparent when we read a text produced in an earlier historical period. The cultural conditions in these two settings may be extremely different. Many of the interests of the first readers may no longer be relevant for a contemporary audience, but be replaced by other concerns. (Recall the compass image in the John Donne poem at the beginning of Chapter 9; it would have seemed intriguing to readers in the early 1600s partly because it mixed romance with 'technology'. Nowadays, the Internet might work as a kind of parallel image for lovers' union when they are apart.)

With recently written texts, context applies in other ways. There may be quite obvious geographical and national factors. An American text that addresses local affairs may be received with much less interest if reprinted in Australia. However, the effects of context can also work in a more subtle manner.

Throughout our study of writing structures and strategies we have been noting that texts do more than provide information. They also represent and evaluate subject matter, frequently making readers understand the material in quite specific terms. We could say that a text often presumes a certain kind of **authority** over its topic. It seems to imply that its representation of the subject is, if not the only possible way of depicting it, at least a correct and truthful way of doing so. This kind of presumption seems to be basic to a wide range of non-fictional genres, from academic research to administrative reports to news articles. In addition, fictional genres, such as novels and films, may also set up an air of reality.

An awareness of the processes of representation in the textual structures and strategies we have been examining might make us a little sceptical about the absolute reliability of such a presumption. Nonetheless, the point remains that many genres make this sort of move in trying to establish their standing and authority with readers.

Such authority puts pressure on the reader to agree with the text, to see things in its terms. When this influence has effect, readers are *positioned* to accept the text's viewpoint on the subject matter. They may be persuaded, or indeed more or less forced by the text to go along with its representation and evaluative attitude. On the other hand, readers might disagree with its meanings—but often this requires a deliberate effort on their part.

Hence a text sets its readers in varying positions of understanding and power. They are compelled and coaxed (often quite subtly) to accept its viewpoint or they may be motivated to question it. The text begins to affect readers' understanding of the social context and their place in it.

If a text persuades its reader to agree with it, then we could say that the reader is adopting a similar evaluative attitude towards the subject matter. In other words, text and reader are sharing a compatible social perspective on the issue. The text has, in effect, *placed the reader within its point of view on the topic.*

This positioning process can be summed up by stating that a text not only supplies its subject matter or issue, but also offers the reader the terms in which it is to be interpreted. As well as relating to the text, these terms may extend to the reader's understanding of his or her social situation. Hence textual strategies, meanings and viewpoints can also affect people's ideas about their social contexts. In short, we can say that **texts socialise readers**.

Critical analysis

A key point in our developing approach to texts has become that the analysis of strategies of representation can reveal a text's presumptions of authority, the way it can get readers to take its evaluative attitudes for their own.

This socialising effect emerges as the most important consequence of the idea of genre that was raised in the previous chapter. In a sense, genre is the 'biggest' or most involved concept with which we have dealt. By thinking of it as a *process*, we saw that genre incorporates the full range of textual features, strategies and conventions that have been discussed, from issues of structure and organisation to choice of perspective and subject matter, to questions of evaluative attitude, language style and figurative language.

Because it covers all these elements, genre determines the way the audience is positioned to understand a text. Familiarity with a genre (through previous readings) sets up expectations about what a new text will be trying to do. Usually, we anticipate that texts such as academic essays, business letters or newspaper articles, will conform to generic conventions. Thus a genre can prepare readers to understand a text in a certain way before they have finished reading it—and perhaps even before they have started to read it.

The kind of understanding that genre initiates is always related to a social viewpoint towards the subject matter. Accordingly, through the strategies of representation which they activate, genres and texts make readers understand their topics in specific social terms. In this process, the attitudes and beliefs that underlie these terms are reinforced (or, as we will see, possibly challenged).

Our principal aim in analysing language is to uncover the *socialisation and attitude formation* that go on in texts. If we read language actively and critically, it becomes a revealing, important way to examine and question the social presumptions of different genres and strategies of representation.

Case study: fashion

In this section we will try to practise the kind of critical analysis which has been described above. We will survey a range of social texts, from advertisements to academic essays. The topic for all the texts is 'fashion'. However, as will be seen, what fashion is and means changes considerably as we move from text to text and cut across genres and representational strategies. This kind of textual and generic variation reflects the cultural diversity of fashion's significance and meaning.

What is fashion? A simple definition can be gained by turning to the *Macquarie Dictionary*: 'prevailing custom or style or dress, etiquette, procedure, etc.; manner, way, mode; the make or form of anything'. This suggests a rather general meaning for fashion as the 'prevailing' style. As we might expect, the dictionary definition offers little insight into specific conceptions and modes of fashion. For example, different things prevail in different contexts. What rap musicians see as fashionable would seem to vary a great deal from the perceptions of lawyers or accountants.

Our working definition could therefore be that while a prevailing style, fashion is part of social reality but does not really have a single meaning or function. It means various things in different contexts, and as we will see, it can even *do* various things in different contexts.

Because we are acting as textual critics (rather than as anthropologists, historians, sociologists or authorities on fashion), our approach to fashion's meanings and functions is via texts. The starting premiss for this method is that one way of getting at fashion's significance is to analyse texts that represent it in various ways through different language strategies. Textual analysis should reveal these differences and their effects on readers' understanding of how fashion works in society and what it means.

Let's start by looking at the following dress rules. These texts are being used to explain and enforce policies of group membership. They seek to impose acceptable forms of behaviour and appearance. Hence, they not only convey meanings, they also (and perhaps most importantly) attempt to *do things to readers*. In this way, they are part of the genre of legal texts, which tries to assert power over readers, controlling their actions and thoughts by reinforcing norms of behaviour and understanding. Fashion is being evaluated as a pivotal aspect of social regulation.

7.2 Dress Guidelines

To assist in maintaining a satisfactory standard within the Members Reserve, dress regulations apply. While the Trust may vary dress requirements, Members are responsible for ensuring an acceptable standard. Your co-operation is appreciated.

The following guidelines may assist:

FOOTBALL STADIUM:
Males: Neat casual attire—shoes with socks, dress shorts, shirt with collar (No thongs, sandals or T-shirts).
Females: Neat casual attire (No thongs or bare feet). **No revealing attire.**

CRICKET GROUND:
Members Pavilion
Males: Shirt with collar, long trousers, socks and shoes, (Shorts, sandals, and thongs are not permitted.)
Females: Blouse with slacks, skirt or dress. (Shorts are not permitted.) No revealing attire.

M.A. Noble and Ladies Stand

Males: Neat casual attire, shoes with socks, dress shorts, shirt with collar (No thongs, sandals or T-shirts).

Females: Neat casual attire (No thongs or bare feet).
           No revealing attire.

** Dress guidelines apply to children but discretion will be used.

NOTE: **Members are reminded that the dress and behaviour standards of both Members and Guests are your responsibility.**

Bowling Club

By-law 5. Uniforms. Women.

5.2.   White sports frock with full belt or Princess-lined frock (belt optional). Not more than 38cm from the ground. Long or short sleeves not less that 10cm underarm seam. Attachments of any kind to lengthen sleeves are not permitted. Only sports style frock as approved by the Association shall be worn.

5.2.a.2. Culottes with shirt. White culottes to have box pleats centre back and centre front with elastic in back band. White shirt. Culottes and shirt to be of the same non-transparent material. The wearing of culottes and shirt is optional. Only culottes and shirt as approved by the Association shall be worn.

5.2.c.   Hats. White sports hat, closed crown. Width of brim optional. Hats optional for twilight and night bowls. Players may remove their hats in clubhouse on the authority of the presiding officer.

5.5.   Non-compliance with any of the above provisions shall render the member liable to disqualification or suspension for such time as the Executive Committee shall determine.

If we consider the style of the rules, we note that they are presented as orders rather than as texts that are simply giving information. Strictly speaking, the grammar of the rules is incorrect because verbs are not used. However, there seems to be an implicit command, 'You will wear', at the beginning of each one. As orders, the rules are trying to enjoin the official evaluative attitudes to dress on readers. They speak at, rather than for the reader—though if the reader is a satisfied member of the group, the rules may speak for, as well as at him or her.

In the cricket ground rules, we can note that a number of social distinctions and categories are being reinforced. First of all, there is the distinction between genders. There are different rules for males and females, including an apparent concern over any visible appearance of women's bodies. Phrases such as 'No ... bare feet' and 'No revealing attire' (repeated and in bold type) are used only in the rules for women, not in relation to men. This awareness of women's physical presence seems to suggest that the authorising members are themselves male.

Second, there are allusions to distinctions in social hierarchy. Shared taste is assumed in the repeated phrase, 'neat casual attire'. No explanation of what 'neat casual' means is offered. Instead, the text sets up an in-group, a 'we' who already know what it denotes. The ability to interpret the text in the 'correct' way (that is, as the cricket ground deems correct) is a prerequisite of group membership. 'We'—who read and dress correctly—make up the members as opposed to 'them', the non-members, who either wear thongs and T-shirts or misread the rules. Even within the members there is an order of rank, suggested by the difference between the rules for the two grandstands. The stricter dress rules in force for the members' stand show that clothes and texts about them can be used to indicate and enforce status.

The bowling club rules illustrate an intensification of these effects. They comprise a strictly detailed set of forms and fashions, especially for women, which would reinforce, on the one hand, the power of the association, the presiding officers and the executive committee, and on the other, the conformity of members. The rules apply not only to what members can wear but what they can do and where they can do it. For example, clause 5.2.c. explains when someone can take her hat off when indoors.

Again, the interpretation of the text becomes grounds for power to be exercised over members. In clause 5.5, 'Non-compliance with any of the above provisions', there is some ambiguity over what someone may be disciplined for. The notion of 'non-compliance' suggests that an offence can result as much from not reading the provisions properly as from wearing the wrong kind or cut of clothes. We could say that obedient reading and dressing have become parallel social actions and that the executive committee has assumed the power to punish those who do not read or dress as it expects. This possibility reveals that textual power (through the reading and writing of texts) can be as strong as effects of fashion regarding the membership of social groups.

The next text we will examine works against the genre of dress rules. Indeed, without that genre, this text, an advertisement from a women's magazine, would lose a lot of its meaning, since it sets itself to *contradict* ('contra-dict' or 'speak against') the evaluative attitude of dress rules.

This isn't P.E. class.

This is your life.
And there are no rules.

And there are no grades.

And there are no more
ugly little uniforms.

We can show you the Elite™ Aerobic Thong. We can show you the Elite Aerobic
Brief Short. But we can't possibly show you everything Nike makes for women. So to see
more of it, call for your free copy of the Nike Women's Source Book.

1-800-642-1190.

Although the Nike advertisement seems to emphasise rebellion and individuality rather than group membership, it does have some similar effects to the dress rules. Like them, it sets up certain ident-ities for both the reader and the authors. All three texts designate and address a 'you', either an individual or a group member. In each case this identity seems to have something attractive about it—the security of group allegiance or personal independence— which may encourage the reader to accept it. The texts also ident-ify the authors of the text as the association or the company, a 'we' who speaks in person to the audience.

Yet in contrast to the others, the advertisement speaks not so much 'at', as on behalf of the audience, seeming to adopt rather than supply its voice and evaluative attitude to rules. The text declares itself as anti-rules and identifies the reader quite specifically as a post-school female. It suggests that a key way to become an adult woman is to forget about rules and choose one's own clothes. Fashion acts as *the* means of forming one's identity.

If we continue to analyse the text, however, a paradox starts to emerge. In the small print, we note an ironic effect. The advertisement has promised individuality but now supplies another type of group identity as the 'Nike woman'.

It seems to veer back towards the rules from which it had so strongly separated itself, even suggesting that the reader get a copy of the rule book, the *Nike Women's Source Book*. In the guise of individuality, the text ends up offering the uniform you wear and the group identity you have when you're not wearing a uniform or having a group identity.

The relationship between the first three texts is, then, rather unusual. Although in some respects they belong to different genres (advertisements, rules) and pronounce contrasting evaluative attitudes to fashion, they also have strongly similar conceptions of the links between fashion and personal identity. We can uncover this similarity and its social implications through the process of critical analysis.

Exercise

Analyse the verbal strategies of a fashion advertisement in a magazine to establish the social identity and position it sets up for readers. Can you rewrite the advertisement (perhaps as a parody) in such a way that the identity and position will be reversed?

The next three texts are magazine and newspaper articles. They are examples of how the genre of journalism functions. As suggested earlier, news articles often have a double effect: they provide information, but they also tell readers how to interpret what they read. The factual tones used in the news genre offer an evaluative attitude to the subject matter that can be hard to resist.

The first article, titled 'Job Strategies', begins by pinpointing an identity for the reader and urging her to adopt it: 'If you're like most professional women...' The text invokes a contemporary, Equal Opportunity workplace and professional character that many women (especially among the magazine's readers) would accept. Indeed, the reader would have to reject social changes over the last twenty-five years to deny the identity that is offered ('No, I'm not like most professional women and I don't want to be').

Job strategies

WORKPLACE DON'TS

If you're like most professional women, you not only work hard at your job, you work hard at *dressing* for your job. So it's natural to wonder how a badly dressed colleague can get away with it. The truth is, she can't. Managers and personnel directors are well aware of who's dressed appropriately and who isn't—it's part of their job—and in these recessionary times, the one who comes up lacking is usually the first to go. Here, the biggest faux pas we've heard of in recent months.

Out of place in the workplace

A researcher for a large Midwest ad agency gave a presentation on demographic trends wearing a short white dress, white lace hose and white boots. Even without the boots, her look would have been a Don't. In a presentation of this sort, the *information* should be the focus of attention. A tailored dress or suit in a dark neutral, even red, would have been a smart choice.

A first-year law associate in a Los Angeles firm came to work wearing what her colleagues called 'rodeo clothes'—fringed leather jacket, suede skirt and cowboy boots. The look was so comment provoking and so out of place that several women partners took her aside to offer guidelines on how to dress for the job.

Susan W. Miller, a Los Angeles career counselor, recalls a woman who showed up for one of her Friday seminars in a sweatshirt and jeans. 'Fridays are casual, dress-down days for a lot of companies, but I had people there from several

firms. This woman looked, and felt, badly out of place.' Even if Friday is a casual day at your job, dress up if your work takes you outside, urges Miller. 'You're representing your company wherever you go.'

'The worst faux pas I ever saw was a woman in a knit outfit that was far too tight,' recalls Crystal Ettridge, vice president of a Washington DC temp agency. Few working women set out to dress in such a skimpy or suggestive manner. If you've put on weight, put the outfit aside until it fits again. If it has shrunk, give it away. If you wear clothing with stretch choose pieces for comfort, not cling.

Perhaps because of the nature of her company, the personnel administrator for a Dallas cosmetics company focuses on makeup Don'ts. A big one: 'blue or green eye shadow from lid to brow'. Equally disastrous are the bi- and tricolor variations in colors to match the outfit. A better choice if you wear shadow: a dab on the lid with neutral brown or gray tones.

A do except for . . .

The mistake many well-dressed women make: too much perfume. 'You want to be remembered for yourself, not the scent you're wearing,' says Cecile Baltazar, human resources manager at a Los Angeles law firm. Better to spritz just a little in the morning and reapply later in the day.

Shoes are another source of trouble. A Dallas administrator re-calls a businesswoman who wore see-through plastic slingbacks with her tailored suits. Then there are the scuffed-up, down-at-the-heel pumps that have never seen a shine. It's a mistake to think colleagues don't notice.

Creative licence
Even at 'anything goes' jobs, everything *doesn't* go. Look to your colleagues and supervisors for a clue to how short, tight or bohemian to go. The ad saleswoman for a Seattle rock radio station who came to work in a thigh-high black leather mini and a Van Halen T-shirt was roundly declared out-of-bounds. 'We *are* a radio station,' says the personnel manager, acknowledging the creative ambience, 'but that was too much.'

Three things that always say 'do'
• Tailored clothing
• Good grooming
• Well-maintained shoes

Here's how they looked on a Phoenix training manager described by Carol Warner, the recruiter who hired her: 'She wore a tailored, gray tweed suit and low-heeled pumps. Her blunt-cut hair was an above-the-shoulder length, her makeup was just enough to flatter her features, and she wore clear polish on her short, well-groomed nails. She looked put-together and professional.'

Source: Glamour, March 1992

The article contends that, to be successful, readers should dress the way it describes. It gives a number of mini-narratives of various women's failures at work due to their dress. Within the tones of friendly warning—like the advertisement, the text appears to speak with, rather than at the audience—it is again offering a set of dress rules. The article seems progressive by talking about the reader as a professional woman, yet, in the end, its effect is to reinforce a sexist perspective that the key to a woman's success is how she looks. (Would an article on young male professionals raise these kinds of issues?) The last sentence reveals its central conceptual metaphor that for women professionalism *is* appearance: 'She looked put-together and professional.'

The text also implies that women are constantly being looked at, by themselves and by others. This implication is developed in the next article, 'Fashion Workshop'. Again speaking as a wise older sister, the text sets up rules of appearance. It gives numerous tips on spring suits but, more significantly, it reinforces certain ideas about the proper shape of women's bodies. The text instructs the reader to scrutinise her physical self. For example, look at the paragraph titled 'Flattery check': 'If you're short or heavy, fullest pants are dicey choices; seek out those with some taper'; or, under 'The news: fit-and-flare' heading: 'Surprise! *This silhouette* can *flatter fullish hips* .... If your bust is large, choose a single- (rather than double-) breasted jacket.'

Fashion Workshop

Need a suit this spring? Think womanly menswear—or just womanly

- One trend likely to be around for a while: the pants suit, predictably popular in this season of hemline variety. Choices vary in pants width from the newer style, softly full, to the more familiar trim and narrow. What's consistent is their menswear inspiration (longer jackets, trouser-style pants) and womanly execution (often via color—white, ivory, deep pastels, rather than the usual narrow range of neutrals). In the same vein: tailored shorts suits. And you can invent a pants/shorts suit by pairing up your own pieces in same or same-family hues.
- The smartest go-withs for any pants suit now: spare top (or no top, if jacket permits); heels. Think of a bra top/bustier beneath a pants suit for evening—or go for the more modest 'bare' of stretch sheer. The point: When the theme is classic, the details are feminine.
- Flattery check: If you're short or heavy, fullest pants are dicey choices; seek out those with some taper (though you *can* afford to go slightly fuller if fabric is flowing—like washed silk or crepe) . . .
- A 'suit' can be out-and-out *pretty*. Last year's dress-plus-jacket was the straight shift and long jacket. That look is still around (an easy update: belt the shift), but the newest interpretations boast more built-in style—a dress with shape (pleats, a waist, a top that's snug and figure-defining), a jacket that's anything but basic. (You'll see this modified-bolero shape in a number of jackets and sweaters now, part of a mini trend in Spanish-inspired clothes.) Look for other nontraditional jackets, too—shirt-styled or sleekly fitted.
- Flattery facts: Much depends on dress/jacket shape. Straight shifts are still the most universally figure-friendly choices; most can be belted without compromising on flattery. Hip-length jackets flatter full hips more than either cropped, or long double-breasted styles. See 'jacket' and 'skirt' sections for more strategies.
- The best shoes for most dress/jacket combos? Heels rather than flats—but low (1"-plus) is fine.

The news: fit-and-flare

It's a curvy silhouette in its extreme to make the point: fitted jacket, nipped-in waist, a skirt with body.

- *You'll find this silhouette* in a range of fabrics/moods—from work wool to evening silk, from matched, as here, to un-. (This particular incarnation also owes its timeliness to this season's softened-up-menswear trend—a double-breasted jacket with curves, businesslike fabric atop bare skin.
- Surprise! *This silhouette can flatter fullish hips.* The key: skirt fabric that's gentle, not stiff. If your bust is large, choose a single- (rather than double-) breasted jacket.
- This womanly silhouette calls for some heel—though just a little is fine.

Source: Glamour, May 1992

The perspective in these excerpts focuses on the body and, in effect, instructs readers to inspect and measure themselves closely before trying to mould and manipulate their body shapes. It suggests that there is an ideal woman's body to which the audience should aspire. Fashion has become the key to one's self-image and sexuality, at both work and leisure.

Desirable Denim

Denim has come a long way from the ranches of the American West and the Californian goldfields. The staple attire of working men throughout the world, it has become the great standby for off-duty wear—whether for young or old, city or country folk, toffs or plebs. It is the simplest and most egalitarian fabric.

But gradually this humble cotton twill has gained class. In the latest designer collections, denim is the surprise element, whether blue or brightly coloured, embroidered or covered in rhinestones.

Chanel designer Karl Lagerfeld started the trend last year with his clever mixes of denim, tweed and grosgrain. For Lagerfeld, denim is a weapon in his war against the conventions of fashion, whereby garments and accessories have their natural settings—chiffon for evening, denim for fun. Chanel's powder-blue frayed denim skirt looks more formal than many classic suits.

In the coming spring/summer collections, denim is the fabric of choice for evening wear. And very chic it looks, too. Italian designer Gianni Versace, a master of the un-orthodox, has inspired many with his sexy combinations of floral organza evening skirts with denim shirts, sexy satin and silk bustier tops with denim shirts and jeans.

Among other top designers who used denim as a glamour item were Armani, who mixed long denim skirts with beautiful organza shirts in his diffusion range. Errenno, and Ralph Lauren, who made denim elegant with his long, straight skirt topped with a starched denim shirt which has leg-of-mutton sleeves; the shirt tied under the bust. Ungaro favoured chic 70s-style denim trouser-suits with white piping.

Designer denim is a hot item, but classic blue jeans are also making a come-back. After declining demand in the late 1980s, when there was a lull in innovation after the acid wash craze, sales are again climbing. Levis and Lee have launched rival marketing campaigns and Lee Cooper is re-entering the market.

Marketing men say sales are broadening across a wider age group as the baby-boom generation gets older. Jeans are, together with rock music, something parents now have in common with their children.

'Denim is the one thing everyone owns,' says American designer Donna Karan, who uses it extensively.

'It makes you look younger,' adds Franco Moschino, who has been using denim in his collections for years.

A sign of the increasing respect-ability of jeans is a recent change in dress rules at the Adelaide Casino to allow entry to jeans-clad punters. That's quite a change from the days where jeans were a symbol of teenage rebellion, but denim is the one fabric that has the capacity to keep re-inventing itself.

Source: Anne Lim,
The Weekend Australian,
16–17 May 1992

The third journalistic text, titled 'Desirable denim', repeatedly invokes the excitement of a social life for those who are stylishly dressed: 'denim is the fabric of choice [whose choice?] for evening wear. And very chic it looks, too.' Fashion becomes the key to social success, and many positive words and phrases are used to reinforce its importance: 'class, surprise, fun, sexy, glamour, a hot item, makes you look younger'.

The evaluative attitude running through these texts is ambiguous. While it remains positive to fashion, it seems quite judgemental towards readers. It sounds the warning that readers are unlikely to shape up physically, professionally, socially (and so, inevitably, psychologically) unless they are very careful. While commending fashion, the texts set up a program of self-scrutiny for the reader.

The following excerpt, from Miles Franklin's *My Brilliant Career*, demonstrates the way fashion is often used in fictional narrative. Perhaps the key function of dress in this genre is as a means of characterisation. It works as a metaphorical concept for personality. In this respect, fictional narrative exploits the same links between fashion and identity that have emerged in the non-fictional texts. But whereas those texts seemed to suppress a full awareness of the links (even as they forged them), fiction often foregrounds them in portraying characters:

> Miss Sarah Beecham, and then Miss Derrick brought herself and her dress in with great style and airs. She was garbed in a sea-green silk, and had jewellery on her neck, arms, and hair. Her self-confident mien was suggestive of the conquest of many masculine hearts. She was a big handsome woman. Beside her, I in my crushed white muslin dress was as over-shadowed as a little white handkerchief would be in comparison to a gorgeous shawl heavily wrought in silks and velvet. She was given the best seat as though she were a princess. She sat down with great indifference, twirled a bracelet around her wrist, languidly opened her fan, and closed her eyes as she wafted it slowly to and fro.

In Franklin's novel, then, Miss Derrick's powerful character is signified by her lavish clothes, jewellery and gestures. In comparison, the narrator in a simple white dress is almost unnoticed: the 'crushed white muslin' seems to suggest her crushed spirit. As our earlier readings of narrative in Chapter 3 suggested, however, the narrator's perspective can work ironically. Here, the evaluative attitude seems ambivalent, for along with the narrator's envy, the detail to Miss

Derrick seems exaggerated. It focuses on her appearance and gestures to slightly comic or ironic effect, undercutting the initial impression she makes.

Through all the fashion texts considered so far, the recurring metaphorical concept has been the link between fashion and identity. By analysing them in terms of their evaluative attitudes and figurative language, we can see that fashion works as way of identifying oneself as a group member or an outsider, as a good worker, as law-abiding, sexually attractive, self-contented, and so on. These texts not only present these ideas but position readers to accept them as legitimate social values. The informative tone of the journalistic genre may work to disguise these socialising effects. But all the texts reinforce various social norms and attitudes for their audience.

The final four passages we will consider are taken from academic studies of fashion. Each adopts the combination of expository and argumentative approaches to material which we have seen is a distinctive feature of academic writing. The four texts share a generic, evaluative attitude that fashion is complex and must be examined closely, that it has a history and a range of cultural meanings. At the same time, each one is proposing and trying to support a different thesis about what these meanings and history might be.

The first excerpt is taken from a sociological study of the 'fashioned self', by Joanne Finkelstein:

The Fashioned Self

The symbolic content of the necktie seems enriched by its ostensible lack of function. It is unarguably decorative, being worn largely as a sign both of the individual's sense of aesthetics and claims of social propriety. It remains an item of clothing that requires a degree of skilled tailoring and costly human labour in its manufacture and so, at its best, it is a relatively expensive item of clothing that allows the wearer to demonstrate a degree of idiosyncratic personal style. The necktie loses value when it is poorly made, if it hangs too long or not long enough, or if it is worn inappropriately, say, while engaging in active or dirty work. The necktie is a sign of conspicuous immobility because it is shown to its best effect when the wearer is inactive, idle, even motionless. It is a fragile and unreliable accessory in so far as it can betray one's aspirations as effectively as it publicizes them, yet, it is an accessory weighted down by the importance of first impressions; as Fraser has commented, the tie is used to transmit 'minor social messages' (1981: 232). To apply Hollander's thesis to an analysis of the necktie is to see definitions of masculinity and male identity through that item of clothing. In the industrialized world where a man's social identity is submerged in the business suit or the uniform work clothes, the necktie can be made into a talisman of individuality and imbued with an exorbitant burden of identity claims.

Currently, men wear ties as part of their customary apparel; in contrast, women occasionally wear them, such as when fashion dictates. The tie varies in appearance, its size, texture, colour and shape reflect trends in fashions as well as personal preferences. Sometimes the tie is snake-thin and made of leather, or abundant, floral and cut from soft silk. Much has been made of the necktie as a flag or signpost to the wearer's mood, intentions and character. The necktie can be an emblem of social attachment, say, to a school or private club; as well, it can advertise its designer origins with references within its pattern to the well-known logos of, say, Cardin and Givenchy. This trend can be contrasted with the designer labels of most quality garments which remain inside. Some ties are more eloquent than others. Generally, the paler the tie, the more important the social occasion where it is worn,

the white bowtie being the most formal. The pale tie is shown to full advantage when it is immaculately clean, unblemished. In this pristine state, it proves the adroitness of the wearer; after all, he must have refined table manners and social skills because no drip nor morsel of food has stained it. Other ties signify various meanings; the bold red tie, commonly seen against the dark suit, is purportedly eloquent of a man's sexual energy, and the American black string-tie, held by an ornamental torquoise clasp, is used to identify regional origin and to gather to its wearer the characteristics associated with the cowboy who tamed the wild west and fore-shadowed America world hegemony (see Lurie 1983). The bowtie draws attention to the head and lower part of the face, it especially highlights the mouth, which is supposedly the organ through which intelligence is demonstrated. Thus, the bowtie is thought to be favoured by those men who have elected the importance of the mind over the body.

Source: Joanne Finkelstein, 1991

The text focuses on the necktie as an important cultural symbol used mainly by men to say things about themselves. This point forms the thesis of the text. The dominant conceptual metaphor running through the passage is that fashion is a kind of language. Neckties speak and send different kinds of messages: 'The necktie can be an emblem ... Some tie are more eloquent than others ... Other ties signify various meanings ...' The author analyses different types of ties, reading them as if they are texts that express masculinity, wealth, sexuality, and so on. The evaluative attitude seems neither approving nor encouraging. It's not as if the text is aiming to get the reader to start wearing ties. Rather the motive is explanatory: the text uses a range of descriptive and expository structures to support its thesis through examples, evidence and interpretation.

The following piece, from a history of underwear by Elizabeth Ewing, is again expository. However, instead of relying wholly on description, it also uses a narrative structure to recount the history of changes in underwear styles. Again, it is not recommending a particular style over others but traces developments through different periods. Its thesis is founded on this narrative structure: underwear alters according to changing social standards.

Underwear: A History

Among the recent fashions that have influenced underwear the most important was the mini-skirt. It was at its height (literally) from 1967 until well into 1969, when a violent winter-time swing to the maxi dealt it a strong, if partial, body-blow. From these two extremes there emerged, half way through 1970, the midi-length, coming to varying points on the calf. The importance of this lies not in a mere juggling with hemlines, but in the fact that it expresses a new, softer, more feminine look, a shapely figure with a defined natural waistline and something like a return to elegance. It indicates a reaction from blatant, defiant freedom and has social echoes in the contemporary trend of thought. It is also, for a change, a fashion for all ages, not only for the young.

The mini was outstanding in the fact that for the first time ever it revealed female limbs up to an including the thighs. Previously the knees had been the limit—and when they were unveiled for the first times less than fifty years ago that was the word which horrified older and more staid people applied to the fashion. The progressive revelation of the female body has, however, been proceeding briskly in fashions of recent years, with general acceptance.

So far as underwear was concerned the mini made stockings, established for centuries, an outmoded idea because they stopped short of the newly-exposed thighs. With them the suspender, proud achievement of less than a century ago, also met its Waterloo. Tights, more reminiscent of fifteenth- and sixteenth-century male fashion than of anything in the woman's world, took over. With them the pantee-girdle and pantee-corselette became the new foundationwear classics. The girdle and corselette thus became two-legged. That is still the latest underwear revolution and the crystal ball does not reveal anything beyond it. Following the lines of the body as closely as any garment could, these new underpinnings have brought the wheel full cycle from the whalebone stays of history. To complete the cycle, even the word 'corset' now fails to describe the pantees, pantee-corselettes and girdles that are generally worn. The word foundationwear is the most acceptable of the suggestions made in the search for a suitable description, and a number of leading stores have re-named their corset departments 'foundationwear departments'. Other verbal innovations include 'underfashions' and 'body fashions', but both are too generally applicable to underwear to replace the word 'corset' which remains irreplaceable and therefore now much more needed than is the traditional form of the garment itself.

Source: Elizabeth Ewing, 1972

228 Structures and Strategies

No reference is made to specific designers in this excerpt. To emphasise the subject matter, underwear and the mini-skirt are themselves presented as the main characters in the narrative. They are depicted as actively doing things to women's bodies: 'The mini . . . revealed female limbs'; 'Tights . . . took over.'

The next two texts exemplify many of the important features of academic writing as a synthesis of different styles, genres and strategies. They combine description, narration and exposition to present arguments on the effects of fashion on people. The first one makes a case that there can be no escape from fashion, since it's as pervasive as culture itself. It surveys a range of different types of dressers and maintains that they all are highly conscious of fashion. Even the unfashionable need to be aware of fashion trends to make sure they avoid them.

Adorned in Dreams

In all societies the body is 'dressed', and everywhere dress and adornment play symbolic, communicative and aesthetic roles. Dress is always 'unspeakably meaningful'. The earliest forms of 'clothing' seem to have been adornments such as body painting, ornaments, scarifications (scarring), tattooing, masks and often constricting neck and waist bands. Many of these deformed, reformed or otherwise modified the body. The bodies of men and of children, not just those of women, were altered—there seems to be a widespread human desire to transcend the body's limitations.

Dress in general seems then to fulfil a number of social, aesthetic and psychological functions; indeed it knots them together, and can express all simultaneously. This is true of modern as of ancient dress. What is added to dress as we ourselves know it in the West is *fashion*.

The growth of the European city in the early stages of what is known as mercantile capitalism at the end of the Middle Ages saw the birth of fashionable dress, that is of something qualitatively new and different.

Fashion is dress in which the key feature is rapid and continual changing of styles. Fashion, in a sense *is* change, and in modern Western societies no clothes are outside fashion; fashion sets the terms of *all* sartorial behaviour—even uniforms have been designed by Paris dressmakers; even nuns have shortened their skirts; even the poor seldom go in rags—they wear cheap versions of the fashions that went out a few years ago and are therefore to be found in second-hand shops and jumble sales. Dress still differs in detail from one community to another—middle-aged women in the English 'provinces' or in the American Midwest, or in Southern

Italy or in Finland don't look exactly like one another, and they look still less like the fashion freaks of Paris or Tokyo. Nevertheless they are less different than they probably feel, for their way of dressing is inevitably determined by fashion. At 'punk' secondhand fashion stalls in the small market towns of the South of France it is possible to see both trendy young holiday makers and elderly peasants buying print 'granny frocks' from the 1940s; to the young they represent 'retro-chic', to the older women what still seems to them a suitable style. But the granny frocks themselves are dim replicas, or sometimes caricatures, of frocks originally designed by Chanel or Lucien Lelong in the late 1930s. They began life as fashion garments and not as some form of traditional peasant dress.

Even the determindely *un*fashionable wear clothes that manifestly represent a reaction against what *is* in fashion. To be unfashionable is not to escape the whole discourse, or to get outside the parameters. Indeed the most dowdy clothes may at any moment suddenly get taken up and become, perversely, all the rage. Harold Macmillan, Prime Minister of Britain in the late 1950s and early 1960s, used to wear a shapeless, knitted cardigan—it was part of his country gentleman's persona of 'unflappability'. This (which was also and perhaps even more influentially worn by Rex Harrison as Professor Higgins in the film *My Fair Lady*) became for a season the smart item that every young woman 'had' to have. Since Macmillan himself possibly used the garment semi-deliberately as one of the stage props for his public self, its transformation into a fashion was a kind of double parody.

Source: Elizabeth Wilson, 1985

The extract also offers a general thesis concerning the 'social, aesthetic and psychological functions' of fashion. This passage is taken from the beginning of Elizabeth Wilson's book *Adorned in Dreams*, and this position in a larger study ensures its introductory function. The passage attempts to demonstrate the general range of the book's subject matter and approach.

The final text is much more focused than an introductory excerpt. It is taken from one of the middle chapters of W.F. Haug's *Critique of Commodity Aesthetics*. As expected, this part of the book concentrates on developing and illustrating its argument. It does not have a generalising purpose and is not trying to set up or prepare the way for a wider argument. Instead, it applies a specific case, the Hush Puppies brand name, to make a point about the manipulation and control of consumers exerted by companies through using catchy phrases and advertising.

Critique of Commodity Aesthetics

Commodity aesthetics—its comprehensive meaning; 'Hush Puppies' and the spread of the fashionable dog; subject-object relation as conditoned by commodity aesthetics; natural history of capitalism

In 1943, as a wartime economy measure, the US Government required the meat industry to introduce new skinning methods for piglets, as the basis for the valorization of the hides in the leather and footwear trades. One leather and shoe company developed machines specifically for this purpose. This enterprise grew into one of the world's largest shoe empires—Wolverine World Wide Inc., Rockford (Michigan)—which sold more than 120 million pairs of shoes between 1959 and 1971 under the trade name of 'Hush Puppies' and the basset-hound symbol. Since 1963 there has been a licensed subsidiary in the Federal Republic which, up to 1971, had sold more than 6 million pairs in that country alone. The reason why the company does not run out of pigskin, 'which is after all only a "waste product"', is due to the continuing popularity of barbecues which cost the lives of millions of American piglets'. The brand symbol, the dog and the name, is known to more than half the people in the Federal Republic, and by as much as two-thirds of the under-thirties, and is thus known to more people than most 'well-known' politicians.

In answer to the question of how the company arrived at the trademark, they tell a story worth remembering as revealing evidence of the capitalist spirit. In 1958, somewhere in the American Deep South, the sales director is said to have come across a group of people eating popcorn, and throwing some to their barking dogs with the words, 'Hush puppies!'. Watching this scene, a good idea came to him. It might profit his firm to offer something to pacify another kind of noisy 'dog'. This, of course, was the public—the world of buyers. During consumer research potential buyers were given seven names from which to choose. 'Hush Puppies' scored lowest. Yet the name was selected because it pleased the retailers, on whose sales business the company now depended. The point is that the 'user' came last in the sales department's calculations, and success has proved them right: the user's judgement could easily be remoulded, and bought off by the dog-symbol.

Source: W.F. Haug, 1986

For this text, fashion has little to do with self-expression, as raised in the excerpts by Finkelstein and Wilson, and in most of the non-academic texts we considered earlier. Rather, fashion and dress are important instances of the workings of consumer capitalism. The text evaluates capitalism critically, including the sales director's dismissive attitude to consumers: 'It might profit his firm to offer something to pacify another kind of noisy "dog". This, of course, was the public—the world of buyers.' This is used as evidence of the socio-economic system's exploitative effects.

In these passages from scholarly studies, the major motive and strategy are to present certain information and interpretations of it to readers. An equally important concern, however, is to challenge, and perhaps change, readers' understanding of what fashion means. The four texts each use examples and evidence to construct their case through descriptive and narrative structures, and to attempt to make their case seem persuasive and convincing.

But there is often more to academic texts than the presentation of a researched argument. In addition to using the generic conventions of well-organised thesis and supporting evidence, academic texts may have their own political and social intentions, their own cultural and historical arguments to make, as exemplified by the last excerpt arguing against the role of fashion in capitalist societies. Just as we tried to analyse and uncover the evaluative attitudes of more general social texts on fashion, so in our study of academic texts it is necessary to examine the strategies they use to transform research into specific *intellectual* and *social* perspectives on their topics.

Thus it is necessary to think about the links between language and society at a number of levels and across the many genres that we encounter:

1 All texts are written and read in social contexts and represent social attitudes to their subject matter.
2 Texts don't simply convey 'pure' information but influence and determine readers' understanding of such information.
3 Through language strategies, texts position readers with certain roles and identities that affect their conception of their social context.

Exercise

Using some of the research indexes and catalogues that are available in your campus library, locate and assemble a range of academic, journalistic, governmental, administrative and other kinds of texts (including advertisements) on a topic such as *crime*, *health*, or *leisure*. Write a 1,500-word analytical essay on the generic strategies and structures that these texts use to represent the topic.

You might address the following kinds of questions in your analysis: Is there a particular evaluative attitude towards the topic that recurs through the texts? Are there conflicting attitudes? What kinds of attitudes may be omitted? In what ways do these texts position readers to understand the topic in certain social terms?

Works cited

Ewing, Elizabeth (1972) *Underwear: A History*, Theatre Arts Books, New York

Finkelstein, Joanne (1991) *The Fashioned Self*, Polity, Cambridge

Franklin, Miles (1979) *My Brilliant Career*, Angus and Robertson, Sydney

Haug, W. F. (1986) *Critique of Commodity Aesthetics*, translator, Robert Bock, Polity, Cambridge

'Job Strategies' and 'Fashion Workshop' (1992) *Glamour*, March

Lim, Anne (1992) 'Desirable Denim', *The Weekend Australian,* 16–17 May

Sydney Cricket and Sports Ground Trust (1994) *Members' Handbook: Sydney Cricket Ground, Sydney Football Stadium*

Wilson, Elizabeth (1985) *Adorned in Dreams: Fashion and Modernity*, Virago, London

Index